NATIONAL PERFORMANCE
Representing Quebec from Expo 67 to Céline Dion

National Performance

*Representing Quebec from
Expo 67 to Céline Dion*

Erin Hurley

UNIVERSITY OF TORONTO PRESS
Toronto Buffalo London

ISBN 978-1-4426-4095-5

Printed on acid-free, 100% post-consumer recycled paper
with vegetable-based inks.

Cultural Spaces

Library and Archives Canada Cataloguing in Publication

Hurley, Erin
National performance : representing Quebec from Expo 67 to
Céline Dion / Erin Hurley.

(Cultural spaces)
Includes bibliographical references and index.
ISBN 978-1-4426-4095-5

1. Theater and society – Québec (Province). 2. Theater audiences –
Québec (Province) – Psychology. 3. Performing arts – Social aspects –
Québec (Province). 4. Performing arts – Audiences – Québec (Province).
5. Nationalism – Québec (Province). I. Title. II. Series: Cultural spaces

PN2305.Q4.H87 2011   792.09714   C2010-903628-X

University of Toronto Press acknowledges the financial assistance
to its publishing program of the Canada Council for the Arts and the
Ontario Arts Council.

 Canada Council   Conseil des Arts   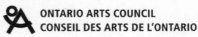 ONTARIO ARTS COUNCIL
for the Arts   du Canada   CONSEIL DES ARTS DE L'ONTARIO

This book has been published with the help of a grant from the Canadian
Federation for the Humanities and Social Sciences, through the Aid to
Scholarly Publications Programme, using funds provided by the Social Sciences
and Humanities Research Council of Canada.

University of Toronto Press acknowledges the financial support for its
publishing activities of the Government of Canada through the Canada
Book Fund.

Contents

Acknowledgments

As a PhD candidate in theatre at the City University of New York – The Graduate Center, I convinced my eventual dissertation advisor, Marvin Carlson, to do an individual reading course with me on Québécois drama. During each session Marvin would ask me, 'What makes this play Québécois?' It is a question I've been trying to answer in one way or another with respect to all manner of 'Québécois' cultural forms ever since. Since setting me on that path, Marvin has been a supportive guide and his work an important research corpus for me. Jill Dolan and Patricia Ticineto Clough also graciously sat on my dissertation committee. Writing under Marvin, Jill, and Patricia's tutelage allowed me to build up a real and interconnected sense of the fields in which my research into Québécois theatre and national performatives sits. Jill is an excellent friend and mentor to me; she commented on the first chapter of this book, has selflessly offered invaluable professional advice and opportunities, and for many of us is a model of progressive, activist pedagogy and research.

Many women have contributed directly to the current manuscript, several of them my research assistants, first at the University of British Columbia and then at McGill University. Megan Dallimore gathered materials on Céline Dion and popular music audiences; Laura Fisher compiled the results to the survey on Céline Dion, which Cléa Desjardins facilitated technically and Annie Gobour helped translate; Laura Fisher and Naomi Levine commented insightfully on each of the chapters as they came out of the printer and copyedited with precision and aplomb. Naomi was an important, patient, and savvy interlocutor during my most intensive period of book writing; she helped me formulate a number of key arguments in the Micone, Carbone 14, and Dion chapters. I am grateful for her intellectual generosity. She also prepared the index.

Anna Roth Trowbridge helped get the References in order and, most recently, Amanda Clarke searched out permissions, proofread, and took other tasks off my desk so that I might complete this one.

Many others sustained me and the writing in significant ways. Jen Harvie, a fellow-traveller in the realm of national performance and long-time dear friend, has inspired my work and myself, and been a model of critical generosity and love. Jill Lane had long, intellectually nourishing conversations with me in the early stages of this research. Laura Moss, Kirsty Johnston, Mary Chapman, and Leslie Paris offered insights, friendly support, editing skills, tea, and playdates during my time in Vancouver. Kirsty generously read the book proposal, the Expo chapter, and pushed me in my use of cultural geography. Laura also commented on the Expo chapter, and Mary read too many versions of the book proposal. In Montreal, Derek Nystrom kindly served as my guide to neo-Marxism; he helped me find the core of chapter 1 and of the Tremblay chapter by reading and discussing them with me when they were just bad, inchoate drafts. Monica Popescu, too, commented usefully on the Tremblay chapter. Sara Warner engaged me on the Céline Dion chapter. Attentive listeners at conferences of the American Society for Theatre Research, the Canadian Association for Theatre Research, and the American Council for Quebec Studies helped me advance my thinking on the topic. I am grateful to the University of Calgary's Performance Studies Speaker Series and the University of Lethbridge's Women Scholars Speaker Series for giving me the chance to float my ideas about Céline Dion before engaged, multi- and interdisciplinary groups.

Institutional supports have also been essential to writing this book. McGill University's Department of English offers a one-semester research leave to pre-tenure faculty from which this project benefited. The Centre for Research in Women's Studies and Gender Relations at the University of British Columbia also enabled a semester-long research leave to make inroads into the literature on women, nation, and Céline Dion when I was their UBC Scholar. McGill and UBC both granted me some financial support for conference travel and research-related expenses. At the University of Toronto Press, Siobhan McMenemy was a thorough and savvy editor of the manuscript; Ryan van Huijstee guided me expertly through the publication process. I am indebted as well to the two anonymous readers for the University of Toronto Press; their nuanced and balanced reports, which engaged seriously and carefully with the conceptual and practical interests of the book, served as important guides to the book's final revisions. The University of Toronto Press's Manuscript Review

Committee also provided a detailed report full of useful information, including wonderful suggestions for illustrations. The manuscript was honoured by the Northeast Modern Language Association's Book Prize for 2009. Feedback from the anonymous reader for NEMLA arrived at a crucial moment in the book's revisions.

Thank you to those who assisted me in finding, getting copies of, and granting permission to reproduce the photographs in this volume: Sue Turmel, Coordonnatrice campagnes et commandites at le Théâtre du Nouveau Monde; Nathalie Le Coz; Julie Fecteau, archivist in the Service des bibliothèques et archives at the Université de Sherbrooke; Marielle Lavertu, archivist at la Bibliothèque et Archives nationales du Québec; Collections Canada; Kris Lingle of AEG Worldwide; Catherine Hobbs and Emily Monks-Leeson at Library and Archives Canada; Michel Vaïs; Josée Lefebvre at Usine-C/Carbone 14; Danielle Gagnon at the Théâtre du Rideau Vert; Karine Hachey and Isabelle Roy at the Cirque du Soleil.

Sections of my discussion of Marco Micone's dramatic trilogy in chapter 4 first appeared in my article, 'Devenir Autre: The Languages of Marco Micone's culture immigrée,' published in Theatre Research in Canada / Recherches théâtrales au Canada 25: 1–2 (2004). They are reprinted by permission of Theatre Research in Canada / Recherches théâtrales au Canada, c/o Graduate Drama Centre, University of Toronto, 214 College Street, 3rd Floor, Toronto, ON M5T 2Z9. Tel: 416-978-7984; Fax: 416-971-1378; Email: tric.rtac@utoronto.ca; Web: http://www.lib.unb.ca/Texts/TRIC/.

For her invaluable kinship work with my two young children, I am deeply grateful to Cassandra Whyte. Her labours helped make mine possible.

My most significant debts – and those I am most happy to have the opportunity to acknowledge here – are to my family. My parents, Brenda and Morrison Hurley, have supported – and I hope derived some pleasure from – my career in theatre through a number of stages, from its early days in performance (mercifully now abandoned) to its more recent incarnation in scholarship. I thank from the bottom of my heart my husband, Mark Elkin, for his abiding love, quick wit, and quicker laughter, as well as his geographical flexibility. I dedicate this book to our two children, Hugh and Beatrice Elkin.

NATIONAL PERFORMANCE
Representing Quebec from Expo 67 to Céline Dion

chapter one

Introduction

From 27 April to 29 October 1967, Quebec hosted fifty million visitors at the 1967 World's Fair and Exposition, catapulting the region onto the world stage. Key to Quebec's dramatic entrance was the Quebec Pavilion. By day, its mirrored façade reflected the Pavilions of Ontario and France that flanked it (Fig. 1.1). Its reflections evoked the Confederation of the Canadas – Upper Canada (Ontario) and Lower Canada (Quebec) – with Nova Scotia and New Brunswick into the Dominion of Canada in 1867 – the centenary of which Expo 67 celebrated. They also flagged Quebec's aspirations to independent nation-state status by positioning Quebec as a peer among nations. By night, the reflections on the pavilion's envelope gave way to the interior's illuminated exhibits (Fig. 1.2). Inside were revealed a modern, industrial nation's technologies, arts, and inventions, the tools for building a durable state. Expo visitors could see the engines for constructing Quebec's national bid during this politically insurgent period.

The Quebec Pavilion has been usefully read as metaphor for an increasingly urgent Québécois national project. In this analysis, the pavilion is deemed 'national' (i.e., Québécois) inasmuch as its surface *reflects* national characteristics, values, and histories, or to the extent that its interior *constructs* the same. This conventional reading of Expo 67's representational labours indicates the dominance of these two linking figures in scholarship on national performance: reflection and construction. By 'representational labours' I intend representations that have a referential relation to an existing (if variable) idea of nation; they may support or contest that idea and they are decoded through analysis of signifier (the representation) and signified (the nation). However, the example of Expo also directs our attention to the performance's oft-overlooked

1.1 Quebec Pavilion and minirail by day at Expo 67.
© Government of Canada. Reproduced with the permission of the Minister of Public
Works and Government Services Canada (2009). Source: Library and Archives Canada /
Canadian Corporation for the 1967 World Exhibition fonds.

emotional labours – the production, management, and distribution of
connections through affective appeals. For the Quebec Pavilion gave not
only a *sign* of Quebec's national status in its ideological encodings, but
also a *sense* of *québécité* (Quebec-ness) in its intense affective address. The
pavilion's 'total environment' featured fully soundtracked, uninterrupted pedestrian circuits often surrounded by moving images by Québécois filmmakers that encompassed the visual field. It immersed visitors

1.2 Quebec Pavilion at night at Expo 67.
© Government of Canada. Reproduced with the permission of the Minister of Public
Works and Government Services Canada (2009). Source: Library and Archives Canada /
Canadian Corporation for the 1967 World Exhibition fonds.

in a thrilling experience of modernity and technological innovation *à la québécoise.*

National Performance: Representing Quebec from Expo 67 to Céline Dion offers a new way of perceiving theatrical and cultural performances as 'national' by attending to this affective experience. As readings of the Quebec Pavilion illustrate, the traditional focus on a performance object's representational labours vis-à-vis the nation leads scholars to rely on the figures of reflection and construction to define how performance stands in for nation. My attention to performance's emotional labours vis-à-vis nation – the ways in which their forms implicate audiences corporeally and affectively, the intensity and range of responses they elicit – activates an expanded taxonomy of figures for theorizing performance-nation relations. Developing the hermeneutic possibilities beyond the figures of reflection and construction, *National Performance* offers three new keywords for theorizing performance as national: simulation, metonymy, and affection. Each figure anchors one chapter and is elaborated through its workings in a particular case-study drawn from my research in modern Québécois theatrical and cultural performance; these include: the 1967 World's Fair and Exposition (construction), Michel Tremblay's play *Les belles-sœurs* (reflection), immigrant and polyglot author Marco Micone's manifesto poem and dramatic trilogy (simulation), Carbone 14's image-theatre (metonymy), and pop diva Céline Dion's popular music (affection). Ultimately, I suggest that the category of emotional labour provides performance scholars with an alternate point of departure for perceiving the national, one which relies less on how performances stand in for the nation than on how performances weave shared emotional repertoires. As a result of this renewed attention to a kind of labour often obscured or hidden from public awareness, women's roles in national processes also come into view. Moreover, their roles are expanded beyond those to which they have often been condemned – as figures or symbols of nation, like England's Britannia or France's Marianne, for instance; they emerge, rather as actors.

A note on what I mean by performance is in order here, for it not only defines the range of aesthetic objects I analyse in the following pages, it also indicates the critical vocabulary and approach I use. In the first instance, I use 'performance' as an umbrella category, one that encompasses the full range of embodied practices and events 'from ritual to theatre and back,' in the famed words of Richard Schechner, one of the founders of Performance Studies (1988, 106–52). This definition of performance as a broad spectrum of human actions that are framed or displayed allows me to examine not only the performing arts – theatre, dance, and music to be precise – but also the heightened social and entertainment environment of a World's Fair and the public displays of identity and allegiance provoked by literary scandals. The umbrella term enables investigating the common conceptual rubrics – like reflection and construction – which would understand such varied 'strips of behaviour' (Schechner 1985, 35) as nonetheless representing a 'nation.' In the second, my use of performance points to the theoretical tools of Performance Studies, a field rich in nuanced examinations of representation and focused on the lived effects of invented 'realities.' Performance Studies is a particularly apt disciplinary vantage point from which to examine the real effects of what Michael Taussig calls 'the really made-up' – 'the political art and social power of make-believe'; it takes seriously the affective and lived reality that representation offers to its audiences (1993, ix). Performance Studies does not espouse or practice a single critical method; rather, it draws on an array of methods from fieldwork to archival exegesis to Marxist analysis to feminist praxis (and beyond) as needed and appropriate to the particular instance of performance at issue in order to calibrate the relation between real and really made-up, between reality and reality-effects. However, one unifying feature of the critical practices of Performance Studies is that they tend to inquire into the social and/or political effects of representational practices and to investigate their premises, paying particular attention to power relations. A successful assessment of performance's role in making, sustaining, and/or complicating ideas of nation requires close attention to how the fictions of performance create new worlds and persuade audiences of their reality, as well as how audiences interpret such an invented reality. Among the methods at the disposal of the Performance Studies scholar, I have drawn most frequently on formal analysis of the different generic features of the performances at issue (e.g., realist drama, dance, manifesto), semiotic analysis of the several and often contradictory 'languages of the stage' including gesture, design, sound and the like, and reception theory.

In each of the case studies that follow, those figural relations of performance to nation are coded to a certain extent in the event's formal apparatus; for instance, realist plays (unsurprisingly) posit a metaphorical truth-relation between their representations and their real-world models, a relation that understands theatre to reflect a pre-existing, stable referent: the nation. Excavating these codes requires a close-reading approach to the performance texts, one that seeks to describe the performance's formal operations, to assemble what Robyn Warhol describes as a 'semiotics of *how* [these] cultural texts convey meaning [specifically the meaningfulness of performance to national formations], rather than of what they mean to say.' In this approach I borrow from Warhol who, in *Having a Good Cry*, distinguishes between the analysis of dramatic structures and conventions described here, and what she calls the 'old formalist method for conquering ambiguity and paradox to arrive at a unified meaning for a (great) text' in which, I might add, form and context are mutually reinforcing (2003, 25). Rather, like Warhol, I am interested in the meanings generated from the interaction of performance forms with their audiences. Thus, in addition to a close attention to the performances' formal operations, I attend to the performances' uptake in order to assess how performance-nation relations are coded in varying modes

of interpretation by a range of interpretive communities including theatre critics, prize juries, and soft-rock listeners. To do so, I conduct discursive analyses of critical reception, paying special attention to the reading
strategies employed, their default assumptions and enabling conditions.
The goal of these analyses is less to determine the success of a performance's conveyance of meaning to an audience (discovered in a mutually
reinforcing reading of the performance's meaning by performance text
and reception community); rather, its purpose is to query how, why, and
on what basis a performance is read as national, sometimes regardless of
the performance's own contrary indications.

I am interested in unearthing the habits of thought that structure
contradictory perceptions of the 'national' in cultural production and
critical reception. This leads me to an analysis of the mimetic figures
subtending production and reception contracts in historical moments at
which they come into conflict in modern Quebec – that conflict providing to at least some degree what ethnolinguist Richard Bauman dubs the
'heightened communication' or sense of self-reflexiveness that defines
performance (1989, 263). Investigating consonant and mismatched
figures in production and reception is one way to approach putatively
national performances that miss or exceed their mark, and putatively
non-national readers who misrecognize the representations of their dis-
enfranchisement in theatrical and cultural performance. By what representational labours do certain performances come to be recognized as
national? What happens when audiences are *not* good or, in reception
theory's terms, 'ideal' readers?

The critical taxonomy I develop in the following pages, tested in its
internationally resonant case studies, models a finely grained approach
to the study of performance-nation links by accounting for those links'
variations in dimension, duration and level of activation by different
interpretive communities. These relational subtleties are critical for
interpreting the changing sociopolitical situations produced by decolonization, multicultural state policies, and late capitalism that typify
contemporary nations. These conditions, in which classical notions of
nation as a people with a shared history, language, and territory must
be reconfigured to account for sub- and supranational identities and
networks, are matched by modern theatrical and cultural performance's
mixed modes and hybridized aesthetic vocabularies. Neither 'nation'
nor 'performance' allows for transparent reference between the two
terms such that one might perfectly stand in for the other. Further, nation and performance's increasingly encompassing orbits draw in ever

more radically diversified audiences who bring their own modes of interpretation to bear on performance-nation links. *National Performance* offers figures that more aptly capture the often torqued and sometimes strained relations across difference in performance production and reception. Here again, these alternate figures to the dominant (reflection and construction) liberate woman – as fictional figure and lived reality – from a limited and stereotyped form of national 'service.'

Modern Quebec wrestles with precisely these sociopolitical conditions, sharing the challenges and potentialities of other postcolonial and settler nations, particularly in the Americas. Further, in its attempts to alter its status from subnational entity (a province within Canada) to sovereign nation-state – attempts which have entailed significant social, political and economic reform – Quebec has often relied on theatrical and cultural performance to cement the idea of Quebec-as-nation. In the past half-century, the dominant ideologies of Québécois nationalism have shifted from cultural nationalism to transculturalism to globalism, transforming notions of *québécité* (Quebec-ness). This same period has witnessed an efflorescence of theatrical and cultural production characterized by experiments with form and language, an enthusiastic global audience, and controversy over its national credentials. Each of the performances examined in *National Performance* has focused the international spotlight on Quebec: for instance, Carbone 14's productions have anchored international theatre festivals; Céline Dion is the best-selling female music artist of all time (and the third-best celebrity golfer in the world!); Michel Tremblay's plays have been translated into twenty-six languages and produced worldwide. Moreover, each has been subject to intense public scrutiny in Quebec over whether it produces legitimate and fecund or illegitimate and sterile national surrogates; controversy has marked the careers of Tremblay, Dion, and playwright Marco Micone as surely as it greeted the unveiling of the Quebec Pavilion at Expo 67.

Moreover, the legitimation controversies provoked by many of my examples point to the continuing necessity of retaining the nation as a category of analysis. It is because of this palpable and persuasive lived reality of the national fact, the banality and intimacy of its experience as identified by Michael Billig (1995), that I train my eyes on the nation form, even in political and economic conditions that traverse and imperil its efficacy and power. The nation remains a signal pole for identity-formation. Moreover, its state institutions function as operative and sometimes oppressive gatekeepers to people's movements and enfranchisement. With that acknowledgment of the nation-state's real power, I willingly

concede that the nation is an insufficient category for the kinds of multiple and moving identities that typify the contemporary world, as scholars of transnationalism and diaspora performance culture like Aparna
Dharwadker (2003), May Joseph (1999), and Joseph Roach (1996) have
proven. Indeed, it is the nation's insufficiency to fully capture the subject that requires a new way of conceptualizing its relation to performance and thence to identity. As important for this study, a recent spate of
monographs on national theatre traditions by Jen Harvie (2005), Alan
Filewod (2002), Steve Wilmer (2002), Helen Gilbert (1998), and Loren
Kruger (1992) testify to the enduring significance of the national category for theatre and performance scholars. I work here, then, to examine the kinds of relations forged between performance and nation, to
elucidate how ideas of performance and nation legitimize one another.

In keeping with the book's overarching goal to revise the terms by
which performance defines its relationships to the nation, each chapter
considers performances that act as lightning rods for public discussion
of *québécité*, a changing sensibility of Québécois nation-ness, in the second half of the twentieth century. The case studies limn the contours of
cultural production in modern Quebec – from avant-garde to popular,
architectural to musical, local to global. The range of objects across the
high-culture/low-culture register allows me to investigate performance's
official roles in nation formation as well as its unofficial, informal, and
eccentric uses in the momentary crystallizing of national subjectivities. I
also choose objects that push at the margins of how nation, culture, and
national culture are commonly understood (in linguistic, geographical,
and memorial terms, for example), forcing new thinking on the performance-nation dynamic.

The first three chapters elaborate how models of national mimesis as
metaphor (reflection and construction) establish themselves as primary
modes for reading theatrical and cultural performance. Chapter 2, 'Marginals, Metaphors, and Mimesis,' lays out the conceptual and historical
groundwork for this study, offering examples of Québécois performance
that often go unrecognized as such on the international circuit. My in-
vestigations of these more common figures of nationalization in the examples of Expo 67 (chapter 3) and Michel Tremblay's first-produced and
best-known play, *Les belles-sœurs* (chapter 4) reveal the feminized ground
on which these figures operate. The last three chapters propose alternative modes for figuring the performance-nation relationship where that
link is increasingly oblique and strained. Here I analyse the dramatic and
critical oeuvre of Marco Micone (chapter 5), the devised productions

of the image-theatre troupe Carbone 14 (chapter 6), and the musical stylings of Céline Dion (chapter 7). The turned mimetic figures of these last chapters – simulation, metonymy, and affection, respectively – illuminate the affective response performance generates in order to examine its emotional labours vis-à-vis nation. The concluding chapter, 'Feminist (Re)production,' takes the example of feminist theatre practice from the 1970s and 80s to re-examine the concepts central to this study and to national mimesis: production and reproduction.

In sum, *National Performance* proposes a new perspective for reading 'nation-ness' in theatrical and cultural performance using performance-based conceptual vocabularies, specifically those clustering around mimesis. In so doing, it redefines the terms available for thinking the performance-nation relationship, highlights their political problematics, and uncovers their gendered dimensions. My goal is to open the field of national theatre and performance studies to new objects and modes of interpretation. The paths I offer here alter not only what can be recognized as national (in this case, as Québécois) but also the conditions of perception for national performance.

chapter two

Marginals, Metaphors, and Mimesis

2007 was a big year for Québécois cultural production. Over ten million people worldwide bought a ticket to a Cirque du Soleil show. Céline Dion closed her sold-out, five-year run at Las Vegas's Caesars Palace Hotel and Casino theatre, the Colosseum. (And none too soon, given the devastating effects of the global financial crisis of the late 2000s on entertainment tourism generally and Las Vegas in particular.) Director Denis Marleau's *Fantasmagories technologiques* were the theatrical highlight of the international theatre and dance festival, the Festival transamériques (formerly the Festival de théâtre des amériques). Choreographer Édouard Locke's company, La La La Human Steps, returned to the stage after a lengthy absence with *Amjad,* a new piece inspired by iconic romantic ballets. Another Montreal-based contemporary dance choreographer, Marie Chouinard, was awarded the Grand Prix du Conseil des Arts de Montréal and made an Officer of the Order of Canada. And Robert Lepage landed a contract to stage opera's most challenging work – Wagner's *Der Ring des Nibelungen* – at its most prestigious North American venue, New York's Metropolitan Opera.

Most of these names will likely mean something to you, even if you do not live in, come from, or pay much attention to Quebec. For instance, La La La Human Steps, the hyperkinetic dance troupe founded in 1980, pioneered a gravity-defying kind of extreme dance style that garnered the troupe two New York Dance and Performance Awards (1983 and 1986). Along with Ginette Laurin's Ô Vertigo danse, La La La has toured the *nouveau bouger montréalais* on dance and theatre festival circuits in major capitals of Europe, Asia, and America and in coproductions with Paris's Théâtre de la Ville, Amsterdam's Het Muziektheater, Vienna's ImPulsTanz, and Seoul's LG Arts Centre, among others, for the past thirty years. They built the *nouveau bouger*'s reputation for inventive visuals, athletic and high-risk movement, plus intimate and provocative subjects contained within a dramatic narrative scaffolding. Denis Marleau, one of contemporary theatre's leading directors (Féral 1998), has also made his mark on the international scene; his production of Lessing's *Nathan le Sage* opened the 1997 Avignon Festival and his *Urfaust* was selected for Weimar 99, 1999's 'Cultural Capital of Europe.' He was made a Chevalier des Arts et des Lettres by France's Ministry of Culture in 2002. Having forged his style in the 1980s using an innovative mix of theatre and 'la nouvelle danse,' Marleau has since turned to a minimalist scenography and movement repertoire. Indeed, his most recent productions have effectively eliminated live, present actors from his stage in an effort to focus the creative and reception processes on the word (Marleau and Jasmin 2004; Jacques 2005, 2006; Therrien 2008). *Fantasmagories technologiques* featured actors' previously recorded performances projected on dummies and masks, making for a kind of video-installation theatre. In his experimentation with new technologies and his focus on the voice, Marleau is joined by Marie Brassard, the actor, writer, and producer who first came into prominence for her collective creation work with Robert Lepage. (She co-authored *Polygraphe* [1987] with Lepage and participated centrally in the creation of his troupe's germinal works *La Trilogie des dragons* [1985] and *Les sept branches de la rivière Ota* [1994].) She is now as well known for her recent solo performance work – *Jimmy, créature de rêve* (2001), *La noirceur* (2003), *Peepshow* (2005), and *L'invisible* (2008) – in which she experiments with a vocoder (voice encoder) machine to produce a range of different characters created out of how they sound. And of course the international reach and market penetration of Céline Dion and the Cirque du Soleil make it practically impossible to not have them mean something to you.

Yet many of these examples – however well known – are not necessarily well known *as Québécois* on the international stage. As Carl Wilson points out in his excellent book, *Let's Talk about Love: A Journey to the End of Taste* (2007), Americans in particular often mistake Dion for French or indefinably 'other,' and rather less frequently make the connection to Quebec. I cannot tell you the number of times I have heard people describe the Cirque du Soleil as 'French' (i.e., from France). (The most memorable occasion was after giving a paper on the troupe at the Modern Language Association's annual conference.) This misperception is not so surprising when one considers that: the Cirque produces in a circus tradition that does not have especially deep roots in Quebec cul-

ture; the limited amount of language spoken during their shows happens in an invented language accompanied by a world-beat soundtrack;
and their performance worlds are populated by an international cast of
performers. Thus, the Cirque du Soleil's performance codes do not bear
recognizable markers of *québécité* as defined by location, language, genre
of performance, and content (see Fig. 2.1). The Cirque is a national
stealth-figure whose work does not fit into the generally accepted criteria
for inclusion in national theatre history.

As a way into those criteria and their limitations, let us take the example of theatre and film director, actor, producer, and writer Robert
Lepage, the only Québécois artist except playwright Michel Tremblay
to boast a significant response to his work by Anglophone scholars. His
'national' status proves ambivalent if read according to the four dominant criteria by which theatre historians select which theatres, productions, and personnel might be included in a national theatre history as
presented by S. E. Wilmer (2003). By Wilmer's criteria – criteria, I should
specify, that are descriptive of work in the field, not prescriptive of its
future practice – Robert Lepage rates as Québécois by virtue of only one.
As a francophone member of the dominant ethnic and linguistic group
in Quebec, Lepage meets the criterion of 'ethnicity' and is therefore
on solid ground for inclusion in a Québécois national theatre history.
Although based in Quebec City at his multidisciplinary creation-research
centre, La Caserne, and thus meeting the basic 'geography' criterion
Wilmer spies in most national theatre histories, Lepage challenges that
same national index by his near-constant globetrotting (Hunt 1989; Fricker 2008) and his artistic affiliations with other nation-states' national
institutions like Canada's National Arts Centre, England's Royal National Theatre, and Sweden's Dramaten.[1] As to language, Wilmer's second
category of the national, Lepage's productions have consistently used
more than one language, and often languages not strongly associated
with Quebec (e.g., Czech and Japanese in *The Seven Streams of the River
Ota*). In addition, he has increased the purchase of other 'languages of
the stage,' in Patrice Pavis's felicitous terminology (1982), by emphasizing the visual aspects of theatrical production. Some contend that his
creative approach and image-theatre style add up to a distinctly Québécois 'aesthetic,' another of Wilmer's categories. Certainly, within Canada
Lepage and his image-theatre compatriots, like Marleau, the troupe Carbone 14, and their protégés in Pigeons International are often contrasted
with the common look and feel of English-speaking Canadian text-based
theatre; here commentators emphasize image-theatre workers' creative

2.1 The 'Slave Cage' act in *Kà* by Robert Lepage for the Cirque du Soleil at
the MGM Grand, Las Vegas – an example of Québécois cultural products
exceeding the borders of the Québécois territory.
Photo: Tomas Muscionico. Costumes: Marie-Chantal Vaillancourt.
© 2004 Cirque du Soleil.

processes built on devising and gestural vocabularies. Within a larger frame of analysis, however, their aesthetic resonates with those of Robert Wilson, Ariane Mnouchkine, and Peter Brook, thereby relativizing the suggestion of Lepage and his colleagues' specifically Québécois aesthetic (Innes 2005).

That artists like Lepage and the Cirque might be illegible as Québécois on the international stage is one thing. Indeed, many have commented on how ambiguous local markers increase the chances of international success. However, their *québécité* is often at issue in Quebec as well, even among those who acknowledge and even celebrate these artists' Québécois roots. Here again, the Cirque du Soleil, Robert Lepage, and Céline Dion are emblematic. In public statements and press releases, current and recent Quebec governments have lauded these companies' international work as exemplary of a uniquely Québécois creativity and ingenuity. Quebec governments have, moreover, formalized the link between Quebec and these artists by deploying Lepage, the Cirque, and Dion as Quebec's international representatives, naming them 'cultural ambassadors' (Harvie and Hurley 1999). Moreover, advocates for the performing arts in Quebec capitalize on that rhetoric in making their representations to provincial and federal funding bodies. To take but one example, in 2005 the Conseil québécois du théâtre, the Regroupement québécois de la danse, and the Conseil québécois de la musique presented to Canada's Minister of Foreign Affairs a document supporting the desirability of increased (or at least sustained) international touring by Québécois performing artists; it was entitled *Les arts de la scène, grands ambassadeurs de l'identité canadienne à l'étranger* (*Les arts de la scène* 2005). Yet, precisely because of their international reach as well as the 'globalizing' of their product that that kind of reach requires, the Cirque and Dion in particular are often cast as 'American' or at least as less fully or unambiguously 'Québécois.' In Céline Dion's case, for example, her musical performances avoid particularizing national resonances. Even her public image – as glamorous pop diva and contented *mère de famille* – is ambiguously linked to a Québécois national imaginary. If she is often positioned by the Quebec government as an exemplary *Québécoise*, she is as frequently taken for an abjected national body with which one disidentifies to secure one's *québécité*. Dion's national authenticity problems circulate around criticisms that she has sold out to transnational capital interests; that having succumbed to the global pop market, learned English, and relocated outside of Quebec she is no longer truly *Québécoise*; and that her overproduced English-language music does not sound

Québécois because it comes from an Anglo-American musical tradition. These factors render Dion unrecognizable as Québécois despite being, nonetheless, *Québécoise.*

It is the resistance these well known Québécois productions manifest to being readily legible as Québécois via their stage signs that interests me here. How do performances come to mean and matter as Québécois? Further, and a greater challenge, how do they come to do that when they do not appear to be distinctly Québécois? To meet such a challenge, this book both provides a critical history of performances commonly associated with *québécité* and assesses historiographic practices in studies of national performance. I follow the twisted routes by which emblematic cultural productions arrive at *québécité* and come to redefine it. Attention to such trajectories exposes a larger issue for national theatre and performance historiography, namely, the grounds for inclusion in a national theatre history. At first glance my chosen examples may seem self-evident as likely candidates for inclusion in a national narrative – Expo 67, Michel Tremblay's *Les belles-sœurs,* Marco Micone's oeuvre, Carbone 14's dance-theatre, and Céline Dion. However, they were not nearly so apparently Québécois at the time of their enthronement. Rather, they precipitated significant public discussion over the meanings and values of *québécité* in changing social, political, and economic landscapes across the past forty years. In addition, they required critics and audiences to develop new reading strategies, which account for their formal innovations and assess anew theatrical *québécité.* In the period covered by this book, the coordinates shift from rural to urban to cosmopolitan, from the French language to a Québécois vernacular, from farmers to working-class heroes to women to immigrants, and from an insular self-sustaining economy and culture to an increasingly transnational one.

My larger project, then, is to broaden the framework of national theatre historiography by pursuing which performances are designated Québécois, and why. In this line of inquiry I join theatre historians and historiographers like S.E. Wilmer, Bruce McConachie, and Alan Filewod, each of whom has theorized the conditions of production for *national* theatre history specifically, its conceptual foundations, its narrative tendencies, and its often restricted compass. For instance, Filewod's groundbreaking work, *Performing Canada: The Nation Enacted in the Imagined Theatre,* rethinks 'the conceptual foundations of Canadian theatre and, by extension, the Canadian nation which that theatre performs' (2002, x). Offering Marc Lescarbot's pageant *Le Théâtre de Neptune en la Nouvelle France* (1606) as the prototype of the relationship between 'theatre' and

'Canada,' Filewod claims that Canadian theatre marks and masks that which constitutes the postcolonial nation: the absence of an authentic identity claim and the displacement of those who might possess one, namely, aboriginals. In some respects, *National Performance* is a feminist, Québécois rejoinder to Filewod's project, as it marks and *un*masks the infrastructure of 'national' performance, namely emotional labour and women (as both figures and actual people).

As manifest in the example of Robert Lepage above, the criteria for national selection Wilmer identifies are insufficient measures of *québécité* that, in the end, tend to lean rather heavily on Wilmer's criterion of 'ethnicity' as guarantor of nation-ness. How then to deal with unruly or reluctant or non-normative Québécois productions? By what measure might they be deemed national without making recourse to the dubious category of ethnicity? *National Performance* answers the nationality question in ways that refuse the usual criteria of national performance. In a departure from previous scholarship on the national question, I investigate the relationships national theatre history presumes between cultural production and nation, relationships that form the conceptual grounds on which those national designations are made. What conceptual mechanisms allow for the linking of performance to nation? For instance, does the celebrated choreography of Marie Chouinard stand in a relation of homology, analogy, metaphor, or metonymy to Quebec? And what are the consequences of those terms of engagement? In short, I examine the representational contracts that theatre historians and cultural commentators strike between performance and nation to take a given production, playwright, or event into the national fold.

In many ways, my project's worrying over the means by which certain people, institutions, and cultural products attain the status of national while others are exiled to sub- or non-national status is a very Québécois critical preoccupation. In 'Culture and Its Values,' Sherry Simon identifies 'a persistent core of critical activity' in Quebec since at least the end of the nineteenth century: the 'articulation of the link between representation and value, between literary and social configurations' (1991a, 167). Moreover, and more pointedly, in Quebec the question is of enduring and real interest. One need only recall the responses to Michel Tremblay and Robert Lepage's recent critical comments about the *indépendantiste* cause as practised by the Parti Québécois under the leadership of André Boisclair. In April 2006 both lamented the party's emphasis on the economy over culture as the key indicator of Quebec's readiness to assume sovereignty. For Tremblay, this represented an estrangement from and bastardization of *indépendantisme*'s fundamental principles; Lepage allowed that he was 'less convinced than before' of the validity and possibility of the sovereigntist cause. Victor Lévy-Beaulieu, author, publisher, and long-time self-appointed guardian of literary *québécité*, launched an immediate attack in one of Montreal's newspapers, *La Presse*. 'It doesn't surprise me that those people who are known the world over forget where they're from, forget their roots. It's a case of early senility' (Beauchemin and Péloquin 2006, A13).[2] While several responses were less punitive than VLB's and many even supported Tremblay and Lepage's reservations, that Tremblay and Lepage's remarks made headlines and sparked debate in the editorial pages of the largest French-language daily in North America speaks to the volatility and import of the national question. Moreover, this debate is but the most recent in a performance genealogy of theatrical and literary scandals concerned with a similar constellation of issues – origins, language, political values, and their relation to literary and theatrical value (Hurley 2009b). Although national legitimation crises are not everyday occurrences in Quebec, they do occur rather regularly and with a never-diminishing urgency. (Most recently, a plan by the Commission des champs de bataille nationaux to re-enact the Battle of the Plains of Abraham in the summer of 2009 to commemorate the 250th anniversary of its occurrence was scuttled in response to a significant public outcry and some menacing comments. This 1759 battle of the Seven Years War saw British General James Wolfe's army defeat General the Marquis de Montcalm's French army and thus secure Britain's colonial domination over what would eventually become the Dominion of Canada; in Quebec the battle is called 'la Conquête' (see Radio-Canada.ca 2009).) Their recurrence testifies to the debate's continuing felt necessity and has produced some finely grained attributions of *québécité* that merit greater attention.

The historical and continuing importance of the performing arts to Québécois national movements and imaginaries – be they cultural nationalist, corporate transnational, or transcultural/multicultural – recommends Québécois performance as a fruitful location for this investigation. In Quebec, performance's national labours are enacted in more pressurized conditions than they are in established, internationally recognized nation-states. Quebec is what political scientists call a 'small nation'; it perceives itself as a national community, based on a common history, territory, language, and culture, yet it lacks a state that would ratify this self-concept. Rather, it is ensconced within a larger state apparatus, the Dominion of Canada, in relation to whose population the 'small nation' is a minority. Statelessness is a matter of degree, however. Although Quebec lacks a sovereign state designation, within Canada's federal system it functions in many respects as a quasi-independent territory. Its provincial leaders since the 1960s have bolstered a sense and practice of Quebec's national status by maximizing its control over the policy sectors within provincial jurisdiction, including education, natural resources, and, significantly, culture.[3]

The period on which this book focuses, from the mid-1960s to the mid-2000s, has been a critical one in Quebec's national formation marked by changing ideologies of *québécité* in response to altered hemispheric economic relations and an increasingly globalized cultural field. The 1960s are generally deemed the decade of an expressly *modern* Quebec's birth. Its first six years are commonly referred to as the Quiet Revolution and are characterized by the transformation of Quebec society into a modern welfare state with a liberalized economy, a secular outlook, and nationalized energy and banking institutions. It was in 1967 that France's President Charles de Gaulle proclaimed, 'Vive le Québec libre!' from the balcony of Montreal's City Hall, providing a rallying cry of Québécois *indépendantistes*. The following day, de Gaulle visited the 1967 World's Fair and Exposition, Expo 67, held in and around Montreal's Old Port. In part an expression of Québécois pride and national futurity – as we'll see in the next chapter – Expo 67 was brought into being as the capstone celebration of the Dominion of Canada's centennial year. The 1960s also witness the emergence of the notion of *québécité* that is central to this study. In his etymology of the term, historian Jocelyn Létourneau locates its genesis in the Quiet Revolution, during which time the idea of Quebec-as-nation solidified in cultural, political, social, and economic practices. He asserts that *québécité* is 'a project/process of (re) construction of Quebec that develops in reaction (read: in opposition) to the project/process of the country's Canadianization' (2006, 159).[4] *Québécité*'s political aspect found its organized expression in the Parti québécois, founded in 1968.

Since this foundational decade of *québécisation*, two referenda on sovereignty have been called, demonstrating again the national project's continued vitality. The first was held in 1980 and the second in 1995, the latter defeated by less than 1 per cent of the vote. Having failed thus far to secure the Quebec nation with a sovereign Quebec state, successive Quebec governments have sought constitutional recognition of the province's distinct cultural and linguistic status.[5] On the international circuit, Quebec asserts the status of a proto-nation-state by implementing a form of 'paradiplomacy,' institutionalizing its powers in the international sphere, as granted by the Canadian federal government (Thérien, Bélanger and Gosselin 1993, 260).[6] In the political sphere, the Quebec government boasts representatives abroad in established foreign delegations. As of 2008, the Ministry of International Relations had established a diplomatic network of twenty-five 'general delegations,' 'delegations,' 'bureaus,' and 'trade branches' throughout Western Europe, francophone Africa, Asia, and the Americas ('Offices Abroad'). In the commercial sphere, it ratifies *ententes*, agreements that bind upon the province and a foreign government and pertain, for instance, to economic and cultural matters (Thérien et.al. 1993, 262–3).

Like other nations without a state, Quebec relies on cultural production to vouch for its national status; for instance, the Quebec government enacts affiliations with international peers through international cultural networks, particularly those travelled by Québécois cultural products, a practice that began in earnest during the preparatory stages of Expo 67. Historian Magali Deleuze writes of the period from the late 1950s through 1967, 'The Quebecois began building individual ties with certain African and North African [magrébin] countries: visits by journalists and intellectuals, university invitations, commercial exchanges of business people' (2008, 50). At home, cultural institutions have benefited from significant governmental, philanthropic, and audience support, resulting in a vibrant cultural scene. Since the mid-twentieth century, Quebec theatre has institutionalized, professionalized, and nationalized. The Centre d'essai des auteurs dramatiques, now called simply the Centre des auteurs dramatiques (Playwrights' Centre) (founded 1965) supports playwrights' creative development through workshopping, reading, and archiving plays by Québécois dramatists; the Conseil des arts de la région métropolitaine (Metropolitan Regional Arts Council) has provided financial support to artists in the form of grants since 1956. A period of durable infrastructure provision for the performing arts changed the face of mid-twentieth century urban centres. The curtain went up on Montreal's major regional theatre, the Théâtre du Nouveau Monde (Theatre of the New World) in 1951; Place des Arts – a multi-space performance venue – was erected downtown Montreal in 1963; Quebec City inaugurated the Grand Théâtre de Québec in 1971 (Beauchamp 2003). Training schools like the Conservatoire de musique et d'art dramatique, a network of performing arts schools opened in 1942, Montreal's École nationale de théâtre du Canada (National Theatre School) (founded 1961), and the École nationale du Cirque (National Circus School), also

in Montreal (founded 1981) offer professional training in the performing arts, furnishing a kind of personnel infrastructure. (Union des artistes, the theatrical union, has supported that personnel since 1937.)
Scholarly organizations and learned journals soon followed: the Société
québécoise d'études théâtrales (Quebec Society for Theatre Studies)
(founded in 1976) publishes *Annuaire théâtral*; *Cahiers de théâtre Jeu* becomes the journal of record for Québécois theatre shortly after its first
volume appears in 1976. Québécois theatre also nationalizes: the Théâtre d'aujourd'hui (Theatre of Today) mounts exclusively Québécois
plays; major writers and publishing houses collaborate on translations
of the European repertoire into Québécois (see Brisset 1996; Ladouceur
2005).

Although other parts of Canada experienced a similar efflorescence
of the performing arts and erected their own monuments, training programs, and societies during this period (see Rubin 1996), as a small nation, Quebec's building spree had differently inflected stakes. For small
nations, establishing the nation's existence, its reality, if you will, is especially pressing. Their nations must be established as 'real' to make a persuasive case for statehood, but because they lack a state to legitimate and
enforce the national fact, small nations' fictional status is underscored.
Since the political realm cannot offer its own proofs of the nation's reality, the fictions of cultural production frequently bear the burden of
proving *le fait national* (see Handler 1988). Viewed from this angle, the
vital role of cultural production in the national project in Quebec is clear:
cultural production depicts the nation's attributes onstage; this makes
'the nation' those depictions' ultimate referee and guarantor of meaning. Granting the nation referent status through performance effectively
establishes the off-stage 'nation' as fact. Thus the relation between cultural production and nation is mimetic in nature: culture represents nation. Hence, too, the criteria Wilmer draws out of his analysis of national
theatre histories: 'national' cultural productions mirror a nation's geography, language(s), aesthetic(s) and ethnicity(ies). It is this naively
mimetic relationship between cultural production and ideas of nation
– most evident in but by no means limited to small nations like Quebec –
that *National Performance* strives to complicate.

To illuminate what I am calling 'national mimesis,' the concept that
stands at the centre of my argument, as well as its stakes to small nations
like Quebec, let me take an example from the archives of Québécois
theatre history. In a 1949 address at the Université de Montréal entitled
'Pour un théâtre national et populaire,' playwright and burlesque actor

Gratien Gélinas advocated the creation of an indigenous, French-Canadian national drama, saying '*a theatre must be national first and foremost*' (1949, 41). His assertion ran counter to the prevailing theatrical practice at the time when high culture was dominated by French classics and popular culture featured U.S. musicals and popular entertainments.[7] Gélinas proposed replacing representations of customs, manners, and social worlds foreign to Quebec with depictions of 'national' life in local accents. His argument runs as follows: Theatre is the marriage of the stage and the public. In this marriage ('une communion totale' [a complete communion]), the spouses 'must not only come together in the same auditorium, but must also unite, mix together to live the same drama/story' (1949, 36). This theatrical-marital harmony is most completely achieved when the author and the public are 'of the same essence, the same stock, the same past, the same present, the same future' (1949, 37). As evidence of this perfect union, 'the man in the audience *see[s] himself* and murmur[s] the words of the man onstage *from the same emotional place as the actor and at the same time* as him' (Ibid.) The story these well-matched spouses share will be told in '*the most pure dramatic form* – not the only dramatic form but rather the most pure [: ...] *that which would represent the public it addresses in the most direct possible manner*' (1949, 35. Emphasis in original).

'Pour un théâtre national et populaire' exemplifies the dominant mode of categorizing and measuring Quebec-ness in scholarship on national performance: a performance's resemblance to the nation – in language, theme, or character – betokens its nationality.[8] Gélinas privileged sameness, even identity, among author, actor, and audience as a basis for a national theatre. Author, actor, and audience share features upon which nations are built: soul, ethnicity, history, way of life, and a collective sense of futurity. Gélinas discovers the most perfect expression of that similarity in realist drama, where the audience would be represented onstage by characters like themselves and situations resembling their own. A performance's nation-ness would be measured, then, by a standard of 'likeness' or resemblance to social reality. Theatre and nation would stand in an iconic mimetic relation in which 'the icon represents its object "mainly by similarity" between the sign-vehicle and its signified' (Elam 1988, 21). With iconicity as the governing principle, the nation is privileged as the dominant term, the referent and guarantor of performance's national meaning.

But what of those who would be national but do not share the same 'essence, the same stock, the same past' as those depicted on stage? By what routes might those cultural productions whose roots are less pure or deep, whose images are less straightforwardly reflective of the national fact nonetheless be deemed national? The theatrical concept of mimesis serves well in this instance too because mimesis operates via other, less-acknowledged and less-theorized ways in addition to its function as iconic imitation. Elin Diamond explains, '*mimesis* denotes both the activity of representing and the result of it – both a doing and a thing done; both the generative embodied activity of representing (including improvising in music and dance) and a (true) representation (of a model)' (1997, v). By extension, 'national mimesis' is the activity of representing the nation as well as the result of it (an image of the nation). As in the Gélinas example, it is around the idea of a '(true) representation (of a model)' that national mimesis has tended to function in the scholarly literature on national performance. A play's or character's nation-ness is established according to the accuracy of its depiction or re-presentation of a 'real-life,' local referent. This accords with Gélinas's vision whose insularity derives from its insistence on faithful reproduction. This kind of vision prompts Bruce McConachie to call for histories of national theatre and performance traditions that avoid what he names 'monoculturalism,' the 'belief that the culture of their country is ... singular, with its own roots of origin and its unique historical branches.' What paradigms for historical narrative, he asks, are 'better at nudging the prose of historians into structures that recognize that matters of cultural influence and significance must involve all peoples within a country and many outside of it?' (McConachie 2001, 120).

Fortunately, mimesis is not limited to a reproductive or imitative iconic mode. The means by which one thing (say, theatre) comes to stand in for another (say, nation) varies. In the language of semiotics, the relation between signifier and signified may be indexical or symbolic. Indexical signs are 'causally connected with their objects, often physically or through contiguity'; the connection between a symbolic sign and its signified is pure convention (Elam 1988, 21–2). Thus, indexical and symbolic figures like metonymy and simulation may be based in dissimilarity or usage instead of on resemblance. My focus on such turned mimetic figures, figures which organize the following chapters, challenges received practices in the field of national performance history. It opens the national field to marginalized constituencies and cultural productions that, because they are not culturally dominant, are not immediately recognizable as nationally 'authentic.'

The preferred, iconic figural relations between performance and nation mask some rather high stakes not only for Quebec and theatrical performance's mutual legitimation but also for women and other feminized marginal figures. The iconic representational contracts that link performance to nation in Quebec work through (but not often for) women. Feminist theatre historians and historiographers Tracy C. Davis, Susan Bennett, Diana Taylor, and Charlotte Canning have laid bare the often unarticulated yet fully active assumptions about cultural value and authority that privilege male agents and subtend much theatre history. In an effort to rectify this imbalance, each of these historians encourages a far-reaching theoretical project: changing the practice of writing history. For instance, Canning urges 'understanding history as a performance' as such an understanding will 'enable feminists to reveal its performative, that is the iterations and reiterations that make it appear natural and stable, in order to use that understanding to effect ongoing transformation and change' (Canning 2001, 230). Bennett imagines a 'detailed dissection of those categories which have attained particular significance in the articulation of Western theatre history' (2000, 56). Taylor's *Disappearing Acts* (1997) takes up this challenge by dissecting the category of the nation in order to uproot its gendered and misogynist discourses. In the vein of work by Joan Landes and Lynn Hunt on female national figureheads like France's Marianne, Taylor reads the ways in which women are used in national narratives but are not served by them. She highlights as an example a type common to many national histories – woman as metaphor for endangered or vulnerable homeland. In Quebec, woman-as-metaphor-for-nation recurs most insistently in narratives of the Conquest, in which the French colonial territory of present-day Quebec is 'raped' and trapped in an unwanted marriage to English Canada in 1759. French Canada's enforced inclusion in a federal system established and run by Anglo-Canadians cements the gendered relations of dominance and submission between what the novelist Hugh MacLennan memorably allegorized as 'the two solitudes' (1945) for the next two hundred and fifty years. To mention just one instance of where this trope is prominent, Québécois adaptations of Shakespeare from the Quiet Revolution period to the early twenty-first century derive much of their dramatic impact from this scenario (Drouin 2005). In these examples, female figures' diegetic pain – and female actors' on-stage labour – furnishes audiences with the vicarious experience of nation-ness.

If we are to reconceive national performance in terms that may not only use but also serve women and other feminized marginals, we must expand our purview to include the gendered relations assumed between performance and nation. Following Gélinas, in the mirror of a national drama the spectator 'sees himself and not another,' thereby securing in its representation the spectator's sense of national identity (Gélinas 1949, 35). One risk of this model is what Peggy Phelan calls the 'me-ism' of realist representation. 'Unable to see oneself reflected in a corresponding image of the Same, the spectator can reject the representation as "not about me." Or worse, the spectator can valorize the representation which fails to reflect her likeness, as one with "universal appeal" or "transcendent power"' (Phelan 1993, 11). Realism's 'me-ism' leaves little room for a national self that is not already culturally dominant, thereby shunting to the nation's sidelines women and marginalized others. Another risk for those whose actuality is evacuated in their use as national metaphors is how the iconic relationship reduces the other to the same; in the space of the theatre, arguably the space of the Other *par excellence*, Gélinas would have Québécois audiences see 'not another.' Recall that the marital union Gélinas prescribes between the stage and auditorium is between men, a homosocial contract: 'The man in the audience *see[s] himself* and murmur[s] the words of the man onstage' (1949, 37).

As Tania Modleski asserts, 'the process of creating metaphoric equivalencies' results in 'the obliteration of human differences' (1997, 61). Here we might consider Quebec's historical and often problematic identification with Black peoples, particularly African-Americans, where those populations' marginal status vis-à-vis colonial and state power made them useful metaphoric equivalents for Québécois marginality vis-à-vis Canada. The image of Québécois as the 'white niggers of America,' as activist author Pierre Vallières put it (1968, 1971), sits alongside that of Québécois as oppressed female figures. What unites these subject positions is their marginality. In the 'Quebec is female' and 'Quebec is black' metaphors, 'Quebec,' 'female' and 'black' share a category of meaning – marginality – that enables the significant differences among the three terms to be overlooked in favour of seeing their resemblances. The strategies by which we link theatre to nation – particularly through the rhetorical figure of metaphor – thus tend to produce a fairly stable repertoire of 'de souche' (old stock) male figures of theatrical nationness. Therefore, expanding national theatre history's figural taxonomy beyond figures based in iconicity or resemblance clarifies the costs of current practices and points to ways of conceptualizing national performance in feminist, anti-racist, and otherwise non-reductive terms. As part of this effort, and as indicated in the Introduction, *National Performance* offers three new figures for theorizing the performance-nation relation: metonymy, simulation, and what I call 'affection' to denote a primarily affective relation that sidesteps to some degree the other figures' reference and indication.

Nation-performance relations are likewise gendered in the roles in which they tend to cast nation and cultural production. By simply and faithfully imitating national features in the iconic mode, cultural production mimics; it dissembles, but does not create. In a word, cultural production reproduces, an activity associated (generally negatively) with women, femininity, and performance since at least Plato (see Barish 1981; Jackson 2004). Significantly, reproduction is also the dominant mode by which women participate in national processes according to political theorists Nira Yuval-Davis and Floya Anthias. Women reproduce members of national collectives by bearing children (a form of reproduction the Quebec government endorses with pro-natalist policies like 'baby bonuses,' extended parental leave programs, and a state-subsidized day-care system); they reproduce the nation ideologically by transmitting its culture in the form of language, religion, history, songs, and other forms of folk expression; and finally women are often called upon to symbolize ethnic/national differences by wearing customary dress and keeping other kinds of tradition associated with the *ethnie* (Yuval-Davis and Anthias 1989, 1–15). Despite women's biological, ideological, and symbolic centrality to national projects, women 'are often excluded from the collective "we" of the body politic, and retain an object rather than a subject position' (Yuval-Davis 1997, 47). As but one example of this dynamic, women in Quebec won the right to vote in provincial elections and to run for municipal office only in 1940, twenty-two years after they had been enfranchised in Canada's federal elections.

Women's object position within national mimesis is crudely concretized in the trope of Quebec's rape where, as Taylor writes of the same trope in Argentina, 'violence against women disappears and reappears as pure metaphor' (1997, 10). To recast her position in the terms I used to define mimesis – where it is both an activity and its result –, 'woman' in this scenario is 'a thing done' (Diamond 1997, v). In less crude terms, she is an object and an image, the after-effect of the act of representation. I will call this her 'representational labour' on the nation's behalf. Representational labour is the work aesthetic representations do to furnish the materials upon which national identities might be built; these images function in a manner similar to political representation, acting as the public's substitutes. Gélinas's program for a Québécois national drama relies on the theatre's representational labours: in its language, settings, characters, and themes, a national drama would mirror local conditions, peoples, and interests. In their representational labour, women bear the symbolic burden of proving the national fact. But women serve crucially in another type of national labour that I will call 'emotional labour,' following sociologist Arlie Hochschild's usage (2003). To explain emotional labour, let us return to that image of raped, female nation, the female national surrogate in pain; in addition to representing the nation, it also furnishes audiences with the felt sense of nation-ness – an experience of group identity under threat and imprisoned in abusive conditions. This is not to recuperate the national rape script. On the contrary, I wish to highlight the importance of vicarious experience, of the sensations and affects that the performing arts can generate and for which audiences buy tickets. I shall use it as a wedge to force open the standard representational contracts between performance and nation that (re)produce nation-ness on such unequal terms.

Feminist studies of emotional labour have isolated its primary contributions as that of building networks and forming communities. Emotional labour makes, manages, and distributes relationships through affective appeals; it draws people and objects, real and imaginary, into affective webs. By allying audiences emotionally with the on-stage action, or providing vicarious experience – often of emotionality itself – or prompting thrill responses, for instance, emotional labour creates what Jill Lane terms 'national sentiment' in her deft analysis of blackface performance's national labours in anti-colonial Cuba (2005). As in national mimesis's representational labour, 'Woman' and actual women are key functionaries. They facilitate affective ties and act as repositories of national sentiment.

Significantly, Gélinas himself gestures toward emotional labour in an address otherwise firmly entrenched in the visibility politics of theatre's representational labour vis-à-vis Quebec. In fact, he establishes emotional labour as representational labour's necessary pre-condition. For Gélinas, it is the emotional union of stage and public that allows national theatre to exist: 'for theatre to exist the author and the spectator must melt and dissolve one into the other' (1949, 37). Recall too that these partners murmur the play's lines simultaneously, as though 'du même cœur' (from the same heart). This sensation of semblance is one aspect of emotional labour. As in Gélinas's example, these affective webs form the substrate of national performance; they create the conditions of possibility for reading certain performances as 'ours,' and, thus, as 'national.' In addition to providing symbolic materials to the nation in its representational labours, then, performance's enacted imitations also furnish the nation's connective tissue.

The category of emotional labour helps us to rethink familiar performance-nation relations. Certainly performance inheres in representational systems and, as such, forges connections through reference and indication; it is by virtue of this kind of relation that theatre in particular offers, in Peter Handke's delightful phraseology, a brightness pretending to be another brightness, a chair pretending to be another chair, and so on (quoted in Carlson 1989, 4). However, the performing arts also hold open the possibility of a strong emotional connection that is substantially non-referential. For instance, popular music listeners do not necessarily thrill to power ballads for their narrative content; instead, their goose-bumps may result from an affect-inducing formal apparatus. Art's 'usefulness' to national projects comes not only in its referential capacities but also through its more basic affective linking functionality; feelings produce alliances, identifications, and dis-identifications among participants in relation to common objects. This perspective allows historians of national performance to consider how performances that do not signify as national come to matter as such nonetheless. On what (affective) grounds are those attachments forged? This is a critical move that displaces the centrality of 'aboutness' in national reading strategies, in which evidence of the relation between performance and nation is in performance's iconic 'record of time and place' (Lecker 1995, 32).[9] In cases where resemblance, reference, or aboutness, is exhausted or undeterminable – as in the case of the Cirque du Soleil with which this chapter opened – attention to emotional labour can provide another way into reading performances as national or nationalizing. Its production of affective ties may help account for 'inappropriate' and 'unanticipated' attachments, such as in instances of cross-identification (of anglophone or allophone Québécois identifying as members of the historically francophone category of 'Québécois') or even identification that goes against self-interest. It opens the door to thinking through how people may produce themselves as national in conditions that militate against it (as in the case of illegal immigrants); and how one may identify *with* the nation (its values, types, etc.) without identifying *as* national.[10]

In studies of national theatre and performance traditions, performance's representational labour has been skilfully analyzed; its emotional labour, on the other hand, has been largely overlooked. This oversight derives, in part, from the less obvious nature of emotional labour's operations and effects. As Shannon Jackson points out, emotional labour

functions via 'operations whose efficacy relies on a condition that paradoxically keeps them unrecognized' (2003, 708). This oversight derives
as well from emotional labour's ideological and practical feminization.
Not only is emotional labour allied with what is traditionally seen as
women's domains and 'natural' talents, but also its public-sphere workforce is predominantly female. For example, according to 2004 data col-
lected by Statistics Canada, Quebec's service-industry-sector workforce
is 54.2 per cent female and 45.8 per cent male; in the health and social
services field (also know as the 'caring professions'), 79.1 per cent of the
workforce is female to 20.9 per cent male (Québec, Institut de la statistique 2005). To adequately address how performance might have conse-
quence in national spheres necessitates illuminating the often gendered
labours – both imaginative and practical – that lay the groundwork of
national representations and their interpretations.

In the following chapters, then, I chart a critical history of performance's national labours – both productive and reproductive – in modern
Quebec. In so doing, I expand the range of figures currently in use to describe and analyze cultural production's roles vis-à-vis national projects
beyond the iconic figures of 'reflection' and 'construction,' the two most
common conceptual rubrics by which performance becomes national.
As importantly, I write in the hope that this work may mark and measure
the costs of the current representational economy in national performance studies, particularly in terms of gender, in my attention to some of
the less-spectacular emotional labours that suture subject/citizen to state.
In that marking, I find that the gendered aspects of national labour – its
representational labours and more centrally its emotional labours – are
constitutive of the naturalized fiction of nation-ness. I suggest, too, that
excavating (reproductive) emotional labour as the groundwork for (productive) representational labour provides performance scholars with an
alternate point of departure for perceiving the national. This excavation
revalues the performance-femininity-emotionality nexus in an area of
study often dominated by masculinist presumptions and concerns. Emotional labour's critical efficacy lies in its potential enfranchisement of a
more diverse national populace, and in its acknowledgment of the often
unmarked, feminized work that creates the conditions of possibility from
which national reference might emerge.

chapter three

National Construction: Quebec's Modernity at Expo 67

Quinze cent et trente-quatre: le Québec reçoit son premier touriste, Jacques Cartier ... Mille neuf cent soixante-sept: cinquante millions de Jacques Cartiers découvrent une terre inconnue – Terre des hommes.

(Carle 1967)

[Fifteen hundred and thirty-four: Quebec hosts its first tourist, Jacques Cartier ... Nineteen hundred and sixty-seven: fifty million Jacques Cartiers discover an unknown land – Man and His World.]

Thus begins Gilles Carle's documentary film on the 1967 World's Fair and Exposition, 'Terre des hommes/Man and His World,' held in Montreal from 28 April to 27 October 1967. Carle's invocation of the tropes of discovery and tourism is not particularly remarkable in the context of world's fairs and their publicity. Indeed, fair-goers have often been exhorted to discover the wonders of the world and venture into the land of tomorrow. Nor are these tropes uncommon in myths of national origin, particularly in the Americas where *terra incognita* – unknown lands – were 'discovered' by European 'explorers' and then claimed as possessions of European colonial powers (Greenblatt 1991). However, Carle has reversed the tropes' usual order; Nouvelle France's most renowned explorer is cast as tourist and Expo 67's crowds play discoverers.

In most origin stories, discovery precedes tourism. Indeed, it is the discovery narrative that transforms the New World's unknown and presumptively empty landmasses into social and political territories, in this case into 'Nouvelle France.' Only once the land is claimed and named can it then welcome foreign visitors who are not 'founders.' Carle's reversal is significant for several reasons. First, calling Cartier a 'tourist' establishes Quebec's territorial identity and integrity prior to the arrival of the Europeans. This offers a new origin story for Quebec in which the territory was not discovered by French explorers in 1534 and then ceded to the colonial power of Great Britain with the signing of the Treaty of Paris in 1763; rather it is (re)discovered and (re)colonized by its own people in the 1960s. *Terre des hommes* acts as a new *terre inconnue,* a *new* 'New World.' *Terre des hommes* names the world of the fair, of course. But it also implies a world whose shape and meaning is constructed by 'Man,' figuratively and literally. In his constructionist emphasis, Carle takes up and twists Expo 67's official ideology. Expo's theme of 'Terre des hommes/Man and His World,' chosen at a summit of intellectuals convened for that purpose at Montebello in 1963 (Martin 1968), drew on Antoine de Saint-Exupéry's philosophical treatise of the same title, whose central idea can be found in the following passage: 'to be a man ... is to feel that through one's own contribution one helps to build the world' (quoted in 'Expo 67: an experiment' 1966, 170). With *Terre des hommes*, Québécois would be not only contributors to building *the* world, but would become builders of their *own* world. That world would take the form of a national, independent, modern, and urban entity.

Carle's reversal is also significant in that it replays in miniature the signal move of 1960s Québécois social and political ideology: the conversion of *le pays* into *la nation*. The shift here is from Quebec as a cultural entity (a people) to Quebec as a nation-state (a particular societal organization of such a people). Put differently, Quebec moves from being a land/country (a physical geography) to a nation (a social/cultural geography). Political scientist Diane Lamoureux argues the necessity of what I would call constructionist labour to Quebec's nationalist project of transforming *pays* into *nation*. In *L'amère patrie*,[1] she analyzes the 'conscious humanization of the territory' undertaken in an effort to 'spatialize' the political project; this profound 'refaçonnement' (refashioning) of the land would do two things: (1) endow the national project with geographical heft, and (2) give the territory political currency. In this chapter, I extend her analysis of the physical labours of 'mastery, occupation, and structuring' undertaken in the 1960s by focusing on the representational and emotional labours mobilized in the name of re-annexing Quebec for Québécois (Lamoureux 2001, 92). Expo 67's symbolic re-annexation of Quebec by and for Québécois – evidenced generally in its geographical layout and modernist aesthetic, and specifically in the semiotics of the Quebec Pavilion – was largely successful. Political scientist Denis Monière affirms the widespread conviction that 'even if it is difficult to prove empirically,' Expo 67 'participated in a change of mentalities' among Québécois that gave some additional force to *québécité* (2008, 14). Historian Ivan Carel links this change in mentalities to the trope of discovery: 'In the historical consciousness of Québécois, the summer of Expo 67 marked and in some way symbolized the discovery of the world and of the self for a people giving themselves a new identity' (2008, 101). And, of course, many point to General de Gaulle's famous, if somewhat ambiguous, exclamation of 'Vive le Québec libre' during his visit to Montreal coincident with the summer of Expo 67 (24 July 1967 from the balcony of Montreal's Hôtel de Ville, to be precise). In this chapter, I follow two of the 'proofs' Expo itself seemed to offer to a consolidating *québécité*: first, a proof of capacity for constructing a new, resolutely urban environment and social landscape (converting *pays* to *nation*) and second, the proof of affective experience induced by the Quebec Pavilion's immersive environments and guided by its hostesses. The latter, I maintain, literally and figuratively enlivened the former to produce a compelling reality-effect of *québécité* reliant on cultural production's representational labours and women's emotional labours.

Re-colonizing Quebec in the name of Québécois, reconceiving it in a new, modern mode, takes work. Quebec-as-nation had to be constructed because it had no political reality. It was a province integrated into a federal political system whose francophone inhabitants' primary identification was linguistic, rather than territorial or statist. Before approximately 1960, francophone residents of Quebec identified as French Canadian/ *canadien-français*, as did their counterparts in other Canadian provinces (e.g., franco-ontariens and franco-manitobans).[2] The appellation indicated a shared language among French speakers across the country and even throughout the continent stemming from the period of French colonial expansion in North America from the sixteenth through eighteenth centuries, when French settlements stretched over the continent along the St Lawrence and Mississippi Rivers from the Gaspé to Louisiana. As Canadian francophones became more invested in political self-determination, the continental vision of *l'Amérique française* gave way to a national, territorial vision.[3] Of the rationale behind centralization in Quebec, political scientist Louis Balthazar notes, 'Nowhere but in Quebec could an elaborate network of communication and institutions that would allow a population to *live in French* and assert a specific French Canadian identity be created. Nowhere but in Quebec could francophones control a government of their own and use it fully to promote their own objectives' (1987, 30; emphasis in original). In other words, the French-Canadian identity would be politically viable only as Québécois. By 1964, Quebec Premier Jean Lesage could proclaim, 'Quebec has become the political expression of French Canada and plays the role of a homeland for all those in the country who speak our language' (quoted in Balthazar 1987, 29–30). Residents of the homeland would call themselves *Québécois*, thereby linking their collective identity with a particular territory (see Sénécal 1992). Only in this clearly bounded territory could Québécois be *maîtres chez nous* (masters in our own house). This 1962 election-winning slogan for the Quebec Liberals clearly expresses this attitude and goal of 're-colonizing' Quebec for the Québécois.

The built fantasy environment of the 1967 World's Fair would play its part in this re-colonization. Its national mimesis – that of construction, which builds models of future (sought-after) worlds and altered social relations – would help 'suture the real to the really made up' (Taussig 1993, 86). Montreal, and by synecdochic extension, Quebec, would become tied to the model, independent, and resolutely urban environment constructed for Expo 67. *Terre des hommes* literally forged a new national origin out of dredged earth, a fabricated urban environment, the national overcoding of the Quebec Pavilion's fairground location, and the narrative organization of its exhibits. Its reality-effect, if you will, was to give *québécité* a lived and affective dimension.

That modern Quebec's refashioned origins would be discovered in the *new* New World of a world's fair and exposition is entirely appropriate. World's fairs are in the business of reinforcing the nation as sociopolitical fact by producing marvellous 'New Worlds.' By encapsulating and organizing exhibits from numerous countries in a single site, international expositions offer a miniaturized explanatory blueprint of the world. These 'symbolic universes,' as Robert W. Rydell calls them, have been privileged sites for exploring the relationship of 'man' to 'his' world since their inception, not coincidentally during the period of western industrialization and high nationalism in the mid-nineteenth century (1984, 2). They index these relationships through displays of manufacturing, industry, commerce, and cultural production.

World's fairs testify to humanity's desire to create new worlds not only via symbolic representation but also through altering geography. In keeping with the mythology of the discovery of the Americas, North American world's fairs have often created land where none existed and/or memorialized the acts of discovery and annexation that constitute the Americas. For example, the Columbian World's Fair of 1893 in Chicago was held on a filled-in former swamp on the banks of Lake Michigan (now the University of Chicago campus). The 1915 Panama Pacific International Exposition was erected on reclaimed land on the south bank of San Francisco Bay and celebrated the completion of the Panama Canal. Although it did not create new land, the Louisiana Purchase Exposition of 1904 commemorated the addition of new land to the United States: the purchase of the French territory of Louisiana by U.S. President Thomas Jefferson.

Expo 67's symbolic universe inhabited a *terre* that was likewise a new creation. Two islands were constructed in the St Lawrence River out of 6,825,000 tons of rock and earth excavated from the new metro lines in Montreal and dredged from the St Lawrence (Fig. 3.1). Crews erected Île Notre-Dame along the wall of the St Lawrence canal and doubled the size of the parkland of Île Sainte-Hélène, adding just over 700 new acres in total ('Expo 67: an experiment' 1966, 170). Although hotly contested by the urban planners in the city government, this choice granted the planning committee a truly new world, unencumbered by the histories of settlement and land use that had prevented using the first proposed site (the working-class Montreal neighbourhood of Pointe-Saint-Charles). Moreover, the constructed island site gave geographical expression to an already circulating metaphor used to represent Quebec's nation-ness: the constructed islands of Expo 67 would stand in for the island of a French Quebec floating in the sea of English-speaking North America. This metaphor was extended in the Quebec Pavilion as well, whose guide explains, 'The Pavilion presents itself first as an immense glass house completely surrounded by water. It is an islet in an island. Just like the French-Canadian civilization is an islet swimming in the vast North American continent' (quoted in Curien 2003, 219). In the symbolic universe and altered geography of *Terre des hommes*, Quebec rewrites its story of origin and asserts a different, aggrandized location in the new New World order. In its fabricated natural environment, with its own pavilion distinct from Canada's, and an additional, separate pavilion showcasing Quebec's industries, the province is symbolically promoted to nation-state status, a peer among fellow nation-exhibitors competing for recognition on the world market. The Quebec Pavilion, the official representation of Quebec at the fair, occupied its own promontory jutting out from Île Notre-Dame into the interior lake used for regattas and other water sports during the exposition. Its sovereignty and position offset (or even countered) the fact that Expo 67 was also the capstone celebration of Canada's centenary and was funded in large measure by the

3.1 Aerial View of Île Notre-Dame and Île Ste-Hélène at Expo 67. The Quebec
Pavilion is on Île Notre-Dame (at the right of the photo); it is the building
on the inland lake with the flat, square roof and sits next to the multipeaked
roof of the Ontario Pavilion. The lower, white peaked roofs surrounding the
inverted pyramid structure (the 'Katamavik') beside and below the Ontario
Pavilion is the Canada Pavilion, the largest one at Expo 67.

© Government of Canada. Reproduced with the permission of the Minister of Public
Works and Government Services Canada (2009). Source: Library and Archives Canada /
Canadian Corporation for the 1967 World Exhibition fonds.

federal government. 'The whole exposition contributed to underlining that Quebec was a completely different political entity: *nowhere* did it appear as a part of Canada. A reflection of the pavilion erected on its own promontory, the exposition itself presented an independent Quebec ... Moreover, traditional Quebec, with its gorgeous countrysides, peaceful villages, and Catholic peasants, shone in its almost total absence,' concludes anthropologist Pauline Curien from her historical reconstruction and searching analysis of the Quebec Pavilion (Curien 2008, 95–6).

The construction of the island sites also created a convincing narrative of national capacity; it served as a microcosm or experiment in converting *pays*, a natural territory, into *nation*, a social organization. Where Jacques Cartier discovered an untamed natural environment, the Québécois 'discoverers' would narrate their modern origin story from the locus of this mastered, and wholly constructed, urban environment. However, the fair's symbolic universe, its newly constructed environment, and the narrative of national competence it enabled, also reveal the public entrenchment of associations that have substantively informed Québécois historiography and studies of Québécois cultural production ever since. These associations lace together modernity, nationality, and urbanity – each gendered male – in a teleologically ordered origin story, and pit themselves against the tissue of tradition, regionalism, and ruralism – all gendered female. Because these opposing associations not only are central to understanding Expo 67's national mimesis as construction, but also provide the parameters for national mimesis in Quebec more generally, let me sketch out how these marked categories operate in the dominant political and academic discourses of the 1960s. Subsequently, I'll point to the ways in which their clean divisions are already troubled at Expo, a troubling that opens up alternate models for national historiography which will be pursued throughout this book. It appears that at the same moment that the Quebec intelligentsia and technocrats disavow (or at the very least, soft-pedal) the region's rural roots, cultural traditions, and kinship model of civil society, the gendered labour that typifies those zones returns to knit together the modern fair and the urban nation.

In its interweaving of nationalism, modernity, and urbanism, Expo 67 exemplifies the spirit of the Quiet Revolution – the period generally understood to be the decade or so following the death of conservative, Union nationale Quebec Premier Maurice Duplessis in 1959 and characterized by the transformation of Quebec society into a modern welfare state with a liberalized economy and a secular outlook. As sociologist Marcel Martel observes, the Quiet Revolution modernized Quebec society by means of state apparatuses (Martel 1997, 107). Quebec's alacritous entry into modernity encompassed the secularization of the health, education, and welfare/social service sectors (which had formerly been the exclusive purview of the Catholic Church). In turn this secularization opened up space for a university-trained class of professionals and technocrats in the newly created government bureaucracy. Modernity's hallmarks are easily recognizable in this project: professionalization (specialist knowledge), technocratic governance, rationalization (adjustments in the means of achieving certain ends such that they are reached more efficiently), and bureaucratization (structure to support these efforts).

What has made Quebec's modernity so interesting to so many is that it is generally considered to have arrived 'late' historically, and then to have taken root and overturned previous social and political modalities quickly and completely. This view of modernity is inscribed within a developmental narrative which orders the world according to a hierarchy of modes of production (primary [agrarian], secondary [industrial], and tertiary [service economy]) and assigns them places in an historical schema reaching from 'ancient' to 'modern,' whereby 'modern' is 'secular, innovative, economically productive, and democratic' (Rosaldo 1995, xiii). Viewed from this angle, the Quiet Revolution advances Quebec society in time. Indeed, the challenge, articulated by a great number of economic historians and sociologists of the period, including Maurice Séguin, Pierre Harvey, and Marcel Rioux, was *rattrapage* or 'catching up' with the more advanced economies of its neighbours, and particularly that of Ontario.[4]

The *rattrapage* thesis argued that mid-century Quebec was caught in a kind of arrested development – economically, socially, and politically. It generally laid the blame for Quebec's backwardness at the feet of a conservative clerico-nationalism propounded by the Catholic Church since the end of the nineteenth century and backed with particular vigour by Maurice Duplessis's provincial governments from 1936 to 1939 and 1944 to 1959. Early twentieth-century nationalist ideology promoted the 'survival' of French-Canadian culture via *un repli sur soi* (a protectionist turning inward). To protect against assimilation, *la survivance* proposed geographic and intellectual isolation/insulation from anglophone North American neighbours, their language, and their ways of life. Instead, it encouraged 'returning to the land,' a large family, transmission of the French language, devotion to the Catholic Church, and agrarian communities centred around a parish. For example, the Church and the government worked together to evangelize what was called the 'colonization movement,' a notable pre–Quiet Revolution example of human labour reworking the natural terrain into a national geography; the land was produced as arable and the population reproduced both *tout court* and as French-Canadian. Parcels of land were distributed to deserving farmers for clearing and cultivation in view of self-sufficiency. Attempts to staunch the exodus to urban centres that had begun just before the turn of the century were multipronged, including government incentives, pastoral letters supporting colonization, and the foundation of the colonization-supporting, Church-sponsored Union catholique des cultivateurs (Catholic Farmers Union) in 1924 and the Ministry of Agriculture-spearheaded Cercles de fermières (Women Farmers Circle) in 1915. Keeping 'our sons on the land and stop[ping] our daughters from deserting the rural parish' was intended to act as a bulwark against the incursion of modernity's foreignness and moral degenerations, strongly associated with urbanism (quoted in Clio Collective 1978, 236). For Duplessis, rural communities offered an ideal society where the Church effectively structured civil society. In addition to presiding over the domains of health and education, the Church involved itself intimately in the daily lives of its adherents. Lamoureux explains, 'All social groups were ensnared in the Church's works with organizations like Scouts and Guides, leisure activities, Catholic student youth and its workers wing, assemblies/groups of farmers and farmers' wives, the unions, etc., of which the common denominator was not only belief but also the protective figure of the chaplain' (2001, 101–2). As Lamoureux also points out, these social institutions ran in large part on women's volunteer labour; for instance, unpaid nuns ran the schools, hospitals, and public charities.

This insular emphasis and defensive posture had the effect of cutting Quebec off from the rest of the industrializing, modernizing, urbanizing world, even as it was constructing its own nationalized territory through its inhabitants' agrarian labours. Indeed, Quebec was perceived as a traditional society *par excellence* (Latouche 1986, 12). In order to catch up with North American pace-setters, Quebec would have to get out from under the skirts of the Church and untie the apron strings that bound them to home and hearth in the form of large and extended families that were the principle social and support network for French Canadians. Historian Jocelyn Létourneau puts the matter baldly: 'All Québécois research and thought of the 1950s and 1960s (NB: that of social scientists) was oriented toward a future that it was necessary to provoke,

toward a modernity one should attain at all costs, and which had been
prevented from happening by a paralyzing past, a past that would henceforth be reviled' (1992, 778).[5] Létourneau's characterization of the period's dominant academic discourse reprises modernity's characteristic
move: a *refus global* or 'total refusal' of what has come before.[6] Fashion-
ing itself as entirely new and innovative, the epoch-making event of the
Quiet Revolution entailed a productive move forward instead of a reproductive return of the same. Brought into the light of progress via an
aggressive modernization program, Quebec would be able to 'grow up'
or 'mature' into a self-actualizing, independent political and social body.
Take as an indicator of this story's widespread uptake the preeminent
Québécois sociologist Fernand Dumont's influential history of Quebec
society, *Genèse de la société québécoise*. Dumont explicitly analogizes Quebec's historical stages (pre-modernity, Quiet Revolution, nation-state status) to stages of life (childhood, adolescence, and adulthood) (Dumont
1996). As the studies of Létourneau, Ronald Rudin, Fernand Ouellet,
and Esther Trépanier among others demonstrate, the *rattrapage* thesis,
with its drive to 'normalcy,' was hugely influential in Québécois sociol-
ogy, history, and arts criticism, each of which 'accepted the premise that
there were certain paths that all societies followed and that material factors were the motor behind social change' (Trépanier 1998).

If in my summary of this foundational, developmental narrative of
modern Quebec society I have emphasized its gendered dimensions,
I have not exaggerated them. In the discourse of this period of *rattrapage*, Quebec's national maturity was resolutely linked to its hetero-mas-
culinization. Traditional ways of life and work were gendered female:
the Church was run by 'men in skirts'; the home was commanded by
women; the farm pivoted around the hearth and required an elaborated
form of domestic labour. As Robert Schwartzwald's careful and foundational work deconstructing modern Québécois national discourses has
decisively shown, these female domains were reproached for having produced *hommes manqués*, specimens of atrophied masculinity whose only
hope for maturity and independence was to 'reconquer and possess his
own territory' (1991, 183; emphasis in original). In the face of clerico-
nationalism's focus on biological reproduction and cultural preserva-
tion, rejecting this past was an insufficient response. The new Québécois
subject strove to manufacture an origin outside of that feminized space;
he would 'be reborn as Québécois, which is to say as a psychologically
normal/healed and decolonized being' (Létourneau 1992, 778). This
kind of auto-genesis required a decisively 'virile' *Québécois* (male gender

intended) to assert what *indépendantiste* leader René Lévesque termed the right of a 'normal people': a modern, sovereign nation-state.

Throwing over tradition's repetitions (its reproductions of people, customs, ways of life), modernity invests in a teleological sense of history – a linear-historical logic of past, present, and future – and develops a consequent ideology of progress. In Quebec, this modernist gesture of 'total refusal' makes the Quiet Revolution the new starting point for Quebec history. In Expo, this narrative discovers its modern, urban Eden.

In its conception and execution, Expo 67 was steeped in the ideology of modernity and its consequent valorization of progress. Writer Gabrielle Roy, in her introduction to *Man and His World*, discloses that the one thing upon which all Montebello conference delegates could agree was that Expo would be about humanity's progress (Faber 1967). That message of progress came across loud and clear. Art historian Johanne Sloan writes, 'at Expo 67 the vision of a common destiny for humankind could be expressed not only via the common rhetoric of humanism, but perhaps even more forcefully, through the recognizably utopian forms and shapes of modern art and architecture ... Expo 67 once again projected an optimistic picture of what a future society might resemble, in visual and material terms.' Expo, therefore, would be a city of the future, a model of humane, modern living. As Sloan notes, several influential critics, among them Reyner Banham, 'took Expo 67 quite seriously as an experiment in crafting a new, emancipatory kind of urban experience' (2007, 82). Where modernity's opposite, 'tradition' was presented, it was generally framed as 'disappearing' – under the welcome boots of progress in the Quebec Pavilion and under the martial boots of a white paternalistic social system in the Indian Pavilion (see Kröller 1997). In the case of Africa Place, which grouped together the fifteen participating African nations into a central, tented, market-like area, tradition was presented as a geographically distant tourist destination.[7]

Not that Expo's investment in progress was unusual for a world's fair. Robert Rydell and John Allwood's work on nineteenth- and early twentieth-century world's fairs amply documents the propensity of every fair to shout its modernity to its patrons – whether in the vaunting of new building techniques, as in the case of the Eiffel Tower at Paris's 1889 Exposition Universelle, or in the selling of corporate America's vision of the future good life, as in the 1964 New York World's Fair (Rydell 1993; Allwood 1977). Nevertheless, Expo 67 took place on a territory deemed to have only recently entered modernity; the notion therefore had particular resonance and political/identitarian value. Moreover, Expo 67's modernity was somewhat differently presented; it was conceptualized as 'story,' with a clearly defined ascending and forward movement. The story of Man and His World, the Canadian Corporation for the 1967 World Exposition writes to potential exhibitors in their promotional booklet, *Canada at Home*, 'must first be told by describing man's attempts to understand his natural environment ... Man adapts to his world – He changes his environment as his skills develop – He adapts to his new environment – And so sets in motion the interesting cycles of material and spiritual change' ('Theme' 1964, n.p.). As such, the fairgrounds were not organized according to nation, as in the 1893 Columbian World's Fair and Exposition's midway, which classed the ethnographic exhibits according to a Darwinian racialist logic. Nor were they grouped according to type – national, commercial (e.g., Bell Telephone, Canadian Pulp and Paper Industry, Kodak), or religious (e.g., Jewish and Christian pavilions) – as at most other world's fairs. Rather, Expo's pavilions were organized thematically to advance the fair's themes clustered around 'Man's' actions and their effects: Man the Creator, Man the Producer, Man the Explorer, Man the Provider, Man and His Health, and Man in the Community. In 'General Information: Methods of Participation and Awards,' an explanatory document distributed to interested participants in 1964, the Canadian Corporation for the 1967 World Exhibition describes the organizing principle: 'From the point of view of physical grouping, the Theme section will form the core or "spine" of the plan. Other pavilions will be located according to their relationship to the Theme buildings, or to geographic, historical and cultural associations, and taking into account architectural factors and the preference of exhibitors' (*Le Canada reçoit* 1964, n.p.).[8]

The theme pavilions also functioned as transfer points for the transport networks that snaked their way through and around the fairgrounds, encouraging visitors, by their circuits and stations, to track the theme's development across the fair. Transport networks included the Expo Express train running at high speed along elevated tracks among the four fair sites – the Montreal mainland, the Cité du havre (Mackay Jetty), and the two island sites – providing a rapid overview of the grounds. The minirail with its small, open carriages with cheerful blue or yellow awnings moved more slowly on raised tracks though at a lower altitude than the Expo Express, encircling certain pavilions and encouraging a closer look at the exposition (Fig. 3.2). On the ground, pedicabs (bicycle cabs) and buses navigated pedestrian walkways; in the water were yacht slips, but also vaporettos (water buses) and hovercraft. In the air, helicopters

3.2 Minirail in front of fountains at Lac des Cygnes during Expo 67.
Notice the city of Montreal in the background.
© Government of Canada. Reproduced with the permission of the Minister of Public
Works and Government Services Canada (2009). Source: Library and Archives Canada /
Canadian Corporation for the 1967 World Exhibition fonds.

shared the skies with an aerial tram, offering yet another perspective on the fair and another means of managing the enormous crowds. The overall impression was of a highly integrated world in motion, a world in which 'man' used 'his' technical skills to experience the exhilaration of movement around and through the architectural statements surrounding 'him.'

Moreover, these transportation systems were part of a conversation, if you will, between the Expo grounds and the city of Montreal. In this dialogue, Montreal boasted some of Expo's successes while it continued to strive to incarnate the modernity and fascination of its constructed, model counterpart. The City of Montreal had just completed what would be the first stage of the underground metro system (1966), whose two lines linked east to west and north to south sides of the city, and spurred commercial development above and below ground along its route.[9] The subterranean expansion of Montreal's commercial sector comprises its famed 'underground city,' while its above-ground mushrooming of tall residential and office towers created a new skyline for the city. Expo's minirails, vaporettos, etc. transformed the new urban commute into a 'ride' (Lortie, Cohen, and Sorkin 2004, 155). This is expressly the case in the design of the meandering minirail route; against city engineers' plans for the minirail route to follow straight lines as in the metro example and emphasizing its efficiency-of-transport, the urban planner to whom the file was given, Steven Staples, was of the opinion 'that its capricious twists would add to the pleasure of the stroll' (quoted in Y. Jasmin 1997, 70).

The Expo fairgrounds themselves were mapped out according to urban planning principles. Expo's chief architect, Édouard Fiset set out the terms by which he wished Expo's environment be read: 'The master plan of the Exhibition stems from an urban composition rather than from a freely contrived landscape with the features of the "English" garden ... The urbanization reveals itself again in the geometric – though not rectilinear – layout of its avenues, in the grouping of the buildings in an endeavour to achieve volumetric equilibrium, in the scale of its squares and open spaces, and in the density of construction' (Fiset 1965, n.p.). Historian Jean-Claude Marsan affirms the successful execution of Fiset's urban plan: 'the general layout ... was distinctly urban ... characterized by the closely knit structure of the built-up areas. This helped to enhance the scale of the plazas, the recesses, and other open spaces and to emphasize the contrast with the natural environment, namely the river and the parks on Notre-Dame and St. Helen's Islands' (Marsan 1981, 367). A model urban space, the fairgrounds related and integrated diverse public facilities – food, lodging, shopping, entertainment, sylvan relaxation, education. Expo's planners used industrial design to highlight this integrated environment via uniform signage and modular street furniture, whose components 'can be used separately or combined in various groupings to emphasize axes and circulation routes or to create rest areas' ('Expo 67: an experiment' 1966, 172).

From the vantage of one utopian public space appeared another (potential) utopian environment across the river: the new Montreal, evidence that Montreal was catching up to its fabricated twin. As Ervin Galantay, architect and chronicler of the city's changes for *The Nation* attests, 'Expo visitors will view Montreal from its most impressive side; looking across the river, they will see the harbor with its majestic grain elevators, recently cleaned for the occasion, and beyond them the competing skyscrapers of the new core with the green hump of Mt. Royal in the background' (1967, 561). Not insignificantly, the Quebec Pavilion boasted 'the best views ... over Expo to the skyline of Montreal,' according to *Architectural Review* critic J.M. Richards (1967, 155). Expo 67's reception in international art and architecture journals confirms its importance for rethinking urban space. Moreover, the vast majority of contemporaneous articles on Expo include substantial discussion – and in some cases, whole features – about Expo's relationship to Montreal's changing urban landscape. World's fair historians John and Margaret Gold aver, 'Expo 67 engaged with its host city more decisively than any exposition since Chicago in 1893' (2005, 122). Of this engagement, architect Michael Sorkin writes, 'There was communication and connection between the collecting style of Expo and the collecting style of the big architectural infrastructure being imposed on the city: each modelled and confirmed the taste of the other' (Lortie, Cohen and Sorkin 2004, 150). Take, for instance Westmount Square designed by Mies Van der Rohe, which opened in December 1967, two months after Expo closed its doors. Its black, reflective, metal and tinted-glass towers elevated above a plaza recall the similarly 'cool' look and placement of Expo's Quebec Pavilion, designed by the firm of Papineau, Gérin-Lajoie, LeBlanc, and Durand. On Expo's Cité du havre site, Moshe Safdie's Habitat 67 – the widely vaunted if ultimately unrealizable vision of urban residential architecture – relied on industrial principles of prefabrication and mass-production for its assemblage of pre-cast concrete apartments (Fig. 3.3). In Montreal, McGill University's Leacock Building (Ray Affleck, 1965) was likewise constructed of interlocking repeatable forms in

3.3 Expobus at Habitat at Expo 67.
© Government of Canada. Reproduced with the permission of the Minister of Public
Works and Government Services Canada (2009). Source: Library and Archives Canada /
Canadian Corporation for the 1967 World Exhibition fonds.

brutalist style, though on a much less ambitious scale than its 'fantasy'
island counterpart. [10]

Lest we ascribe all of the utopian impetus to Expo's alternative city,
let us recall that Montreal itself was subject to experiments in the reorganization of public spaces, their transport connections, and their architectural landmarks before Expo 67 had even been granted to Montreal.
In his chronicle of the city's urban development, Guy R. Legault, the
city's chief urban planner from 1956 until 1987, highlights the catalyz-
ing influence of Place Ville-Marie's cruciform structure, completed in
1962, on Montreal's urban renewal. Funded by U.S. businessman Wil-
liam Zeckendorf and designed by the U.S. architectural firm of I.M. Pei,
Place Ville-Marie provoked a home-grown architectural response, in the
form of Ionel Rudberg's CIL Building (1964) and the CIBC building

(1962), the latter of which competed with Place Ville-Marie to be the Commonwealth's tallest building. 'The three new skyscrapers will henceforth mark the profile of downtown Montreal,' Legault attests (2002, 29). In the lead-up to Expo, no less than three highways and one bridge-tunnel were constructed around and through Montreal – the Décarie (Hwy 15), the Bonaventure (Hwy 10), and the Ville-Marie (Hwy 720) expressways, and the Hippolyte-Lafontaine bridge and tunnel. In its spatial organization, transportation systems, and uses of technology, the City of Montreal evinces industrial modes of production, interconnection, and mobility like Expo 67. Each provides proof of a modern city's secondary (or industrial) economy and its abridging of time and space via transportation and communication technologies. Both cities – the real and the forged – transform into modern, 'world cities' (Galantay 1967).

The Quebec Pavilion offers a second, more condensed example of the complicated relationship between urbanism, modernity, and nationality at play at the fair.[11] While promulgating a progressivist and independent vision of Quebec in its exhibits and their organization, the Quebec Pavilion also moved affective experience front and centre. 'Québécois visitors felt themselves incarnating modern Quebec,' attests Curien (2008, 93). At issue in this next section, then, is the 'real' that the 'really made up' (or representation) of the Quebec Pavilion offers in the larger forged environment of Expo 67; by cultivating spectator sensation (in the total environment of the pavilion) and emotion (in the figures of the hostesses) the Quebec Pavilion provokes a kind of undeniable physiological response that cannot be faked and so is taken for truth, thereby producing national sentiment.

The pavilion's commissioner, Jean Octeau, understood well Quebec's time lag with respect to the rest of Canada and the western world. He writes in a memo to his team of consultants on the project that Quebec cannot hope to compete with its neighbours in the realms of science and technology, and proposes instead that the pavilion highlight the metamorphosis Quebec has been experiencing by displaying the 'collision of tradition and modernity' (quoted in Curien 2003, 197). Thus, Gilles Tremblay's soundtrack for the pavilion juxtaposes nature-sounds (birds singing, water rushing) and sounds of modern life (gears winding, sirens sounding) (Boivin and Hébert 2000, 82). The monumental Quebec Pavilion reprises this developmental narrative of progress and forward movement in an 'uninterrupted circuit,' a regimented path up a combination of an elevator and an ascending, spiralling ramp. The pavilion program informs the visitor that the exhibit 'consist[s] of three stages which illustrate in succession: 1. the natural milieu of Quebec and the challenge it presents to man; 2. man's fight against this natural environment; 3. society and its aspirations: a people's drive toward the future. Three stages characterized by three keywords: CHALLENGE, COMBAT, DRIVE' (quoted in Curien 2003, 197). The 'Élan' or 'Drive' section, situated at the centre of the pavilion, closed with a vision of Quebec in the year 2000.

Each stage occupied its own space, one literally building on top of the other. The elevator that took the visitor through *le Défi* – the shortest of the stages, as though natural obstacles to progress are the least significant aspect of the narrative – would deposit her at *le Combat*, and so on. *Le Combat*, the longest and most articulated section of the exhibit, was divided into seven segments, the first set of which detailed how the natural obstacles – the density of the forests, the soil's resistance to cultivation, the earth's resistance to penetration and extraction – had been overcome via technological advances and human ingenuity. The last two segments, 'Industry' and 'the City,' appeared as the inevitable culmination of the prior manual labour. 'Industry' emphasized the production of commercial goods out of natural resources as well as Québécois inventions (e.g., the snowmobile). The 'City' section began with the city's construction (the city as construction-site), followed by 'Montreal, International City,' then 'Quebec, the Capital City,' and finally 'Sports and Tourism.' The developmental narrative in which modernity, the city, and the nation come together was capped, significantly I think, with 'Rayonnement culturel' or cultural dissemination at the end of *l'Élan*.

The exhibit's organization, elements, and accompanying, explanatory texts reprise the forward movement from *pays* to *nation*. In its inexorable advance towards the year 2000, the exhibit's stages signal the increasing complexity of Québécois society – from rural to urban, from agrarian to industrial – and its provisioning with appropriate tools to manage that complexity (in the form of industrialization and education, for example). Indeed, the very fact of Expo, that it happened on time and with great success, is evidence again of Quebec's maturity and, indeed, was taken as such: 'No longer were we drawers of water. We were capable of making great things,' testifies the president of the Société du patrimoine politique du Québec in hindsight (Monière 2008, 14). Creating Expo's fantasy city required the planning and execution of 'work on roads, drainage, pumping, landfilling, bridges, energy transportation, public transportation, landscaping, design, architecture, public relations, advertising, information for exhibitors, etc.' (Legault 2002, 76). In the example of the director of installations' use of the computerized Critical Path Method to manage all of the Expo building projects we see again the dominance of a technocratic approach to construction (Chamberlin 1967, 35). If Expo is well understood as a cultural event with significant impact on crystallizing a new, forward-looking Québécois identity, it is possibly better understood as an event that marshals (and in some respects, summons) the modern nation's resources, personnel, and apparatuses.

The Quebec Pavilion cultivated a dynamic environment, indicating Quebec's vibrancy, youth, and momentum. The guide to the pavilion states, 'The Quebec Pavilion is not a museum where diverse objects are lined up next to each other. Neither is it an exhibition floor encumbered with multiple stands on which folkloric objects are laid out. Rather, our pavilion offers a show where sounds, lights, and forms evoke more than they illustrate a modern Quebec created following a difficult struggle against an immense and wild territory' (Curien 2003, 218). And indeed, there were comparatively few static exhibits in this 'evocation' of a modern Quebec – even the obligatory birchbark canoe, hackneyed symbol of French Canada's early fur-traders, was suspended from the ceiling and moved with the air currents created by passers-by. More common were films (by the likes of Gilles Carle and Denys Arcand) projected on multiple screens or on groups of white cubes hung together, sound environments (in the glass *Défi* elevator), moving maquettes, illuminated signage, projections, murals on two-story-tall suspended columns, photos, and the like. Curien records that there were 'thirteen films playing continuously, 95 photographic documents, lighted and mechanical animations, murals, and of course historical and contemporary objects' (2008, 95). Most dynamic, however, were the visitors who followed ten- or sixty-minute circuits through the pavilion's 'total environment.' Its uninterrupted pedestrian pathways were flooded with moving, sometimes kaleidoscopic sonic and visual images that encompassed the visitor's sensory field. Music played a key role in the effects of the pavilion's total environment; Gilles Tremblay's soundtrack was broadcast throughout the pavilion to 'assure the coherence of form and content, of the glass and steel structure and the different modular elements (cubist mine, stylized maple) it housed' (Boivin and Hébert 2000, 81-2). Speakers were arranged around the ceiling, inside select cubes, and in a circle prompting at least one 'test-group' of children to be 'filled with joy' and 'literally run after the sounds' on their pre-opening visit (83). An adult visitor, Brigitte Morissette, journalist at *La Patrie* testified to her own affective response to the 'acoustic spectacle': 'At first surprised by the soundtrack,

one soon feels relaxed, overtaken, propulsed by the waves of familiar
or unknown sounds breaking to infinity' (quoted in Boivin and Hébert
2000, 83). Curien, who interviewed Québécois visitors to the Quebec
Pavilion, concludes that even 'the least [or briefest] visit was of a rare
intensity that cannot be measured' (2008, 97). The pavilion's acoustic
and visual environments immersed visitors in a thrilling experience of
modernity and technological innovation in Québécois style.

To this point, I have focused on Expo's *terre*, the way its construction
and semiotic resonances convert *le pays* (a physical geography) into *la
nation* (a political geography). In its representational labours, which
provided new horizons of expectation and a new discourse of national
identity organized around ideas of modernity/futurity and urbanity to
Québécois, Expo 67 re-annexes Quebec in their name. But Carle's film,
with which this chapter opened, emphasized the nation's hosting role as
well. And it is in Expo's hosting function that we see the return of *le pays*'s
feminized traditionalism servicing the new-found *nation*.

Greeting visitors to Expo 67 and introducing them to the wonders
of the Ski Doo in the Quebec Pavilion were the fair's official hostesses,
by many accounts the best aspect of Expo and the foundation of the
Quebec Pavilion (Fig. 3.4). In her exhaustive history of the Quebec Pavilion on which my description above relies, Pauline Curien calls them the
'clous' of the pavilion (Curien 2003, 212). This appellation draws attention at once to their fundamental, connective work of holding the pavilion's social world together as 'nails,' as well as to their more spectacular
role as 'highlight' or featured attraction of the pavilion. Each of these
roles was fundamental to their representational and emotional labour
at the fair. Let me underscore as well the hostesses' role as the primary
'live' communications technology at the fair; while Expo and Montreal's
architectural collections were linked via connective webs of transport
and communication systems, their visitors were connected in large part
through the hospitality work of the hostesses across the fair. The Canadian Corporation for the 1967 World Exhibition hired 235 general
Expo hostesses to greet visitors to the fair, staff information booths on
the grounds, and give guided tours to special guests and visiting digni-
taries. To push the analogy, we might say that these general hostesses
functioned like the Expo Express train, giving visitors an overview of
the fair and mapping the connections among the pavilions. Fashion designer Michel Robichaud appears to have understood this function im-
plicitly; he says that the hostesses' hats were graphic and designed to sit
high on the head so that they might be easy to spot in the large crowds

3.4 Hostess of the Quebec Pavilion on the roof of the Quebec Pavilion and
under the Quebec flag at Expo 67.
© Government of Canada. Reproduced with the permission of the Minister of Public
Works and Government Services Canada (2009). Source: Library and Archives Canada /
Canadian Corporation for the 1967 World Exhibition fonds.

(Robichaud 2007); visitors could thereby find their way about the fair by following the blue, white, and navy wide-striped hats. Each pavilion (national, thematic, or corporate) also hired and trained its own hostesses, providing another level of connective tissue to the fair. The pavilion hostesses were more like the minirail (which passed through the Buckminster Fuller's United States Pavilion, a geodesic dome); they ushered visitors into individual pavilions for a closer look, providing pertinent information along the way. They stood at the pavilion entrance or behind a desk to stamp visitors' 'passports' – one's entry ticket and an Expo 67 innovation – thereby granting them entry into (and a souvenir of) their pavilion. Hostesses in the Telephone Pavilion, for instance, made presentations on future phone technologies while those from the Youth Pavilion, like Louise Roy, animated debates on contemporary issues like the Vietnam War (Roy 2007).

Some pavilions, like Canada's, also had hosts, though they figure not at all in the fair's popular memory, nor in its official or unofficial iconography, both domains where the hostess reigns supreme. Like many performers of this kind of service-industry emotional labour, the hostesses were over-represented in the fair's official iconography as well as in its visual record. An Expo hostess in her blue uniform appears on one of Expo 67's official posters, for instance; the hostesses as a group were a source of fascination for media at the time (see Moser 1967, Anderson 1967b, 'Des hôtesses' 1967, O'Leary 1967). What is more, the hostesses were (or were positioned as) tourist attractions in themselves. The smiling hostess on the poster mentioned above holds a camera; the caption reads, 'Bring your camera / Apportez votre appareil!,' as though it were she one would most want to photograph. Expo was advertised as a place where Montreal's naturally occurring beautiful women would, effectively, be on display – not only as hostesses, but as themselves. The lead for a segment on Expo's hostesses on CBC Radio by John O'Leary, host of the news program *The World at Six*, was typical in this regard: 'Montreal is generally known for its attractive women, but this year the situation has become ridiculous. Aside from the local lovelies, there's Expo with its hostesses' (O'Leary 1967). As in other explorer and tourist narratives, native women could be discovered by foreign visitors. Media reports gleefully charted the heights of skirts worn at Expo; in fact, the Expo hostesses' skirts were raised by one inch in response to the prevailing fashion trend and to the explosion of 'girlwatching' at specified downtown Montreal locations. Don Sauers, author of *The Girl Watcher's Guide* and founder of the American Society of Girl Watchers writes of

Expo's marshalling of the girlwatching phenomenon, 'Expo '67 in Montreal invited us to come up to help them celebrate Girl Watching Week. Would you believe a billboard that said, "Keep Montreal beautiful. Wear a miniskirt." They wrote it, I didn't' (Sauers 2004).[12] An article vaunting Montreal during Expo to readers of *The Nation* also extols the delights of girlwatching, this time at the recently constructed Place Ville-Marie (Galantay 1967, 557). Perhaps unsurprisingly given the context, some hostesses testify to feeling underutilized by Expo visitors, who seemed to look at them as part of the national display instead of approaching them for information or orientation (O'Leary 1967, Moser 1967).

It could be that the hostess's true utility lay elsewhere, as symbol of all that was exciting, vibrant, young, and attractive about the fair and its historical moment. For they have currency to this day as well: Library and Archives Canada built an on-line game of matching hostesses with their country as part of its Expo 67 Virtual Exhibit ('Match the Hostess'). The portal to this Virtual Exhibit, moreover, features an introductory montage of photos from Expo to the tune of the fair's theme-song, 'Un jour, Un jour / Hey Friend, Say Friend.' Its final frame is a picture of seven international hostesses in front of the stand of flags in the Place des Nations ('Introduction,' n.d.). Clearly, the hostesses made Expo 67 memorable to many and still stand in for its singular attractions.

There is something here in the persistent emphasis on the hostesses as among the fair's top attractions, the fair's overarching emphasis on dynamic connections, and the Quebec Pavilion's apotheosis in Sport, Tourism, and Culture that troubles the too-easy, gendered binaries of modernity, urbanism, and nationality versus tradition, ruralism, and regionalism. It seems that in one of the moments widely acknowledged to represent Quebec's ascension into modernity – its arrival on the world stage as at least a symbolically equal national partner – the remnants of a prior social mode are still very active and, indeed, fundamental to the efflorescence of the 'new,' modern mode. This is a mode I call 'emotional labour,' after Arlie Hochschild's foundational analysis of 'women's work' in *The Managed Heart,* first published in 1983. Hochschild defines emotional labour as 'the management of feeling to create a publicly observable facial and bodily display,' which is sold for a wage. Thus, part of the worker's job is to produce and sustain an employer-defined countenance in a bid to create 'the proper state of mind' in one's customers or clients (Hochschild 2003, 9).[13] Testimonies from Expo hostesses confirm that they performed precisely this kind of emotional labour for fair visitors. For instance, Monique Simard, a hostess at the Youth Pavilion, speculates that she was hired mostly for her youthful enthusiasm, linking that personal trait to the job requirement of making visitors to the pavilion equally enthused (Simard 2007). According to the Chief Hostess of Expo 67, Monique Archambault, the practical directives general Expo hostesses followed were to be polite, kind, patient, and above all to provide information ('Des hôtesses' 1967), creating a welcoming and warm environment for their 'guests' – a word that returns over and over in the testimonies and official literature of the fair to describe fair visitors and reinforce the hostesses' hosting function.

The ever-smiling hostesses performed their emotional labour in any number of ways: translating fluently between French and English (bilingualism was a job requirement); smoothing out the rough spots in social interactions among strangers; guiding visitors along the prescribed paths; alleviating visitor discomfort at being confronted with linguistic or aesthetic difference by offering contextual information; planning and hosting evening receptions; and (not least!) looking pretty. The job application form produced by the Canadian Corporation for the 1967 World Exhibition and submitted to 'Miss Hopeful Hostess' at a Montreal address asked for the applicant's age, height, weight, and marital status ('Demande d'emploi' 1963). Just as Expo organizers capitalized on Mme Simard's natural enthusiasm to help create an environment of enthusiasm, here they took advantage of young women's natural features to create an attractive, even sexy, environment. The designer, Michel Robichaud, makes this explicit when he says that the general hostess outfits he designed were cut close to the body because, due to the information available to those doing the hiring, all hostesses had 'a pretty figure' (Robichaud 2007). In addition to being schooled in Canadian and Québécois history, systems of government, and the fair's themes, hostesses were also students to fashion and etiquette consultants on such matters as comportment and customer care. (They were trained in make-up application, grooming, and how to walk.)[14]

As we have seen, the Quebec Pavilion's ideological work consisted largely in branding Quebec as a social geography, as a nation, as against its more usual depiction as a physical geography, *un pays*. The pavilion's hostesses, on the other hand, re-naturalize that national social geography in their hospitality work and social lubrications, imbuing *la nation* with a sense of *le pays*'s longevity, particularity, and irrefutability. Like the other hostesses around the fair, those at the Quebec Pavilion make the pavilion's social world appear as a natural one to its visitors by welcoming them to their 'home' and pointing out (or, in the case of the foreign tourist, establishing) its familiarity. Different from the general Expo hostesses, however, the Quebec Pavilion hostesses needed more than a smile, a map, and strong language skills to render the pavilion environment accessible. Numerous visitors, officials, and hostesses have attested to the difficulty many faced in orienting themselves in the pavilion and interpreting its exhibits. All commentators attribute this challenge to the avant-gardism of the pavilion's design and exhibit organization (see Morasse 2007, for instance). It was widely reported (and not always favourably) as 'futurist,' a word which emphasizes at once its potential for construction's national mimesis as well as its disorienting or defamiliarizing effects. The New World of Quebec as national was, indeed, new and, hence, required additional labour on the part of the hostesses to make the link between the contemporary moment of Quebec and Montreal, as reflected on its exterior glass skin, and its modeled future laid out in the pavilion. The Head Hostess of the Quebec Pavilion, Monique Morissette-Michaud, recalled that many visitors felt 'a little lost' in the unexpected organization of the pavilion, which she describes as a 'performance-installation' (Morissette-Michaud 2007). This disorientation was not limited to foreign visitors or the general public; Morissette-Michaud and Huguette Schwartz, the team leader of the Quebec Pavilion hostesses, recount the story of the visit of Quebec cabinet minister (and eventual Parti québécois leader) René Lévesque, in the company of an official Quebec government delegation. It seems he visited twice. The first time, at the opening of the pavilion, he made his way through the exhibit on his own; he – and his whole party – left confused, pronouncing with some vigour his dissatisfaction. Morissette-Michaud persuaded him to visit a second time, this time with a hostess as his guide (the actress Andrée Saint-Laurent). He left, says Schwartz, 'enchanted.' In this way, the hostesses helped visitors manage the disorientation induced by the pavilion's unusual presentation as well as the surfeit of sensation provoked by its total environment.

As importantly, the hostesses cultivated a reassuring experience of the familiar in their assumption of typically female roles in the pavilion's social world, engaging in activities characteristic of mothers and wives, teachers and flight attendants – hence the emphasis on comportment and etiquette.[15] Of the stereotypical roles hostesses performed, Canadianist Eva-Marie Kröller writes, 'The stylization of Expo hostesses into miniskirted versions of the traditional teacher-and-nurse stereotype reached to comical proportions in a report on a hostess from British Columbia whose medical training came in handy during a flight back "to Vancouver to the P[acific] N[ational] E[xhibition] where she and another hostess *manned* the Expo booth"; when a passenger fell ill, she "found herself the ministering angel in flight"' (Kröller 1997, 42. Emphasis in original). The hostesses' feminized emotional labours created not only *a* 'natural' social world – a world in which women manage and deploy emotions through largely unremarked activities. They also created *our* natural social world, linking the 'really made up' of the Quebec Pavilion's futuristic environment to the real of contemporary Quebec by teasing out the grand narrative of the Quebec Pavilion from its unusual presentation. This world where women ensure affective equilibrium or cohesion in a group and provide a sense of familiarity, locality, and belonging is recognizable to visitors in its affect and its social arrangements, even in conditions where the distinct elements of that social world – the Ski Doo, the mining deeps, the skyline of Montreal and/ or their representations in concrete music and cubist film – were less familiar. Thus, while the hostesses' outfits, professional polish and intellectual preparedness for the modern world differentiated them from their predecessors – the French-Canadian *paysannes* and *habitantes* who settled French Canada – the same kind of work founds both traditional and modern origin stories of Quebec.[16] Here, the 'origins' cast off by Quiet Revolutionaries return in service of the modern nation.

Emotional labour is very old-fashioned work and thus may be associated with pre-industrial modes of production and traditionalist values of conserving a status quo of social relations. Although they were all bilingual college or university students or graduates and part of a new wave of female professionals, the hostesses' on-site behaviours and the constraints within which they operated hardly challenged typical gender roles. As Commissioner General Pierre Dupuy's comments make clear, hostesses were cast by the Expo administration as 'dutiful daughters' and 'ambassadresses.' Of their recruitment and training Dupuy writes, 'They were ours. They were our daughters at their best ... We didn't want a starlet type, dyed-blonde and sophisticated, who wants to impress and looks for adventure. Intelligence, instruction, good manners were essential for being chosen. But we had no objection whatsoever to charm or beauty' (1972, 98). These outreach workers performed what sociologists Nira Yuval-Davis and Floya Anthias identify as women's usual work vis-à-vis national projects: in their information sharing, the hostesses 'participat[ed] centrally in the ideological reproduction of the collectivity and [functioned] as transmitters of its culture'; in their dress, comportment, linguistic competencies, and 'daughter/ambassadress' status,

they 'signif[ied] ... ethnic/national differences' (Yuval-Davis and Anthias 1989). In these respects, the Quebec Pavilion hostess's role was not
significantly different from that of other national pavilion hostesses, also
called upon to wear 'native' or 'traditional' garb, for instance, and thereby form part of the pavilion display. However, that the fair was being held
in Quebec and that Montreal's image (certainly in English-speaking Canada but also to some degree beyond that too) was built on the sexiness
of the city and its inhabitants, put its pavilion hostesses under particular
scrutiny. This links them again to *le pays* and the pre–Quiet Revolution
(hence, pre-'modern') ideology of *la survivance* in which women became
les gardiennes de la race (guardians of the race) by producing numerous
children and ensuring the perpetuation of French-Canadian culture in
their domestic educative efforts, as well as being allegorical figures of the
imperilled nation (LeClerc and West 1997, 7). The hostesses preserve
– and not inconsequentially, are relegated to – *le pays* at the core of the
modern nation. Just as the 'girls' who are 'watched' at Place Ville-Marie
provide a rounder, feminine counterpoint to the phallic structure tower-
ing above them, so too do the hostesses furnish a warm, feminine element to the 'cool' modernity of the fair-city (Wallace 2005).

At the same time as the hostesses provide a living image of the 'pre-
modern' *pays*, from the vantage point of today they might also be read
as projections of the postmodern urban economy and geography. Emotional labour subtends what Michael Hardt and Antonio Negri have
recently identified as the postindustrial service economy of 'Empire.'
Hardt defines affective labour as 'itself and directly the constitution of
communities and collective subjectivities' and places it at the centre of
Empire (Hardt 1999, 89). Expo 67, like the 1976 Olympic Games a decade later and the city's current emphasis on festivals of all kinds, primed
the city's economic pump, tapping into public and private capital for
urban planning needs like transportation systems, housing projects, and
the creation of a tertiary (support/service) sector, particularly in the
form of hotels. Indeed, urban economist Marc V. Levine observes that
Montreal's early and energetic embrace of the service sector as a 'key-
stone for local economic development' took flight with the 'mega-event'
of Expo 67 (2003, 109).

Like Levine, who uncovers the long-term economic folly of such an
investment in mega-events, historian Pierre Linteau cautions against an
overly optimistic reading of Expo's impact on Montreal. He maintains
that while the Expo era 'certainly represents one of the city's recent
strong periods ... it also corresponds with the end of a cycle and even with

the end of a long [post-war] phase of expansion' (2000, 427). Following Expo 67, cultural events like it were increasingly necessary to keep the Montreal economy afloat. For the modern city is modern not only in its mastery over nature, its integrated environment, and its transportation and communication technologies; it is also modern in its displacement of industry to the city's periphery. Here Montreal's experience was decidedly in-step with that of other North American cities moving towards a postindustrial economy; industries moved away from the city's historical economic core along the St Lawrence river to the outlying regions north of the city along its new Highway 40. More damaging was the exodus of corporate headquarters away from Montreal altogether, often to Toronto, within only fifteen years of Place Ville-Marie's development of 1.5 million square feet of office space in view of making Montreal the 'future "Headquarters City" of Canada.' In their wake remained little more than the downtown service economy, particularly the underground plazas stretching out from Place Ville-Marie, which Galantay had identified in 1967 as 'Montreal's best defense against the lure of suburban shopping centers which sap the vitality of the retail core of cities like Detroit or Philadelphia' (1967, 558). These new hearths to which tourists might be drawn form the economic heart of Montreal's postindustrial economy. Since Expo 67 that core has moved more visibly into the public realm in the form of a highly developed tertiary sector hinging on provision of services and a tourist economy. This is why the temporary loss of the Grand Prix in 2008 caused such an uproar, and it provides one explanation for renewed activism for hosting another world's fair. (A federally registered entity is actively promoting 'Expo 17: a World's Fair in Montreal,' and the current [2009] leader of Montreal's municipal opposition party, Benoit Labonté, has also called for another world's fair in 2020 to enliven a sluggish economy ['Expo 17'].) Thus, it seems that Montreal – in its pre-modern, modern, and postmodern modes – cannot help but construct itself around a feminized, and visibly feminine, core.

In its symbolic re-annexation of Quebec for Québécois, Expo 67 crystallized the Quiet Revolution's most durable construction and persuasively moved the 'origin' of Quebec's national story from the 1500s into the 1960s and from the country to the city. Since the Quiet Revolution, and despite economic downturns and changing markets negatively affecting the urban centre, Québécois national ideology has never really looked back to a traditionalist, agrarian ideal. However, the tremendous amount of representational and emotional labour required for the modern narrative's maintenance also attests to that construction's instability. Indeed, in the same decade that the ideology of teleologically ordered progress reached its apotheosis in Expo's symbolic universe, it was also subject to sustained, vigorous critique from an anticolonial perspective. In the theatre, evidence of this critique made a rather spectacular appearance less than one year after Expo's closure.

In its content, style, and the criticism it provoked, Michel Tremblay's bitter comedy, *Les belles-sœurs* (The Sisters-in-Law), encapsulated the competing program for Quebec's modern nationality – anticolonial socialism. Receiving its first full production in August 1968, *Les belles-sœurs* reignited the decade's most pointed debates concerning not only Québécois modernity, but also the nature and efficacy of the relationship between art and national society. Where Quiet Revolutionary discourse favoured the figure of construction as explanatory grid for both modernity and the performance-nation relation, anticolonial nationalist discourse favoured that of reflection, a figure that posits an iconic connection based on resemblance between text and context and that minimizes differences between stage reality and social reality. This turn to reflection might be read as evidence of Québécois confidence in the national construction's successful naturalization. The theatre could now reflect the nation as the nation had a legitimate existence. And indeed, there is merit to the claim that over the course of the 1960s Quebec-as-nation transforms from project into point of reference, from aspiration to signified; even the Quiet Revolution's most strident anticolonial critics exult in the sea-change in Québécois identity by 1968. Moreover, some aspects of Tremblay's play, particularly its resolutely urban setting and its realist mode, might foster that same conclusion about national confidence.

However, as the title implies, *Les belles-sœurs* also depicts an exclusively *female* network of filiations by blood and marriage. Further, the connections suggested by the title manifest themselves in the play as un-self-reflexive tribalism and provincial small-mindedness, both clearly at odds with Quiet Revolutionary ideology. These 'good women' were undeniably unreconstructed *canadiennes-françaises* who just happened to be living in an urban enclave seemingly unaffected by national progress. The figural means by which anticolonial nationalists recuperated Tremblay's characters and the costs of that recuperation to women form the core of the next chapter.

chapter four

National Reflection: Michel Tremblay's
Les belles-sœurs and *le nouveau théâtre québécois*

The period from about 1960 to 1976 in Quebec seems to be typified by rebirth at the hands of Man, and the story of Michel Tremblay's first produced play, *Les belles-sœurs* (The Sisters-in-Law), is easily inscribed in this narrative. The critic who wrote that with *Les belles-sœurs* Tremblay (b. 1942) effectively raised Quebec theatre from the dead was not alone in his ascription of almost supernatural powers to the play, even if this was the most hyperbolic statement to that effect (Basile 1972, 135). Tremblay's two most important early critics, playwright Jean-Claude Germain and *Le Devoir*'s theatre critic Michel Bélair, agreed that 28 August 1968 was the beginning of something new and important in Quebec theatre. In his review of that electrifying opening night, Germain called *Les belles-sœurs* 'the birth of Québécois Theatre' and hailed it as 'a theatre of liberation,' inscribing it in a program of artistic, political, and individual liberation (Germain 1968b, 10; 1968a, 5). For his part, Bélair found in *Les belles-sœurs* the origin of what he would call '*le nouveau théâtre québécois*' (new Québécois theatre) (Bélair 1973).

It is now something of a truism that Tremblay's *succès de scandale* inaugurated a type of theatre that was explicitly and self-consciously Québécois in form, theme, and language. Within five years of its opening, it had already been declared a 'Québécois classic.'[1] In this chapter, I am interested in the figurative means by which *Les belles-sœurs* ascended so rapidly to that originary, classic status. Response to the play emblematizes the dominant version of engagé criticism at the time – in Quebec and beyond – which has largely determined interpretations of this play, and many others, since. Moreover, the source material around performance-to-nation figural relations is especially rich as this period is one of tremendous critical interest in precisely the question that animates this book. With care and persistence, anticolonial cultural critics in particular struggled to define how and where text rubs up against context, and how the former might be relevant to and have an impact on the latter. They sought answers to this question under the particularly pressing circumstances of a burgeoning national independence movement that aimed not only to repossess the territory and products of Quebec – as did the Quiet Revolutionaries – but also to regain possession of Québécois self-worth.

The critical literature surrounding the play, dating from its opening to the most recent publications on it, is dominated by proofs of its national credentials generally in the form of adumbrations of its Québécois characteristics. As in Gélinas's stipulations for a national theatre, the most important evidence of the play's *québécité* is its realism in form, theme, and expression. The majority of Tremblay's critics in the late 1960s and early 1970s emphasized *Les belles-sœurs*'s documentation of the political, economic, and cultural marginalization of *les Québécois*. They posited an iconic connection between text and context: stage and social realities shared a set of visual referents, a list of major concerns, and a popular language of expression. Minimizing the differences between stage reality and social reality, critics attributed to *Les belles-sœurs* an authenticity and political efficacy heretofore unattained.

I suggest that *Les belles-sœurs* holds a more complicated vision of *québécité* than its critics have often allowed. This alternative *québécité* might be read in the differences between play-world and real-world that a reflective reading invested in text-context correspondences tends to suppress. Thus, after sketching the context in which a politicized reading strategy based on reflection responds aptly to infrastructural realities in Québécois theatre and culture at large, I turn to the elements of *Les belles-sœurs* that are unassimilable to and/or unreadable by this analysis: namely, the characters' gender and the play's explicitly theatrical formal elements. To render these elements as Québécois, critics supplemented reflection with metaphor, a figure that still posits an original truth that cultural production represents but which marks the distance between that truth and its representation. With regard to gender, for instance, contemporary critics assumed that the all-female cast stood in for an all-male polity. This shift in interpretive strategy displays the preferred reading strategy's internal inconsistencies. More significantly, it opens the door to alternative readings of *Les belles-sœurs* that take into account not only women's symbolic role in *indépendantisme* but also their actual place within the movement. *Les belles-sœurs* manifests an alternative model of *québécité* in the dramaturgical and political problems its all-female cast poses for critics. This model is articulated in the dual structure of the drama itself and in the series of extended monologues delivered by the five central characters; importantly, it denies a strictly metaphorical relationship between theatre and nation in which the nation is the truth to which theatrical meaning refers.

By reconsidering the efficacy of reflection and metaphor as the primary related figures linking theatre to nation, I do not aspire to 'correct' the play's most compelling and long-lived interpretation; rather, I want to participate in that 'persistent core of critical activity' in Quebec concerned to understand the links between 'literary and social configurations' of which I made note in chapter 2 (Simon 1991a, 167). My difference with these critics is not with their insistence on cultural production's efficacy, nor with the play's realistic markers. Rather, it is with the insistence that the theatre's primary social value resides in its reflective capacities. By focusing instead on *Les belles-sœurs*'s explicitly theatrical elements, I illuminate the stakes of metaphor for anticolonial theorists and argue that the metaphor of Quebec-as-female runs the considerable risk of consuming its object: namely, women.

Les belles-sœurs is the story of Germaine Lauzon, a working-class housewife in Montreal's east end – the city's most densely francophone area and, not coincidentally, one of its poorest. It is 1965 and Germaine has won a million trading stamps in a contest, which will allow her to redecorate her whole house. However, pasting a million stamps into booklets is a big job so Germaine browbeats her daughter Linda into helping her and invites two of her three sisters, Rose Ouimet and Gabrielle Jodoin; her sister-in-law; and some friends and neighbours to a stamp-pasting party.

For a short while all goes according to plan as fifteen women circulate around Germaine's kitchen table swapping stories of their recent activities, sharing strongly held moralistic opinions, and pasting stamps. Soon, however, the stamp-pasting activity and Germaine's too frequent references to her new buying power tap each character's longings for something more than what they have. In a series of monologues that are alternately spiteful, wistful, and comic the *belles-sœurs* hold forth about their lives. Some bemoan their condition, as in the cases of the estranged sisters, Rose Ouimet and the uninvited Pierrette Guérin, who each speaks movingly, angrily, of being trapped and sexually exploited in her relationships with men. Others articulate a post-scarcity vision of a different life in which domestic relations are happy and the home environment beautiful. Indeed, the possibility of attaining domestic beauty provides the pretext for the gathering. Germaine's opening monologue (delivered on the phone to her sister, Rose) adumbrates how she will 'tout meubler ma maison en neuf' (do over the whole house) with the 'belles affaires' (nice things) from the catalogue, including velvet paintings for the living room and kitchen appliances in red with gold stars (Tremblay 1968, 11; 1974, 12).[2] However, the play's set-up also belies its fundamental absurdity. The task required for her dream's actualization – pasting one million stamps into booklets – is ridiculous. That the stamps must be pasted into booklets in order to claim the home goods is senseless; and the enormous number of stamps that need pasting underscores again the silliness of the requirement. What Germaine has won most immediately is a repetitive, boring, and practically endless job. Only after she has performed it to the company's satisfaction will she receive what she really desires.

A movement between banality and fantasy composes the structural basis of *Les belles-sœurs*. It is replicated in the contrasting content and tone of the monologues as well as in the structure of the play as a whole, which alternates between the monologues and rapid-fire, comic dialogue largely about quotidian activities exchanged while pasting stamps. The movement between banality and fantasy is perhaps best expressed in the contrasting odes declaimed in unison by the *belles-sœurs*: Act 1's 'maudite vie plate' quintet and Act 2's 'ode au bingo.' The 'maudite vie plate' (damned boring life) quintet describes the *belles-sœurs*' typical week. It is replete with unrewarding and repetitive domestic labour (Monday is wash day, Tuesday is for ironing, Wednesday for shopping), ungrateful children, absent husbands, constant bickering, and evenings in front of the television. Their life is 'boring' because it is 'without relief,' another translation for 'plate.' The days are not clearly differentiated one from the other, producing a monotonous flatness to the week; if Tuesday differs from Monday because it is ironing day instead of wash day, the nature of the day's central activity is nonetheless unchanged. The life lacks relief in another way: the domestic labour in which these characters are engaged – washing and ironing, but also cooking and cleaning, looking after their children, and the like – is not only repetitive, but it is also incessant, constant; there is no relief from it until the evening television. Finally, the life is 'plate' as in the colloquial usage of the word: it 'stinks.'

If the 'maudite vie plate' quintet demarcates the banal pole of this tragicomedy, the 'ode au bingo' is located at the most excitingly out-of-the-ordinary end of the scale. In it, nine of the women passionately proclaim in chorus their undying love of the Catholic Church's favoured game of chance, bingo: 'Moé, j'aime ça, le bingo. Moé, c'est ben simple, j'adore ça, le bingo! Moé, y'a rien au monde que j'aime plus que le bingo!' (1968, 55). (I love playing bingo. I adore playing bingo! There's nothing in this world that I like more than bingo! [1974, 87].) Bingo summons a joyful, intense emotionality seen nowhere else in the play; of the forty-six sentences that comprise the ode, only three are not punctuated with an exclamation point. It closes with the women asserting that they would be much happier if only there were more of these extraordinary bingos to punctuate their days.

Ultimately, the women's desires for a life with relief – in both its meanings of variation and relaxation – combined with their resentment of Germaine's good fortune, lead them to steal the booklets they have filled with stamps. They deprive Germaine not just of her stamps, of course, but of the only means she has to realize her dream. Stripped of her recourse to fantasy, Germaine is left with her now inescapable 'maudite vie plate'; she cries, 'Mes timbres! Y me reste pus rien! Rien! Rien! Ma belle maison neuve! Mes beaux meubles! Rien! Mes timbres!' (My stamps! There's nothing left! Nothing! Nothing! My beautiful new home! My lovely furniture! Gone! My stamps!) Having glimpsed the dream, Germaine is left again with only another big job; as Linda says before leaving, 'Ça va être une vraie job, toute nettoyer ça!' (1968, 71). (It'll be some job cleaning all that up! [1974, 114].) After a good cry, Germaine pulls herself together to join the others who are singing 'O Canada' offstage. The play closes on the image of Germaine alone on stage, standing at attention with tears in her eyes and singing the Canadian national anthem, while the trading stamps that might have led her out of her little world fall like snow from the sky (Fig. 4.1).[3]

Tremblay's depiction of fifteen women drawn from three generations garnered a remarkable amount of critical, political, and public scrutiny, catapulting the play and its 26-year-old, former typesetter author into the spotlight. Set in a working-class district and populated entirely by women who discuss their daily lives in their native idiom, Les belles-sœurs pointedly reintroduced local sites, issues, and dialects to Quebec theatre. First performed in a political and cultural environment actively searching for ways to represent and promulgate a newly politicized Québécois identity, the play rekindled debates among artists, intellectuals, politicians, and clergy regarding the features of that national identity and its relationship to cultural production. The intensity of focus on Les belles-sœurs and the wide range of institutions weighing in on its merits (or lack thereof)

4.1 Original cast of *Les belles-sœurs*, on the set designed by Réal Ouellette at the Théâtre du Rideau Vert, August 1968. Notice the division of the stage picture with the older generation of women stage right (with the exception of the shamed Angéline Sauvé [Anne-Marie Ducharme] in mourning black and with downcast eyes) and the younger generation, including Pierrette (Luce Guilbeault) in the long, black, halter dress stage left. Germaine (Denise Proulx) stands farthest downstage with her mouth slightly open and in the light coloured housedress; Rose (Denise Filiatrault) is next to her in the polka-dot dress.

Photo: Guy Dubois. Courtesy Archives du Théâtre du Rideau Vert.

signalled the importance of its role in this identity project. So central was his play to the Québécois national movement that Tremblay has been credited with launching 'the biggest blow of Québécois politico-cultural liberation' (Lévesque 1988). This comment from Robert Lévesque – Montreal's chief theatre critic of the 1980s and 1990s – might be viewed as a theatre professional's aggrandizement of his métier as influential beyond its own community. However, Lévesque's hindsight judgment regarding the impact of Tremblay's first foray onto the major metropolitan stage is supported by a review of press coverage of Tremblay's work from 1968 to 1976 conducted by Lorraine Camerlain and Pierre Lavoie. Camerlain and Lavoie's bibliography of works about Michel Tremblay lists over 150 articles or books that reference *Les belles-sœurs*. Their review reveals not only the impact of *Les belles-sœurs* on public consciousness, but also the major parties involved in the constitution, definition, and circulation of a hotly contested *québécité*.[4]

Although opinions of the play's merits varied as widely as the venues in which they appeared, on the whole, debate polarized into two positions: (1) Quiet Revolutionary modernizers who advocated incremental reform, along with clergy who espoused a return to traditional French-Canadian values, and (2) theatre and literature critics and professionals who espoused a revolutionary nationalist position. Underlying both positions was the assumption that theatre reflected society, and that theatre's most significant referent could be found in the present-day 'real world.'[5] In this sense, theatre's representational labour was not to be constructionist or projective. Its role was not to build new worlds, like Expo 67, but rather to draw Québécois' attention to their present conditions. Each camp was concerned for the image of Quebec and the Québécois being projected in Tremblay's work. However, each had different notions of that identity's preferred characteristics. Both understood Tremblay's depiction of Québécois as negative or critical. Yet, each understood differently the value of that depiction to the Quebec nation.

In demographic terms, reformists were generally of the professional middle and upper classes and represented the interests of capital (banking) and government. As we saw in the last chapter, the new Québécois identity they proposed was modern, secular, professional, and French-speaking. The French-Canadian identity depicted in Tremblay's play was just the opposite: working class, nominal Catholics whose spiritual zeal had been diverted into consumerism and who spoke joual – an English-inflected sociolect of French. In marked contrast with those most salutary *Québécoises*, the Expo hostesses, the *belles-sœurs* exhibited the worst of modernity's offerings. While the hostesses are professional, polished, and worldly, the *belles-sœurs* are uneducated, unkempt (they appear in housedresses and, in Linda's case, hair-curlers), and cripplingly insular. They live in the city, but in one of its worst examples of urban squalor; their proximity to the international, in the form of their Italian immigrant neighbours, stokes xenophobic anger and fear. Where the Quiet Revolution emphasized productive action, the sisters-in-law excel at unproductive activities like passively watching the television and consuming (or dreaming of consuming) prefabricated goods. Germaine's stamps are the most obvious example of consumerism gone amok, but she is not alone in her consumerist folly. For instance, Lisette de Courval buttresses her sense of cultural superiority with financially unsustainable trips to Europe and a real mink stole, while her peers content themselves with trips only to their mother-in-laws' houses for Sunday dinner and fake fur coats. Germaine's daughter Linda's friend, Lise Paquette, is similarly concerned with escaping what Lisette calls 'le monde *cheap*.' Lise's desire for a better life 'with money' is more sympathetically presented than Lisette or Germaine's; having fallen pregnant, she struggles with the decision to abort in order to have the chance to make something of herself. Nonetheless, her idea of 'becoming something' is to have 'un char, un beau logement, du beau linge!' (1968, 57) (have a car, a decent place to live, some nice clothes [1974, 91].) Unlike Quiet Revolutionaries who understood themselves to be the architects of the new Quebec, none of the *belles-sœurs* is the engineer of even her own life. All wait for something or someone else to lift them out of their situation – be it the serendipitous windfalls of bingo, crossword contests, and trading stamps; a boyfriend who 'fai[t] d'l'argent comme de l'eau' (1968, 57) (ma[kes] all this money [1974, 91]); or God.

Worse still for reformists who had laboured to construct a new, modern Quebec in their own image, the 'good sisters' were throw-backs to pre–Quiet Revolution feminine ideals. Drawn together by nature and by law, the *belles-sœurs* are ensconced in an elaborate and binding network that Laurent Mailhot, one of *Les belles-sœurs*'s earliest academic critics, typifies as 'the tentacles and shadows of familial relations.' He observes, 'they often speak of sisters-in-law ... and even of "the sister-in-law of one of my sisters-in-law," when it's not of the "husband of the daughter of a childhood friend of ..."' (Mailhot 1970, 99; 98). In Yvette Longpré's extraordinary second-act monologue, these already extended family ties exceed legal family to encompass familiarity. For no apparent reason, Yvette names all of those gathered at her sister-in-law's birthday party the week before. In the catalogue of familiar Québécois first and last names she produces, Yvette sketches a social universe in which everyone knows everyone else. Many of the names can be found on lists of the most common Quebec names, as they come from the territory's relatively small number of original French settlers ('Le programme de recherche').[6] The joke here is that, ultimately, all *Québécois de souche* (old stock Québécois) are related somehow, that there is no escape from family. The joke's dark humour is revealed in the play's nightmare vision of family as suffocating and in the good sisters' perverse performance of traditional values.

According to the *belles-sœurs*, they are models of Christian devotion and feminine self-sacrifice. Thérèse Dubuc, who cares for her ninety-three-year-old, wheelchair-bound mother-in-law, Olivine Dubuc, plays most frequently on the 'cross' she must bear in order to elicit pity from her peers. The others try to out-do each other in their expressions of admiration.

DES-NEIGES VERRETTE: Vous êtes trop bonne, Thérèse! ...
MARIE-ANGE BROUILLETTE: On pourra dire que vous l'avez gagné, vot'ciel, vous! ...
LISETTE DE COURVAL: C'est ben simple, vous m'émouvez jusqu'aux larmes! ...
DES-NEIGES VERRETTE: J'ai rien qu'une chose à vous dire, madame Dubuc, vous êtes une sainte femme! (1968, 21)

[DES-NEIGES: You're too good, Thérèse! ...
MARIE-ANGE: If you ask me, Thérèse, you've got a heavy [cross to bear]! ...
LISETTE: I can't bear it. It makes you want to weep! ...
DES-NEIGES: Mme. Dubuc, all I can say is, you're a real saint (1974, 28–9).]

Tremblay's finely tuned comic build-up to Thérèse's canonization is undercut shortly thereafter when Thérèse betrays the frustration and violence at the core of her relationship to her mother-in-law. After Olivine spills her bowl of water for pasting the stamps, Thérèse smacks her upside the head to calm her down (27). Olivine's cartoonish indestructibility, on which the humour of her role depends, is first introduced at her dramatic, off-stage entrance when she falls down the three flights of stairs to Germaine's apartment. When the others inquire after Olivine's well-being, certain she must be dead, Thérèse brushes off their misplaced concerns, reassuring them that her mother-in-law falls out of her wheelchair ten times a day without serious injury. Although the slap-stick frame in which the Dubucs are presented tempers somewhat this abuse, it nonetheless exposes the family as a site of violence.

The other 'good sisters' are no better at being 'good,' even if their trespasses are less spectacular. The most obvious example of their moral culpability, of course, is that even Germaine's sisters steal her booklets. They argue incessantly among themselves, and Rose in particular does not hesitate to take her own frustrations out on the assembled by dressing them down with her caustic remarks. Germaine, Rose, and Gabrielle are united only in their total rejection of their youngest sister, Pierrette, for leaving the family enclave for her no-good boyfriend – 'Le maudit Johnny! Un vrai démon sorti de l'enfer! C'est de sa faute si est devenue comme a l'est astheur!' (1968, 44). (Goddamn Johnny! He's a devil out of hell! If she turned out the way she did, he's the one to blame [1974, 69].) – and the bright lights and bars of Montreal's Boulevard Saint-Laurent. In the disjoint between their words and their actions, the *belles-sœurs* embody not so much the pre–Quiet Revolutionary feminine ideal, but rather its worst excesses: the corrosive effects of that ideal on family life and the social fabric. In effect, they stage the reason for the 'correction' of the Quiet Revolution.

Perhaps in part because *Les belles-sœurs* laid bare the limited reach of the Quiet Revolution's programs, reformists responded to the play with shock and disgust; they disavowed its portrayal of *québécité* and positioned it as an obstruction to a modern Quebec's entrance onto the international stage. Upon the play's opening, the uproar regarding its image of francophone Québécois found public expression in the literary and editorial pages of *La Presse* and focused on Tremblay's use of joual.[7] In his review of the Théâtre du Rideau Vert production, the paper's long-time theatre critic Martial Dassylva lamented what he considered the waste of Tremblay's obvious talent on an exercise in dramatic joual, and decried its irredeemably foul language (Dassylva 1972, 133-5). The proof of the reformists' reflective interpretive method lies precisely in the force and valence of the response to the play. Had *Les belles-sœurs* been taken up as 'fantasy' or even 'spoof,' there would have been no need to indict its depiction of Quebec society, for that depiction would not have been tied so directly to that society. The play's many realistic markers – setting, language, theme, and so on – guide critics toward at least an initial reading of the play as in the mode of realism, and hence reflective of a specific time and place. Reformists' reflective reading of *Les belles-sœurs* was most explicit when Jean-Louis Barrault's Théâtre des Nations in Paris invited the Rideau Vert to perform the play for Parisian audiences in 1972. The Liberal Quebec government refused to fund the excursion because of its depiction of Québécois as vulgar and ignorant. Quebec's minister of cultural affairs insisted instead on a different play that was 'written in French.'[8]

If Tremblay's *belles-sœurs* were a negative portrait of French Canadians who had not yet 'caught up' with the societal changes wrought during the Quiet Revolution, anticolonial critics would argue that they were nonetheless a *truthful* depiction of many who were not yet fully 'Québécois.' For this second generation of the Quiet Revolution, the symbolic (and sometimes actual) sons of Expo's engineers, 'truth' was representation's key social value. Thus, the worth of a play like *Les belles-sœurs* lay in its searing, if somewhat exaggerated, depictions of an ugly contemporary reality. Concerns over *Les belles-sœurs*'s ugly image gave way to a valorization of its native style. And the discomfort Tremblay's play occasioned in its audience would function as a lever to raise the consciousness of Québécois.

The clearest and most influential expression of this broadly anticolonial philosophy was the cultural journal *Parti pris*. Founded in 1963 by a group of engagé writers, graduate students, and political activists in their twenties, *Parti pris* espoused some of the most rigorous arguments in favour of a secular, socialist, and sovereign Quebec. The *Parti pris* generation based their program for independence on the work of anticolonial theorists and activists including Jean-Paul Sartre, Albert Memmi, Jacques Berque, and Frantz Fanon. In keeping with other anticolonial nationalist projects of the period, *partipristes* sought to reverse the effects of foreign domination in all spheres of activity: in the political sphere (by [English-speaking] Canada), in the economic sphere (by a combination of English-Canadian and U.S. business interests), and in the cultural sphere (by the French). However, while the Quiet Revolution's modernization program focused on rediscovering and re-annexing Quebec's territory, the *partipristes*' anticolonial program honed in on Québécois's self-discovery and self-repossession. For *partipristes*, Quebec independence hinged on Québécois self-realization. The fight for political, economic, and cultural liberation thus began by 'dis-alienat(ing) the everyday life of the nation's people' (Chamberland 1963, 18). Freed of distorting alien influence, the revolutionary subject was reborn as 'l'homme québécois' (Québécois man), a national subject accepting of who 'he' is and rooted in 'his' native soil. With this, Chamberland specifies here the animating principles of the *partipriste* vision of revolution: *reconquête et natalité* (reconquest and birth) (1964a, 58).

However, *l'homme québécois* could not be born again if he lacked full self-knowledge. This epistemological challenge, difficult in most circumstances, was aggravated in Quebec by the Québécois' dispossessions at the hands of non-native governing classes (i.e., U.S. and Canadian corporations, plus anglophone Québécois) and the compensatory ideology propounded by the native governing classes (the clergy and the bourgeoisie). For instance, the myths aggrandizing French Canadians' role in perpetuating the Catholic faith and the French language compensated for and distracted them from their lack of political and economic power. In their 1964 special issue entitled 'Portrait du colonisé' (Portrait of the colonized), *partipristes* indict the traditionalist values and the myths of *canayenété* ([French] Canadian-ness) propagated by the Church, enforced in the family, and supported by provincial governments. *Parti pris*'s new insight, however, was that the values and myths that the Quiet Revolution sought to overthrow were but symptoms of a more fundamental problem: namely, the harsh reality of a colonized Quebec that had largely succeeded in making Québécois dupes of false consciousness and in alienating them from their true selves, the effects of which had not been eradicated by the Quiet Revolution's modernization program.[9] For *partipristes*, the Quiet Revolution failed by misprising the target and then by constructing a neo-colonial power structure largely benefiting the upper classes and the petty bourgeoisie. Only when the conditions in which Québécois lived were exposed *as colonial* could Québécois forge a better reality based on their true identity, *as national.* Actively decorticating the myths that 'mask oppression in the eyes of the oppressed' would thus clear the ground for a socialist-nationalist revolution. Chamberland explains, 'Demystification is a positive weapon in the hand of the oppressed class or nation: it aims to destroy the values imposed by the dominant class, in order to recognize oneself and to realize oneself in the face of one's true needs, one's true desires' (Chamberland 1963, 14; 21). In this task of demystification, cultural production discovered its revolutionary praxis: 'action by unveiling' (R. Major 1979, 72). It would counter those myths' falsehoods with unflinching truth realistically presented.

Many saw the expression of *Parti pris*'s anticolonial cultural philosophy in Tremblay's *Les belles-sœurs.* Like the fully realized Québécois identity proposed by *partipristes*, the new Québécois theatre broke with all signs of foreign cultural domination. Bélair writes, 'Québécois in its form, its language, and in the problems it confronts, the new Québécois theatre is one of the most essential factors in the affirmation of our identity' (Bélair 1973, 11). In accordance with this reading formation, anticolonial critics looked to *Les belles-sœurs* for its truth-telling ability. As is evident from the reformists' negative reactions to *Les belles-sœurs*, the play did attack the still-active pre–Quiet Revolutionary ideology. For instance, in *Le Théâtre Québécois: instrument de contestation sociale et politique,* Jacques Cotnam glimpses revolt in the characters' collective denunciation of outdated images of mothers as submissive and hiding behind religion (1976, 93-4). Moreover, *Les belles-sœurs* conducted its demystifying representational labour via a realist aesthetic. For example, the bulk of the play consists of a series of vivid conversations about the characters' disappointments and the banalities of their lives. The performance codes employed in the original 1968 production likewise conform to the theatrical conventions of realism. The set at the Rideau Vert was littered with kitchen parapher-nalia, and the characters appeared clothed in garments recognizable to the audience as appropriate to their social class. The critic from the Eng-lish-language Montreal paper, *The Gazette*, describes the set of its second production (1969) the following season (again at the Rideau Vert) as follows: 'On stage are an old refrigerator, an old treadle sewing-machine, an old washer-with-wringer; an old gas range, hot-water heater. The only new element is the telephone. Around it are penciled old numbers. The furniture is chrome and leatherette and used. The kitchen sink stands on four pieces of 2x2 and has a fringe of plastic tacked around it. Above and beyond the walls stands a stark forest of television aerials' (Robert-son 1972, 153). In the comedy's thematic concerns, many saw theories of French-Canadian marginality, colonization, and alienation literally acted out on stage. No less than former *partipriste* André Major wrote that *Les belles-sœurs* uncovers 'the real, everyday poverty, the impoverishment and submission, the animality and egotism, all there is in an embryonic, nar-row, and joyless existence' (A. Major 1968, 14). In each of these instanc-es, the mode of reference was empirical, relying on the correspondence of observable phenomena (Fig. 4.2).

The structural device of the unity of time utilized in the play also makes *Les belles-sœurs* a good candidate for this kind of low mimetic or reflective criticism that minimizes the distance between stage reality and social reality. Laurent Mailhot confirms, 'The action of *Les belles-sœurs* is of exactly the same duration as its performance; dramatic time equals real time.' There is an act break, which Mailhot calls 'pure convention' (Mailhot 1970, 100). And by the play's 1972 second-print edition, Trem-

4.2 The 'good sisters' paste stamps into booklets as Germaine supervises in the
first production of *Les belles-soeurs*, directed by André Brassard, August 1968.
Note Lisette de Courval's mink stole and pearls (Hélène Loiselle), the Jesus
figurine on the stovetop stage right, and the water heater in the upstage
left corner.

Photo: Guy Dubois. Courtesy Archives du Théâtre du Rideau Vert.

blay's stage directions indicate that the last six lines of Act 1 shall be repeated at the beginning of Act 2, thereby creating the illusion of un-broken action. The didiskalia read as follows: 'Le deuxième acte com-mence à l'entrée de Pierrette. On refait donc les six dernières répliques du premier acte avant d'enchaîner' (Tremblay 1972, 75). (The second act begins with PIERRETTE's entrance. Hence, the last six lines of Act One are repeated now [Tremblay 1974, 73].) The continuity of time within the stage world and the stage world's synchronization with the audience's world lend themselves to an understanding of the play as a kind of documentary.

The other primary proof of *Les belles-sœurs*'s authentic *québécité* was its use of the joual. Writing in joual (or what they called 'écrire mal' [to write badly]) was also a favoured *partipriste* practice for representing the social with adequate literary representations of speech.[10] Paul Chamber-land, whose own collection of engagé nationalist poems, *Terre Québec*, was published in 1964, links the use of the vernacular to Québécois literature in 'Dire ce que je suis' (To speak what I am): 'There is no meaningful literature except that which is rooted in a reality, a common life – and the writer, the poet is rooted in it only by first basing him/herself in the language of the everyday' (1965, 36). That everyday language was a 'contact zone,' in Mary Louise Pratt's terminology: 'social spaces where cultures meet, clash, and grapple with each other, often in contexts of highly asymmetrical relations of power, such as colonialism, slavery, or their aftermaths as they are lived out in many parts of the world today' (1997, 63). In sociolinguistic terms, joual is a sociolect – a language sys-tem (*langage* in French) which is developed in contact with and response to a dominant language which encompasses it. Joual combines Québé-cois French with urban influences – most notably, English. (Québécois French is the regionalism of French developed after French colonial rule over what was then 'Lower Canada' ended. Severed from spoken continental French, Quebecois retains some of the stylistic characteris-tics of *ancien régime* French. It augmented French vocabulary with new words for natural phenomena encountered in the New World – flora, fauna, weather systems, and the like.) The population shift in the 1950s from the farm to the city is reflected in the rise of Quebecois French's urban variant, joual, which was formed in the linguistically and ethnical-ly mixed urban neighbourhoods of Montreal during the mid-twentieth century. In that environment, its vocabulary expanded once again – this time with urban and workplace references (largely industrial) and with English and English-inflected words (Robert 1995, 118).

As inflammatory as what the joual 'is' – a mixed, oral sociolect – is its function as a kind of self-image for Québécois. In Jean-Claude Germain's terms, joual 'bears in its flesh the scars of life and history.' Its existence 'proves that after 200 years of co-habitation with an English-speaking ruling majority ... the natives are not deaf' (1976, 18). For Germain, joual is evidence of Québécois's continued – if embattled – existence and resilience; it is already the language of defiance and revolt. Joual embodied resistance to French cultural colonialism and English linguistic domination, and functioned as a way of distinguishing *québécité* from *canayenété* and *francité*. Sherry Simon writes that during the period under discussion, 'Québécois literature was largely written in confrontation or in dialogue with English.' She continues, 'Interlinguistic expression of this period of 'decolonization' took the form of a triangular confrontation between the franco-French (the imperial norm), Québécois-French (the language of vernacular authenticity) and English (the agent of linguistic pollution)' (1994, 29). In keeping with this national investment in joual, Bélair calls it 'a faithful mirror of the working class Québécois milieu' (1973, 112).

This second coincidence bound the stage world to the real one ever more tightly. Although Tremblay was not the first dramatist to write dialogue in joual, he was the first dramatist to write an entire play in joual. (Note, though, the didiskalia were written in standard French.) Predecessors like Gratien Gélinas and Marcel Dubé, active playwrights from the 1940s until the late 1960s, had both employed the joual to indicate working-class characters and introduce local color. Tremblay, on the other hand, set his play in its entirety in a working-class milieu populated by characters who can speak *only* joual. Even Lisette de Courval, who strives to surpass 'le monde *cheap*' in which she finds herself by 'perler [*sic*] bien' (speaking well) makes the same grammatical, syntactical, and pronunciation errors as her stamp-stealing compatriots. Her failed choice of language highlights not only the lack of linguistic self-awareness of the sisters-in-law – they do not realize that their speech is impoverished and contaminated – but also the impossibility of their choosing otherwise. The use of joual in *Les belles-sœurs* changes again the theatrical referent – not only to a local, working-class milieu, but also to oral culture instead of literary convention. Winfried Siemerling calls the transmutation of joual into a written language a 'simulated orality,' a new signifying practice that 'often designates here the emergence of presumably authentic identity through the very medium of the dominant symbolic – writing' (2005, 128). This incursion of a vivid orality into the theatre significantly challenges the fundaments of what Bélair calls *le nouveau théâtre québécois*'s nemesis, 'le Grand Théâtre,' or a high-culture, literary model of theatre.

Tremblay's realistic touches and his use of the language of vernacular authenticity neatly coincide with cultural nationalism's desire to reveal a truly native Québécois identity. Although few went so far as *partipriste* Jacques Brault (who believed that only prose could be politically engaged) or André Brochu (who condemned as 'bourgeois' poets overly concerned with style), many in leftist and literary circles during the late 1960s and early 1970s shared the premise that an authentic reflection of social reality required effacing, or at least minimizing, the reminders of the artistry required to create symbolic worlds (quoted in R. Major 1979, 76). Robert Major's *Parti pris: idéologies et littérature* insists that the *partipristes*' cultural program struck a tenuous and exacting balance between affirming literature's political value and celebrating its aesthetic value. Validating literature's praxis entailed careful measurements of the perceived distance between the symbolic universe of the work of art and the lived universe of social reality. In *Parti pris*'s issue on literature and revolution, André Major ties literary praxis to realism's reflections of the contemporary moment, one in which it is an active participant and to which it critically addresses itself: 'Revolutionary works are born of a revolutionary moment. A literature *represents* its era; it lives the era's contradictions and its movement' (A. Major 1964, 57. Emphasis in original). For his part, Bélair naturalizes Tremblay's connection to working-class life, affirming again and again that the world Tremblay describes in his theatre 'was his in the first instance'; he opines, 'Native of a working-class district, Tremblay was unable to tear himself away; his theatre is the striking illustration.' At the same time, Bélair minimizes Tremblay's artistic skill at translating the social world to the stage: 'Tremblay's theatre can therefore establish itself as a faithful transcription of reality: nobody will deny it. In any case, a brief incursion into the working-class districts of Montreal or of any other little town will succeed in proving it immediately. Quebec still has an enormous number of Germaine Lauzons' (Bélair 1973, 121; 114; 121). Both realism as an artistic form and the new Québécois identity are predicated on the ability to know and re-present the truth of a people's identity and experience.

Having suffered the wages of colonialism's more abstract forms of representation – an ideology based on religious principles of piety and self-sacrifice and universalist principles of modernization and humanism – *partipristes* and those inspired by them favoured what Denis Salter has called in another context 'empirically-based, low mimetic types of referentiality' that facilitate nationalist projects (1991, 90); in other words, they valued direct and transparent representation for its clarity of meaning. The closer the symbol lies to the referent, the less room there is for (mis)interpretation. Moreover, low mimetic cultural productions had more utility for the anticolonial movement. Irrefutable reflections of 'how things are' would force spectators to face up to their marginalization and inspire them to do something about it. Revolutionary plays like *Les belles-sœurs* were 'action,' not only by 'unveiling,' but also by provocation. The mirror of representation 'no longer lied'; neither did it engender passivity in those who would gaze into it (Pontaut 1972, iii). Rather, *Les belles-sœurs*'s truthful reflections would activate 'prises de conscience' ('consciousness-raising') in the audience. In the late 1960s and early 1970s, Tremblay himself assigned a consciousness-raising purpose to what he called his 'theatre-*vérité*, slap-in-the-face theatre, "descriptive" theatre.' He insisted, '*Les belles-sœurs* is a political play. It is obvious that when you show people how they are, it is in order to change them' (quoted in Handfield 1970, 27). In another interview he attests, 'My theatre follows current events, and it is in that regard that it is political. It tells people what they really are, it reflects their own image and aims essentially at a consciousness-raising for an eventual unblocking' ('Michel Tremblay' 1972, 20). (Given the clear influence of *Parti pris* aesthetic philosophy in Tremblay's descriptions of his plays, it may be worth mentioning that when he was working as a typesetter, he set all of *Parti pris*'s issues [Arbic 1976].) Where Tremblay's evaluations of his artistic work's social utility were pretty straight-forward, Jean-Claude Germain's ascription of action to *Les belles-sœurs* resonates with the language of resurrection: 'There is only one possible reaction to *Les belles-sœurs*: "No! I don't accept that, not for myself, not for anyone" ... When Tremblay declares that *Les belles-sœurs* is "scary," he is absolutely right. Stripped of all excuses, of all justifications, naked, our reality would scare a dead person. Scare him so much that he might rediscover, in that fear, a taste for living' (Germain 1968b, 4-5). Exposed to frighteningly accurate reflections of the Québécois condition, the dead person will awaken to kill off distorted, externally imposed self-images; in so doing, he will be reanimated as a fully realized *homme québécois*.

Although *Les belles-sœurs*'s dramatic realism and its use of joual lent themselves to positivist arguments regarding the play's *québécité*, when it came to the sisters-in-law themselves, critics required another tactic for adequating Tremblay's fiction with social fact. That this most Québécois of plays was populated entirely by *Québécoises* proved difficult to assimilate to a movement trafficking in masculine symbols of alienation and false consciousness. The very proliferation of female types on stage might have guided some toward a reading of the *belles-sœurs* as 'woman,' for instance, before instead settling on the generic, male-implied referent of *Québécois*. As Mailhot observes, 'Woman completely engulfs the stage of *Les belles-sœurs*. Woman at every age, from every angle ..., in all of her conditions: mother; grandmother; abusive, unsatisfied, or neglected spouse; virgin, pregnant woman; housewife; prostitute; etc.' (1970, 98). Despite the multiple specifications of the category of 'woman,' in the moment of the play's first public reception the characters' gender and the gender-specific nature of their complaints and fantasies expressed in monologues were not taken up.

To maintain the national allegory in the face of the good sisters, critics had to explicitly negotiate the breach between theatre and society that their more empirical proofs of the play's *québécité* papered over. They were forced to supplement their straight reflective reading with metaphor, calling upon the latter to forge similarity out of manifest sex-difference, and complementarity between signifier and (presumed) signified. Thus, the good sisters themselves were not interpreted following the one-to-one correspondence criterion deployed by many in their interpretations of the other elements of the play. Although the set's kitchen sink was presumed to index kitchen sinks all over Montreal's east side, and the characters' mode of expression was lifted wholesale from social context, the female characters were not interpreted as accurate depictions of 'real' women. Instead, they embodied the distorted, imposed self-images of Québécois that Germain's resurrected 'dead person' must vanquish in order to become *l'homme québécois*. Here, even readers like Bélair, disdainful of the 'thematic' interpretations of the previous generation, resorted to a similar metaphorical critical practice when confronted with the good sisters' sexual specificity and their gender-typical fantasies. They are 'representative types as much in their individuality as in their collectivity' (Caron 1968/1972, 143). They were neutered symbols of what Pierre Maheu called the 'revolt' against traditional values which paved the way to the 'revolution' against colonial and capitalist structures (P. Maheu 1963). To one critic, the *belles-sœurs* represented the 'triumph of the tribe over the individual, of frustration over pleasure' (Greffard 1993, 42). To many others, they were symbols of 1968 Quebec's marginality: working class and female to the Anglos' bourgeois comforts and male privilege.[11] We can again count Tremblay himself in this number; in the myriad interviews he granted in the five or so years following *Les belles-sœurs*'s opening night, Tremblay frequently referred to his characters as 'marginals.' He explains, 'I write about marginals ... in my plays because the Québecois [*sic*] are like marginals. They are a people fighting and dreaming of the right to be who and what they are, dreaming to be free' (Pacheco 1974, 55). In this recourse to metaphor, *partipriste* reception displays the fissures within its seemingly tidy (low) mimetic reading strategy.

Like many of his reformist and revolutionary contemporaries, Tremblay expressed Quebec's situation in gendered metaphors. As we saw in chapter 1, the economically marginal, sexually repressed, and culturally backward Quebec of the 1960s was often figured as female. 'She' was allegorized as an unhappy wife, forced to suffer the indignities and abuses of power of her husband, English Canada (see Probyn 1996). In a revealing 1971 interview printed in the first issue of the cultural journal *Nord*, Tremblay critiques colonialism for distorting Québécois's self-image, declaring, 'We are a people who disguised ourselves for years in order to look like another people. It's not a joke! We were transvestites for 300 years' (Cloutier, Laberge, and Gignac 1971, 64). The emphasis on unnatural disguise and its necessary unveiling in quotes like the above dovetails with *partipriste* writings in which, Robert Schwartzwald proves, travesty and homosexuality are deemed symptomatic of Quebec's national underdevelopment (1993).[12] For instance, Maheu's contribution to the 'Portrait du colonisé' issue significantly entitled 'Œdipe colonial' indicts Quebec's matriarchal family system for de-naturing men and for effectively castrating them. Wives' frigidity denied and repressed their husbands' virility; women's mythologized status as saintly mothers made women the ultimate household authority. Together, this separated men from their true (masculine) selves, effectively transforming them into (feminized) metaphor; Québécois became 'le fils de sa femme' (his wife's son), a victim of arrested development (1964, 26). Here, the stakes of demystification and revolution clarify themselves on the terrain of reproduction. Colonial falsity's feminizations not only obscure national and personal truth but could lead to Québécois extinction. A people consisting of 'men in skirts' and castrating women does not reproduce. In the absence and/or perversion of 'proper' sexual relations leading to reproduction, cultural production's symbolic labours are called upon to model more faithful and fruitful types of reproduction.

Consistent with this reading formation, Bélair characterizes Tremblay's precursors of the 1940s and 1950s as sterile: 'Fridolin (by Gratien

Gélinas) and the characters of [Marcel] Dubé did not have descendents; despite all their impact, they snuffed themselves out by not leaving any-one to perpetuate them' (1973, 111). Tremblay, though nobody's artistic son, is clearly positioned by Bélair as the father of the new Québécois theatre's popular or working-class current. The playwright's fecundity results from his work's enmeshment in contemporary, local experi-ence. His work's commitment to what Maheu defined as the world of the Father – 'the universe of durable goods, of the reality of objects, of concrete outcomes, of work and effectiveness; the Father is praxis' (P. Maheu 1964, 25) – contributes to national remasculinization.

As we have seen, for anticolonial critics of this period, the mimetic model that is most fruitful is the one that is also most faithful, namely, empirically based reflection. Given this positive emphasis on one-to-one correspondences, why were the good sisters not read as *Québécoises* or *canadiennes-françaises* by revolutionary critics? To explain metaphor's per-sistence in the case of the good sisters we must address the utility of the metaphor they embodied – Quebec-is-female – to an anticolonial nation-alist project.

The *belles-sœurs* were useful to anticolonial projects in the same way they were to reformist ones: as negative examples of an outmoded and nationally dangerous culture and attitude. Quiet Revolutionary reform-ists fastened on how the good sisters still embraced aspects of *canayenété* that reformists disavowed – like traditionalism and Catholicism – and how they distorted aspects of *québécité* reformists held dear – like moder-nity, urbanity, and *le fait français*. The *belles-sœurs* rebuked in turn *partipriste* visions of *québécité*. Where *partipristes* valorized the working class, the sis-ters-in-law envied a bourgeois lifestyle with all its accoutrements. Where *partipristes* advocated class solidarity through the alliance of intellectuals and professionals with the working classes, the sisters-in-law fantasized about class mobility (Arbic 1975). Where the anticolonial vision was of collective solidarity (of the Québécois people) and autonomy (for Que-bec), the sisters-in-laws' vision was of individual wealth (material plenty) and connection (sexual pleasure). The signal difference between re-formist and anticolonial refusals of the good sisters was in their different mobilizations of them. By restricting the play's performance, reformists disavowed the continued existence of people like the good sisters. Anti-colonial critics, on the other hand, embraced them as Cassandra figures who spoke the truth of the as-yet-unrealized Québécois condition.

More important for my interests in national mimesis, revolutionary critics cast the sisters-in-law as men in drag, as castrated French Canadians, courtesy of metaphor. The *belles-sœurs*, like Quebec and the Québécois subject they represented, were 'naturally' men but had been turned into or had disguised themselves as women under colonial pressures. Revealing this metaphor as metaphor (or, in their terms, 'myth') – that is, as distorted both in source (because colonial, not native) and in form (because metaphorical, not real) – made it possible to imagine overthrowing it. It was through the metaphor of Quebec/Québécois-as-female that 'awakened' Québécois found hope in a new beginning. By casting off this distortion of Quebec identity Québécois would, in the words of critic Adrien Thério, 'begin again to walk like men' (1972, 150). In Maheu's formulation, these new men would liberate themselves from the symbolic Mother who had kept them feminized children. 'By surging anew from her breast,' *l'homme québécois* prepares to fight a battle not against falsifying metaphors, those having been demystified in the 'revolt' stage preceding 'revolution,' but against 'concrete enemies.' This more crucial battle toward Québécois self-realization and national independence 'will with the same stroke launch revolutionary praxis' (P. Maheu 1964, 29). In addition, the Quebec-as-female metaphor gave 'awakened' Québécois the hope of divorce – Quebec from Canada – as inferred through the insistent heterosexualization of majority-minority relations circulating in public culture.

Their recourse to metaphor, of course, effectively eliminated – or at least reduced – the need to wrestle with the good sisters' gender-specific concerns, as they were vividly outlined in the dystopic monologues of Pierrette or of Marie-Ange, who introduces the theme of poverty into the play in its second monologue. Nor would the critical orthodoxy confront the very concrete lack that marked Germaine and Lise's experiences, for instance, for which their rich fantasy lives populated with red and gold kitchen appliances and dreams of 'becoming somebody' would compensate. Rather, the monologues in which these concerns and fantasies were expressed were largely rendered politically unintelligible in the anticolonial interpretation. Although the play is broadly structured in accordance with the unity of time, a fact many critics stressed in an effort to align the play's representations with Quebec's present situation, five extended soliloquies and two choral odes interrupt its narrative action. Critics interested in *Les belles-sœurs* as social realism tripped over these 'secondary' structural elements, these unruly interjections that do not easily integrate themselves into the play's narrative action. In fact, in his review of Bélair's *Michel Tremblay*, Jean-Claude Germain lamented the critic's lack of interest in extra-narrative elements (1972). Tremblay likewise complained of his early reception 'that everybody was discussing the content of my plays, while the form was analyzed very little, so that the writer in me was frustrated' (quoted in Usmiani 1979b, 37). (A notable exception to this tendency was J.-P. Ryngaert's 'Du réalisme à la théâtralité: La dramaturgie de Michel Tremblay dans les Belles-Sœurs et À Toi pour toujours, ta Marie-Lou' [1971], with which I engage more extensively below.) Reintegrating the monologues into the anticolonial interpretation of *Les belles-sœurs* might extend its critique. Attention to the monologues' formal disruptions, their reminders of metaphor's bridging work, highlights the political potential of fantasy. Attention to the monologues' content marks the conditions the play indicts not only as peculiarly Québécois but also as specifically – not just metaphorically – female.

On the level of form, each monologue breaks decisively with the action of the play and, in the play's first staging by Tremblay collaborator, director André Brassard at Montreal's Théâtre du Rideau Vert, each was delivered soliloquy-style under a spotlight and directly to the audience. When the spotlight focused on the monologist, she was no longer a part of the continuous movement of time in the rest of the play; the other characters froze behind her. These monologues are written and performed as temporal gaps or absences in the narrative of the play. They are a time out of time; as soon as they are over, continuous time and narrative resume exactly where they left off, as though the stage clock stopped during the monologue. Contra the period's critical orthodoxy, J.-P. Ryngaert investigated the functions of these explicitly theatrical elements. He finds that 'contrary to classic dramaturgy where the monologue comes after an exit and where the character is generally alone on stage, [Tremblay's monologues in *Les belles-sœurs*] appear in the form of a *flash*, and hence in breach of the action' (1971, 100). The smooth link between stage reality and social reality propagated by critics like Bélair is likewise ruptured in these moments. Their obvious theatricality breaks the realist frame and highlights the distance and difference between the 'real world' and the stage world. The made-up worlds they articulate remind viewers and readers that the stage world is a created and creative alternative reality, regardless of its other resemblances to the quotidian. In other words, they force reading the whole play – not just its monologues or its female characters – as metaphor. The on-stage kitchen sink is not merely an index of 'real' East End kitchen sinks. It may also be a metaphor – for drudgery or for working-class Québécois public spaces, for instance. The temporal disruption of the monologues offers the possibility of taking elements construed as mutually exclusive and rendering them mutually informative. In this alternate reading, *Les belles-sœurs*'s two temporalities (narrative and monologue), its two registers (quotidian/banal and exceptional/poetic), and the two kinds of mimetic readings associated with them (reflection and metaphor) are not only doubled but twinned, necessarily conjoined. For support in this tactic, let us return to Chamberland's crucial articulation of literary text / social context relations in 'Dire ce que je suis.' He writes,

> I brook *no division between poetry and everyday life*; there is no poetic attitude or universe. I do not go from one world to the other, an allegedly better, more consoling, elevated world ... On the contrary, it is important to *speak the banality of everyday life*, of the Québécois quotidian. Rather, the dream and the real interlaced ... At base, I want simply to say, I would like us to not 'change' 'soul' in using poetry: the only true poetry is the poetry of hours 'without history,' of hours 'without poetry.' Let the dream enter by the stairs or the window, establish itself in all rooms and take on the look of usual things: *the customary may thus be illuminated.* (1965, 40-1. Emphasis in original.)

In this forceful articulation of poetry's social value and the quotidian's poetic value, Chamberland refuses an overly neat separation of social reality and symbolic reality. Although his baseline remains the everyday, he revels in its poetry and sees it as infused with the dream. *Les belles-sœurs*, in its toggling between banality and fantasy, seems also to valorize these two realities as equally 'real' and to understand them as interlaced. What dreams might the *belles-sœurs*' reality unleash? And of what realities might the women's dreams, expressed in monologues and odes, be speaking? Finally, how might their dreams illuminate the customary?

Let us first consider how the reality of Rose's everyday life, as 'poeticized' in her desperate second-act monologue, qualifies the metaphorical reading generally ascribed to it, by insisting on its reflection of a woman's reality.

> (*au bord des larmes*) Pis a [ma fille] finira pas comme moé, à quarante-quatre ans, avec une p'tit gars de deux ans sur les bras pis un écœurant de mari qui veut rien comprendre, pis qui demande son dû deux fois par jour, trois cent soixante-cinq jours par année! Quand t'arrive à quarante ans pis que tu t'aparçois que t'as rien en arrière de toé, pis que t'as rien en avant de toé, ça te donne envie de toute crisser là, pis de toute recommencer en

neuf! Mais les femmes, y peuvent pas faire ça ... Les femmes, sont poignées
à'gorge, pis y vont rester de même jusqu'au boute! (1968, 66)

[(*on the verge of tears*) She [my daughter] won't end up like me, forty-four
years old, with a two-year-old kid on her hands ... and a stupid slob of a husband who can't understand a thing, who demands his 'rights' at least twice a
day, three hundred and sixty-five days of the year. When you get to be forty,
and you realize you've got nothing behind you and nothing in front of you,
it makes you want to dump the whole thing and start all over. But a woman
can't do that ... A woman gets grabbed by the throat, and she's gotta stay
that way right to the end! (1974, 105).]

Rose's *cri de cœur* breaks with anticolonial visions of revolution and even
throws into question revolution's likelihood. While *partipristes* looked
forward to divorcing Canada and beginning anew as free men, Rose expresses a rather dimmer view of women's prospects for independence
and of starting over. She clearly understands her plight as a direct result
of her compromised status as a woman. Kept ignorant about marriage's
realities by the Church and her parents, she vows to not let her own
daughter fall into the same trap. Because she is a woman, starting over
is impossible for Rose, literally and metaphorically: literally because she
has few options outside of marriage, and metaphorically because 'she'
(as metaphor and as woman) functions as that which must be thrown
over to assure the rebirth of *l'homme québécois*. In the solution proposed
by revolutionaries, in which Québécois (men) would assume their 'proper' gender role, Rose's desire for a society in which the gender relations
that produced her specifically female powerlessness will be redressed not
only goes unheard; the anticolonial solution actually reinforces the conditions she decries. In this instance, the risk of the metaphorical reading
is that it tramples its object. Reading Rose's monologue as reflection, as
one might read Germaine's kitchen sink, resuscitates the woman who
grounds the national metaphor.

Lise Paquette (the pregnant 'fille-mère'), Pierrette Guérin (the outcast sister), and Marie-Ange Brouillette (a poor and jealous neighbour)
strike a similarly pessimistic chord in their monologues, in which they re-
gret past choices and rage against conditions that foreclosed on making
different choices. What dreams their realities might unleash is not exactly apparent in their monologues' content about squashed dreams. However, attention to the monologue form may allow for these monologues'
more convincing integration into an anticolonial vision of a new, nation-

al point of departure. In the form of these monologues, whose content despairs of a fulfilling – or even satisfactory – future, Laurent Mailhot recuperates the possibility of a new beginning. He writes, '[The monologue] constantly draws attention to that which could have not been, to that which could be otherwise ... Complication without denouement, its structure is expectation, a new beginning (hence, hope), even if its theme is fatality, powerlessness, imprisonment, anguish' (Mailhot 1973, 36). Appearing in a flash, the monologue form interrupts the play's 'everyday' dialogic sequences and infuses its banality with potential.

Les belles-sœurs's rhapsodic monologues likewise interrupt the narrative action but also foreground the desire for something different in their more fantastic content; they point to a life more fundamentally fulfilling *on the level of feeling*. Even if their visions of a better future do not align themselves with the features of an anticolonial vision, they may nonetheless illuminate customary understandings of the 'political' and, as they did via their form, extend an anticolonial vision.

Certainly, the sisters-in-law's fantasies are avowedly not 'political' in any self-conscious, activist way. On the whole they might be persuasively characterized as *revanchist*, or reactionary. Take, for instance, the most compelling articulation of their vision of plenty and pleasure: Act 2's passionate 'l'Ode au bingo,' involving nine of the fifteen women. (The youngest generation of women – Linda, Lise, and Ginette – and the outcast sister, Pierrette, do not participate.) In the choral ode, bingo takes the place of a lover and the game itself the place of sex. The women describe their preparations for the game in stereotypical lover's language: 'J'me prépare deux jours d'avance, chus t'énarvée, chus pas tenable, j'pense rien qu'à ça' (I get ready two days in advance; I'm a nervous wreck, I can't sit still, I can't even think about anything else'). When the day arrives, they dress to the nines and go to the game. Once installed at tables, bingo cards in front of them, their language takes on a decidedly sexual tone. 'Là, c'est bien simple, j'viens folle ! Mon Dieu, que c'est donc excitant, c't'affaire là ! Chus toute à l'envers, j'ai chaud, j'comprends les numéros de travers ... chus dans toutes mes états!' (1968, 55). (I'm telling you, I get so excited I go right off my rocker. I'm all mixed up, I sweat like a pig, I screw up the numbers ... Oh, I get into a terrible state!' [1974, 87–8].) From this moment on, all sentences are short, repetitive, and exclamatory; they build to a climax: 'Vive les chiens de plâtre ! Vive les lamps torchières ! Vive le bingo !' (1968, 55). When the lights come up after the ode, the women need to refresh themselves with Cokes.

The good sisters' apparently un-self-conscious reprisal of General de Gaulle's infamous 1967 declaration, 'Vive le Québec libre,' seems to clarify once again their apolitical stance. In a moment when many Québécois took 'Vive le Québec libre!' as a rallying cry, the sisters-in-law wish long life to ceramic dogs, floor lamps, and a game of chance. Consistent in tone with the other rhapsodic monologues, it is the stuff of heterosexual bourgeois fantasy. However, the coincidence of 'Vive le bingo!' and 'Vive le Québec libre!' points, I think, in two directions worth pursuing. First, it suggests fantasy's purchase on the Québécois national project. That echo of 'Vive le Québec libre' is found in a collective fantasy about winning at bingo places aspirations for political independence in a similarly fantastic, although not unachievable, realm. In each of the optimistic monologues – those of Germaine, Yvette, Des-Neiges Verrette, and Angéline Sauvé – the dream is within reach: Germaine is about to redecorate her house 'toute en neuf' courtesy of her windfall, for instance. Reading their emphasis on fantasy's use-value as a motivator and animating principle draws to the surface an obscured *partipriste* discourse of fantasy. In Chamberland's thought, for instance, fantasy or dream occupied a central place. For him, 'le souhait' (wish) informs the positivist, objective assessment of current colonial conditions. He writes that present 'facts,' with which the anticolonial movement is so preoccupied, are sedimentations of past actions and projects. In other words, what appear now as inert, concrete 'givens' were once a wish. On the basis of this insight, Chamberland calls for privileging the 'the wish over the proof or report' and the 'hypothesis' over the 'facts'; wishes and hypotheses of improved, future conditions have the potential to transform present facts. He writes, 'It is necessary to talk of hypotheses for action whose "verification" must be realized by the transformation of "facts." And the wish outlines only the emotional fringe of an initial decision for transformation, for revolution' (1964a, 55). Thus the 'wish' and 'hypothesis' are at once the national design's launching point and culmination. Here too, the dream and the real are interlaced.

Second, the coincidence of 'Vive le bingo!' and 'Vive le Québec libre!' pushes us to re-examine the (gender-)politics of these otherwise politically unintelligible moments. During the monologues and choral odes, the play's national labour happens more in the register of feeling than in the register of representation, whether read as reflection or as metaphor. Their language of pleasure and 'l'fun,' however frustrated, overwrites an *indépendantiste* language of rights. For example, Des-Neiges Verrette, a middle-aged single woman, soliloquizes about her secret infatuation with a door-to-door brush salesman. Punctuated by exclamation points, her monologue details her love's development over time and its effects on her emotional life. It seems that in his company she is truly happy for the first time in her life. And the risqué stories and jokes he tells her afford other intense feelings, as well as opportunities for physical contact: 'Des fois, [ses histoires osées] sont tellement cochonnes, que j'rougis. La dernière fois qu'y'est v'nu, y m'a pris la main parce que j'avais rougi. J'ai manqué v'nir folle! Ça ma toute revirée à l'envers de sentir sa grosse main su'a mienne! J'ai besoin de lui, astheur!' (Sometimes I blush, [his stories are] so dirty. The last time he came, he took my hand when I blushed. I nearly went out of my mind! My insides went all funny when he put his big hand on mine! I need him so badly!) Just before the stage lights reintegrate Des Neiges into the quotidian world of Germaine's kitchen, she confides, 'J'rêve ... qu'on est marié ! J'ai besoin qu'y vienne me voir ! [...] j'ai besoin ... d'aimer ... (*Elle baisse les yeux et murmure.*) J'ai besoin d'un homme' (1968, 32). (I dream ... that we're married. I need him to come and see me ... I need ... to love someone ... [*She lowers her eyes and murmurs.*] I need a man [1974, 49].) At a moment when Québécois are exhorted to '*be* a man,' Des-Neiges whispers her desire to *have* a man. As nothing else about her characterization allows us to read Des-Neiges as a gay man in travesty, and as the anticolonial position rendered homosexual desire nationally abject (see Schwartzwald 1991), Des-Neiges's 'need' for a man undoes the metaphorical reading of the good sisters as *québécois-manqués*. Instead, it encourages understanding this illicit desire in the same vein as Rose's anger: as peculiarly (heterosexually) female. It resists metaphor's conversion of (sexual) difference into sameness. In the heart of the play's 'fantasy' sequences lurks another set of recalcitrant, and obscured, women's realities.

In another example, Angéline Sauvé rationalizes her secret, illicit barfrequenting by the opportunities it provides for laughter, for spending time with her 'meilleurs amis' (best friends) (none of whom are around Germaine's kitchen table), and for what she calls in good joual, 'l'fun' (51). If Angéline and Des-Neiges's dreams of 'happily ever after' and a good time lack the seriousness of anticolonial dreams of national independence, the visions share an interest in a more egalitarian model of society and in the full acknowledgment of their own desires. The *belles-sœurs* and the *partipristes* both court a more fully realized self, but do so on different registers and with differently gendered attributes.

In its doubled structure, its movement between the quotidian and 'poetry,' and its availability to reflective and metaphorical readings, *Les belles-sœurs* takes its characters' criticisms and desires seriously, even if it cannot find a way to square them completely with the more politicized and masculinist program of decolonization.[13] Madeleine Greffard pinpoints the irreconcilability of the monologues and their social encasement: 'This [interior] voice [of the monologue], held back from the social space where it does not have a place, is isolated in the individual' (1993, 41). Nonetheless, the insistent presence of the monologues and the concerns and wishes they articulate create a shadow-text of possibilities that do not make their way into the orthodox story of the play and its impact, but are not entirely left out either. In this way, Tremblay's *belles-sœurs* flag the work that remains in incorporating the working classes into an independent national vision: namely, dreaming a society that enables emotional fulfillment, equalized gender relations, and 'l'fun.' They also highlight the costs of that vision to women who, once more, are left behind for better, male futures.

Expo 67 and *Les belles-sœurs* expose the most common figurative means by which certain cultural productions become national – namely, metaphor – in its reflective and constructive guises. Both submit to evaluation that measures fidelity – of signifier to signified, of copy to original, where the signified original is a pre-existing notion (if not an actual reality, as in the case of construction) of the nation, of *québécité*. In each example we have seen national metaphor's reasons and risks. National reflection responds to a need to prove a nation's existence; it establishes the nation's anteriority to its reproduction in the performing arts. National construction responds to a need for reclaiming a colonized territory as national, for restarting national history. In both cases, metaphor is a fertile figure. Via its heteronormatively ordered, properly gendered relations, national metaphor generates national offspring – Quebec-as-nation and a Québécois dramatic tradition.

The next three chapters examine mimetic figures rather more resistant to harmonizing signifier-signified relations than was the case for metaphor. The lines that simulation, metonymy, and affection draw between signifier and signified, fiction and fact, art and society are indirect or even twisted. As in all mimetic figures, they name relations of difference. Simulation, metonymy, and affection, however, name relations that refuse verification according to truth criteria, because they do not route themselves through 'originals' or 'sources.' Their reproductions displace 'origins'; simulation operates without them, metonymy historicizes them, and affection undoes them.

chapter five

National Simulation: Marco Micone's
culture immigrée

In *Exiguity: Reflections on the Margins of Literature*, François Paré observes, 'National literatures institute at their margins the fantasy places of their own muting, of their own extinction as a language, their own spaces of exiguity' (1997, 26). Exiguity, here, is an aperture onto difference, a space in which national literatures are no longer themselves and their voices no longer speak with authority. Paré identifies French-speaking cultures outside of Quebec, like Franco-Manitoba or Franco-Alberta, as the signal space of exiguity to the nascent Quebec literary institution of the 1960s and 1970s. And indeed, Paré cites a Québécois literary trope of return to Quebec from 'the undifferentiated outside of exile' beyond Quebec's borders (1997, 26). As we saw in the chapter on Expo 67, forming a national territory in Quebec required leaving behind prior continental attachments, rendering those spaces 'exiguous.'

Tremblay's *belles-sœurs* enact one version of this exiguity in their anglicized speech and their individualist, capitalist desires. They are marginal by virtue of their sex and by virtue of their linguistic and ideological 'taintedness'; their affiliations cannot be neatly secured to a sovereign, secular, and French Quebec. Nonetheless, the good sisters situate themselves more closely to the centre of *québécité* vis-à-vis the even more distant horizon of immigrant difference. On the margins of the good sisters' marginal existence are their Italian neighbours, cast as unclean, sexually promiscuous, and generally strange. For instance, after Des-Neiges remarks on her 'smelly' Italian (female) neighbour, provoking gales of laughter in the assembled, Lisette de Courval insists that Italians do not wear underwear. This contention launches another strand of gossip concerning the supposed promiscuity of the Italian family's daughter (Tremblay 1968, 15–16). While this beat of the play exposes the *belles-sœurs'* ignorance, it also alerts us to the *nouveau théâtre québécois*'s difficulty in accounting for struggles happening on the margins of the franco/anglo binary. In this chapter, I examine the work of Italo-Québécois writer, teacher, and public intellectual Marco Micone (b. 1945), who approaches the issue of ethnic difference from this immigrant space of exiguity and in the mode of simulation. His work writes back to the centre of the Quebec literary institution – including *le nouveau théâtre québécois* – in a process that not only de-centres the centre but uproots it. In so doing, metaphor's national mimesis loses its guarantor – the origin – as well as its standard of measure – the distance between signified and signifier. By marking his literary debts and troubling origins of *québécité*, Micone's oeuvre evinces a feminist politic that undoes the masculinist national fantasy of self-originating.

Like Tremblay's Québécois classics, Micone's neo-Québécois writing is concerned with national identity and difference, and particularly with their linguistic encodings. This focus on language makes sense given that 'language is the mark of nationality in literature' (Godard 1987, 131). Its logic is also clarified in light of Quebec's lengthy and charged history of what is commonly called 'the language question,' or the concern with French's visibility, power, and perpetuation in Quebec. Unlike Tremblay, however, Micone explicitly takes up being another sign of difference (that is, in addition to the woman) against which the dominant mode of 1960s and 1970s Québécois identity articulated itself. His Italian origin and immigrant status mark him as 'other' to Quebec's reterritorialized, remasculinized self. The 'néo' of 'néo-Québécois' acts as qualifier to the immigrant's claims on 'authentic' *québécité* by highlighting her/his newcomer status. It marks a temporal and spatial border between 'true' or 'original' Québécois and new interlopers. 'Neo-Québécois' are not fully Québécois (hence the qualifier 'neo'). Yet neither are they *not*-Québécois (their new-ness is hyphenated with 'Quebec'). The issue then is in what respect and to what extent are neo-Québécois Québécois? Can one convert from being 'Italian,' for instance, to being 'Québécois'? How does one move along the national identification axis from 'not Québécois' to 'not not-Québécois'? By what means? And is that double negative (the not not-Québécois) as far as an immigrant can go? These questions animate Micone's oeuvre.

In the 1980s, Quebec's exiguity shifts from English Canada to the immigrant in Quebec, the 'other' who lives within the home's borders. It is now a given that the 1980s in Quebec witnessed an explosion of interest in 'the other'; this is the moment in which notions of 'transculture' and 'hybridity' gain momentum in Quebec and stake a claim on the collective imagination of *québécité*. The immigrant figure is increasingly taken up by intellectuals and artists for its fruitful expansion of French Quebec. Daniel Chartier quotes poet Robert Berrouët-Oriol's thoughts on the challenge neo-Québécois writers posed to the Québécois literary institution in the 1980s: "'contemporary Québécois literature is still in the process of mourning the discourse of univocal identity." At stake in that era was "the literary field's capacity to welcome the other voice, the voices from here that came from elsewhere, and above all, to knowingly accept that the literary field is worked, transversally, by these mixed voices"' (Chartier 2002, 304). For example, the theatre journal, *Jeu* covers this 'vogue' in special issues, roundtables, and reviews of plays written by neo-Québécois. Sherry Simon helps pioneer the new subfield examining 'écriture migrante,' or 'writing in movement' in spearheading group research projects as well as in individual publications.[1] The transcultural review *Vice versa* publishes in French, Italian, and English from 1983 until 1994, prompting Italo-Québécois poet Filippo Salvatore to proclaim the 1980s 'the time of the three solitudes' (Ireland and Proulx 2004, 2).

Although this celebratory attitude towards neo-Québécois writing has since become the critical norm, the 1980s and early 1990s witnessed considerable turmoil around the question of writing's – and the neo-Québécois figure's – 'normalcy.' In some of the sociopolitical and literary discourses of the period, the immigrant is sited as another, potentially more pernicious, fantasy place of French Quebec's muting and possible extinction. Literary critic Pierre Nepveu worried that the rise of *écriture migrante* could mean 'the "end" of Québécois literature' (quoted in Chartier 2002, 304). In *La Presse*, columnist Nathalie Petrowski likewise worried for the future of Québécois literature in the face of 'transcultural freak[s]' (Petrowski 1993). In what follows, I link the writing of this particular 'transcultural freak' to the heritage of Québécois literature, which is characterised by a fraught yet thoughtful relationship to language and an emphasis on 'coming to voice.' In recalling that heritage, however, Micone's work also reconfigures it. I argue that his dramatic trilogy from the 1980s highlights the margins of Québécois literature and troubles its claims to 'originality'; his 1989 poem 'Speak What' evacuates its centre.

This chapter uses Marco Micone's dramatic trilogy and manifesto-poem from the 1980s to help locate metaphor's limit as the primary figure for national mimesis and to introduce simulation as a more conducive figure for articulating performance-nation relations in the late twentieth and early twenty-first centuries. In its first section, I demonstrate how Micone's *Trilogia* exposes its model, the *nouveau théâtre québécois*, as fabricated; this deconstruction of metaphor's national mimesis opens the door to metaphor's supplanting. In the second section, I read Micone's manifesto-poem 'Speak What' as national simulation. Jean Baudrillard defines simulation as 'the generation by models of a real without origin or reality'; simulation substitutes 'signs of the real for the real itself' producing 'simulacra,' or copies without originals (1983, 2, 4). Ignoring what I argue is the 'essence' of its model, Michèle Lalonde's 1967 poem 'Speak White,' Micone's 'Speak What' simulates *québécité*, providing an alternate entrée into national representation. In this figure, we discover a source of the extinction with which neo-*québécité* was so frequently allied by anxious commentators.

Micone launched his literary career with a triptych of plays concerning the Italian immigrant condition in Quebec: *Gens du silence* (1982), *Addolorata* (1983; 1996), and *Déjà l'agonie* (1986). He has since completely revised his trilogy under the titles *Silences* (2004) and *Migrances suivi de Una Donna* (2005). He has also published a poem ('Speak What,' 1989); a collection of autobiographical *récits* (*Le figuier enchanté*, 1992, awarded the Prix des arcades de Bologne that same year); French translations of Pirandello's *Sei personaggi in cerca d'autore* (1992); Goldoni's *La Locandiera* (1993), *La serva amorosa* (1997), *Le donne di buon umore* (2000), *La vedova scaltra* (2002), and *L'Imprésario de Smyrne* (2008); Shakespeare's *The Taming of the Shrew* (1995); and Gozzi's *Angellino belverde* (1998);[2] and a series of critical essays on the place of immigrants in the Quebec collectivity. In addition, he is also a leading public intellectual, a spokesperson on immigrant issues in Quebec, and a recently retired professor of Italian language and culture at Vanier College in Montreal.

Gens du silence, Addolorata, and *Déjà l'agonie* attempt to give voice to an incipient *néo-Québécois* and allophone-Québécois (other-speaking Québécois) identity by creating a new, hybrid language. At the same time, in their cultural and literary references and borrowings, the plays are positioned as neither completely new nor radically other to the post–Quiet Revolution Québécois dramatic tradition and its linguistic heritage. Referencing the major themes, formal attributes, and political goals of the cultural nationalist *nouveau théâtre québécois* of the 1960s and 1970s, the trilogy both inserts itself into that movement and resignifies it for an allied yet distinct constituency. In so doing, Micone's *Trilogia* also reveals the *nouveau théâtre québécois*'s naturalised linguistic ground as consciously cultivated.

Of the immigrant condition, Micone has written, 'L'immigré est tiraillé entre l'impossibilité de rester tel qu'il était et la difficulté de devenir
autre' (1992, 87–8). (The immigrant is torn between the impossibility
of staying what he is and the difficulty of becoming other.) He chooses
his words carefully. In the above quotation, for instance, Micone deploys
the expression 'être tiraillé entre' to describe the paradoxical position
of the immigrant who is pulled in two different directions; he is torn
between the impossibility of staying who he has been and the difficulty
of becoming other. In its historical usage, the verb 'tirailler' meant 'tirer
peu à la fois et souvent, avec une arme à feu' (Éditions Larousse 1998,
1012). Although its historical associations with both force (the shooting of a gun) and dispersal (scattershot bullets) are not current in the
contemporary, common usage of the verb, they nonetheless encapsulate
the particular history of Montreal's Italian immigrant community – from
which position Micone writes – and trace the general contours of the
immigrant condition, which his 1980s dramatic trilogy and subsequent
cultural interventions contest.

Micone's personal trajectory of forced dispersal stands in for that of
many Italian immigrants to mid-century Montreal. In 1958, at 13 years
old, Micone and his mother immigrated to Montreal from the Molise
region of southern Italy to join his father, who had left Italy seven years
earlier. Compelled by poverty and unemployment to leave an Italy recovering from its recent fascist past, Micone's father joined the growing
Italian diaspora that scattered millions of largely rural people from the
country's south and central regions across the urban, industrial centres
of Europe and the Americas (Painchaud and Poulin 1988, 21–3).[3] In
'Quelques notes sur l'immigration (inédit),' Micone concretises the connection 'tirailler' supposes between shooting and being torn: 'Emigration is not an act taken in full liberty. When it is not guns that chase
unhappy workers, it is poverty' (1979a, 6).

The first tear is ontological; 'torn between the impossibility of remaining as they were and the difficulty of becoming other,' immigrant identity oscillates between being Italian and being Québécois (Micone 1992,
87–8). It is in this foundational rupture and subsequent suspension that
the particularities of Italian migration connect with the generalised experiences of other immigrant communities. Caught between origins –
in their native lands and in their adopted territory – the immigrant's
liminal position is reflected in the terms often used to describe her or
him: '*néo-Québécois*' and 'allophone.' As indicated above, the prefix 'neo'
indicates the immigrant's recent arrival in Quebec. However, recency is

rather expansive in this terminology, as 'neo-Québécois' is often used for adults, like Micone, who arrived as children and for second- and third-generation immigrants. Louise Vigeant in 'Les dessous des préfixes ...' asks, 'As of which generation do immigrants stop being "neo-Québécois"?' (1994, 39). Moreover, as many scholars and demographers attest, neo-Québécois are not new to Quebec. Approximately 350 non-French immigrants accompanied the approximately 9,000 French who settled the St Lawrence River Valley before 1760. Patterns of immigration have shifted over the two intervening centuries, from predominantly French migrants through the early twentieth century, to allophone Italian and southern European migrants from the 1950s through the 1970s, to largely francophone Middle-Eastern, southeast Asian, and Caribbean migrants in the 1980s and 1990s (Lacroix 1996, 165–78).[4]

In the Quebec in which Micone landed, immigration's ontological tear was compounded by a sociological tear; immigrants were suspended not only between Italian (or Greek, or Portuguese, etc.) and Québécois identities, but also between two distinct formations of being Québécois drawn along ethnolinguistic lines: French and English. Already dispossessed of a tangible and present origin in their stranding between here and there, between becoming other and remaining what they were, immigrants were enjoined to re-originate themselves in/as either French or English. Each language 'reveals belonging to a culture, to a society, determines a place on the economic and social hierarchy' (Lacroix 1990, 202). The primary belonging revealed by language was religious. For most, French indicated Catholic affiliation and English indicated Protestant affiliation, a division reflected in Quebec's bifurcated public school system, for instance, with its discrete Catholic and Protestant school boards from 1875 until 1998.[5] As a result, the project of becoming Québécois involved an initial set of decisions around language acquisition that determined which version of Québécois one would become.

However, the 'allophone' category into which Micone and his generation of 'other-speaking' immigrants largely fell gives the lie to the invitation to start over from a Québécois point of origin. 'Allophone' is an omnibus category encased within the franco-anglo (and a presumed Catholic-Protestant) binary that provides the key terms of reference for Québécois identity. The 'allophone' designation, first used in the 1972 Gendron Report on the language question, situates immigrants whose native language is neither French nor English as simply 'other': 'The term "allophone" gives to immigrants and their descendants ... a characteristic definition denuded of all content and reference apart from the opposition between English and French' (Molinaro 1999, 116).[6] Lacking viable origins upon arrival, allophone immigrants find themselves again stranded in a category denied any referential anchor. Micone's dramatic trilogy argues that the primary and most devastating effect of immigration's suspensions between national cultures is silence. With the public reading and publication of *Gens du silence* (Voiceless People) in 1982, Micone became the first Québécois playwright to dramatise the immigrant condition in Montreal. Jean-Michel Lacroix writes that Micone's trilogy 'marks the beginning of immigrant speech on the Québécois stage' (1990, 195). (It is important to note, however, that since the mid-1980s he has been joined by a host of 'neo-Québécois' playwrights who write in French, including Anne-Marie Alonzo, Pan Bouyoucas, Abla Farhoud, Alberto Kurapel, and, most successfully, Wajdi Mouawad, the current [2007–2010] artistic director of *théâtre français* at the National Arts Centre.) *Gens du silence* has been positioned in the critical literature as the beginning of a vogue for the foreign and the exploration of migration (Vaïs and Wickham 1994; Simon 1994, 149–65; Moss 1996a). Acclaimed Le Théâtre de la Manufacture productions of *Addolorata* and *Déjà l'agonie* (translated into English as *Beyond the Ruins*) established Micone's trilogy as an important phase in Québécois dramaturgy. The latter play was short-listed for the Governor General's Award and won the *Journal de Montréal's* Grand Prix. These domestic dramas centre on families comprised of first-, second-, and third-generation immigrants. While the dramatic situations and characters who populate the plays are broadly realistic – they reflect a contemporaneous lived reality – that reality-effect is punctured by Brechtian distancing effects, including narrator figures and direct audience address. Indeed, they are fundamentally dramas of interpretation in which the dramatic tension arises from the clash of world-views and the words that convey them. As one of Micone's most perceptive and earliest critics, Sherry Simon writes, 'the talking matches in Micone's plays are jousts, conflicting versions of reality which confront one another in mutual incomprehension' (1985, 61). Through a series of debates between the central characters, Micone's domestic dramas introduce the reader to the general features of the immigrant condition as they manifest themselves in the particular context of the plays' Italian families. For instance, *Gens du silence* opens with a chorus connecting the particular story of Antonio's emigration from Italy to the larger story of mid-century Italian emigration.

The theme of being silenced by immigration's ontological ruptures and sociological suspensions runs through each play of the trilogy and is most clearly expressed in *Gens du silence*. This play's 'voiceless people' are a family whose history of migration mimics Micone's own. The parents speak in Italian regional dialect at home, learn popular French dialect from their working-class co-workers, and speak only enough English to communicate with their anglophone bosses. Greeted by two distinct *cultures d'accueil* (host cultures), each with its own haphazard and incomplete methods for integrating newcomers into Quebec society, Antonio and Anna send their son, Mario, to English school in the hope that he will ascend to the position of their anglophone bosses; their daughter, Nancy, is sent to French school because '[l]'avenir, c'est pas important pour les femmes' (the future is not important for women) (Micone 1996c, 58; 1997, 51). The results of these choices are twofold: familial disintegration and sociocultural disorientation. The family members are caught between languages, in what Lise Gauvin evocatively calls a '*no man's langue.*' On the road to acculturation, they find themselves culturally dispossessed (Gauvin 2000, 196; Simon 1984, 462). Mario, in particular, suffers from an inability to fully express himself in any language and instead mixes colloquial English and popular French with profanity to communicate. Mario's code-switching, his toggling – sometimes rather vertiginously – between French and English indicates his lack of singular origin; his rootless speech routes itself through doubled, parallel reference points.[7] In this way, his fragmentary bilingualism obviates the kind of singularity of reference on which metaphor relies.

In contrast, Nancy, the daughter who now teaches at an English school, uses French exclusively in the play. She is presented as at once more integrated into Québécois society – having re-originated herself in the majority's language – and as more cognizant of her immigrant status. She recognises that despite what might appear at first glance as a surfeit of languages from which to choose, her community remains voiceless because it does not have a language that adequately speaks to and of its torn experience. Italo-Québécois are masters of no language, and their desire to have a voice – whether in the confines of *Chiuso* (the Italian neighbourhood) or in majority, francophone society – is severely compromised. At the play's climax, she describes the situation to her friend Gino and encapsulates the trilogy's central problematic: 'J'enseigne, moi, Gino, à des adolescents qui portent tous un nom italien et dont la seule culture est celle du silence. Silence sur les origines paysannes de leurs parents et les causes de leur émigration. Silence sur le pays dans lequel ils vivent. Silence sur les raisons de ce silence' (Micone 1996c, 68). (Gino, I teach teenagers who all have Italian names and who have one culture, that of silence. Silence about the peasant origins of their parents. Silence about the manipulation they're victims of. Silence about the country they live in. Silence about the reasons for their silence [Micone 1997, 65].) To break through this silence, immigrants need an alternate mode of expression to reflect their paradoxical condition and to create conditions within which it might operate more positively. Nancy concludes,

> Il faut remplacer la culture du silence par la culture immigrée pour que le paysan en nous se redresse, pour que l'immigrant en nous se souvienne et pour que le québécois en nous commence à vivre. Écris, mais pour que tout le monde te comprenne. C'est seulement si tu écris en français que nous aurons une chance d'être compris et respectés pour ce que nous sommes. (1996c, 68–9)

> [We must replace the culture of silence by immigrant culture, so that the peasant in us stands up, so that the immigrant in us remembers, and so that the Québécois in us can start to live. Write; fine, in a way that everyone can understand you. Young people must find themselves in texts written by someone who lived like them, who understands and wants to help them (1997, 65).][8]

Here, Nancy crystallizes Micone's notion of 'la culture immigrée,' the lynchpin of his oeuvre and his advocacy. In an article entitled 'La culture immigrée comme dépassement des cultures ethniques,' he writes, 'Immigrant culture is one of transition which, because it cannot survive as it is, will, in a situation of true intercultural exchange, be able to make Québécois culture fertile and, in so doing, to perpetuate it' (1996a, 4). Translated variously as 'immigrant culture' and 'emigrated culture,' *la culture immigrée* defines the transitional moment of being neither fully Québécois nor not-Québécois. This mobile space without positive definition is at once a descriptor of the immigrant's paradoxical condition, a critical framework within which to analyze it, an intermediary figure in stagnant language debates between French and English, and a hybrid model of national culture. As in Nancy's monologue above, Micone's *Trilogia* discusses the need for a mode of immigrant expression indexed to the specificities of immigrant experience in Montreal. More importantly, the trilogy offers an example of *la culture immigrée*'s expressive mode in its hybridized French vernacular, one which is forged out of the forced encounter of Italian with French and English words and worlds in the urban matrix of Montreal.

La culture immigrée is expressed in Micone's plays through a French vernacular inflected by Italianisms and anglicisms at the levels of vocabulary, syntax, and accent. This literary contact language has been characterized as 'somewhat artificially popular, sometimes stylized' and as 'a compromise language which reflects the reality of the community without the negative aspects of dialects' (Simon 1985, 60; Pivato 2000, 12). Micone describes 'the French spoken by [his] characters as a French vernacular that is still in flux' (quoted in Caccia 1998c, 191). Capitalizing on the rhetorical power of words, Micone's fluctuating French vernacular is both referential and constructive. Its mixture of 'simplified standard French with bits of patois, English words and Italian expressions' reflects the polyglossic world in which Italian immigrants of the late twentieth century lived in Montreal (Pivato 2000, 12). Micone's literary contact language also constructs a dramatic subject position previously absent on Montreal's stages: the Italo-Québécois.[9]

The strategy of developing alternate literary *langages* to conjure new Québécois subject positions through speech is not unique to Micone. This particular survival tactic of the immigrant condition finds its corollary in Québécois linguistic strategies of the 1960s, spearheaded by the *partipristes* and evident in *le nouveau théâtre québécois*. As we saw in the last chapter, this dramatic movement of the late 1960s and 1970s also strove to match linguistic expression to the French-Canadian condition of that moment. Both joual and Micone's literary speech are sociolects – language systems developed through lived contact with other more dominant languages. For instance, Anna, a first-generation immigrant and the mother of Nancy and Mario in *Gens du silence*, describes herself as working 'dans les guenilles' (in rags) at a sweatshop (Micone 1996c, 72). While this turn of phrase evocatively communicates both her poverty (she is dressed in rags) and the industry in which she is employed (the 'rag trade'), it does so without the benefit of the correct idiomatic expression ('en guenilles'). Significantly, her poverty is communicated in the French meaning of the expression; her exploitative conditions of employment evoked in its English connotations. These associations of French with economic, cultural, and linguistic impoverishment and of English with unethical employment practices repeat those circulated during the cultural nationalist period that informed the language politics of *le nouveau théâtre québécois*. Jean-Claude Germain's characterization of joual as a language that 'bears in its flesh the scars of life and history' provides an equally apt description of Micone's torn vernacular (Germain 1976, 18). In drawing attention to those scars of encounter, each vernacular embodies its history and imagines the expression of a new Québécois subject position formed in that encounter.

In his repetition of this tested Québécois strategy for transforming national identity, however, Micone highlights the fictional or constructed status of Quebec's language of authenticity. Put differently, in the construction of his own literary language for the Italo-Québécois subject, Micone unfounds the presumed reflective relationship between joual and *québécité*. As with Micone's search for a language of authentic expression for his characters, the anticolonial exercise of *reflecting* the quotidian in literary language resulted in the *creation* of joual – through its dissemination and eventual standardization in plays, dictionaries, and acts of translation (Bergeron 1980; Lalonde 1979; Brisset 1996). Joual was an anticolonial attempt to re-root French in the territory of Quebec and as Québécois (Gauvin 2000, 196). Ultimately, the desired coincidence of language, identity, and territory was achieved by an act of state: *la Charte de la langue française* (Bill 101) of 1977. The charter 'aims at making French the language of work and social promotion in business, and the language normally used between speakers of different mother tongues' (Dansereau 1999, 68–9). As important as making the Québécois public sphere French, the legislation aims at the *francisation* (Frenchifying) of allophones. It acts as a bulwark against French's disappearance amidst immigrants' other mother-tongues by legislating the language of business, government, and education. It prevents English from overwhelming French by mandating allophones into French-language education, asking them to re-root themselves in French. Writing from the margins of that now-dominant subject position, Micone confirms the impossibility of a native tongue in Quebec for immigrants and for *Québécois de vieil établissement* alike. For 'Frenchified' immigrants, French is a second origin that, however fully embraced, can never encompass the immigrant's whole experience. He writes in his memoir, *Le figuier enchanté* (The Magic Fig Tree), 'As long as the words of my childhood evoke a world that the words from here cannot grasp, I will remain an immigrant' (1992, 9).[10] For *Québécois de vieil établissement*, the language of cultural authenticity – joual – is revealed as an 'inauthentic,' second planting of language in Quebec. The task of the immigrant to 'become Québécois' turns out to be a repetition of a successful French-Canadian effort (Hurley 2004).

In his dramatic trilogy, Marco Micone reveals that the languages of vernacular authenticity (joual and his own Italo-Québécois patois) on which Quebec's modern origin stories rely are literary constructs, not reflections of native discourse. The more unsettling move with respect to national allegory and its preferred reflection figure, however, is made in his 1989 manifesto-poem entitled 'Speak What,' first published in the Quebec theatre journal *Jeu* (Micone 1989, 83–5).[11] Here, Micone, takes on another key metaphor for Québécois identity: Quebec-as-black. In so doing, he sketches a non-reductive and antiracist theory of national performance.

Dubbed a 'texte poélitique' (poetic-political text), 'Speak What' participates in a well-established Québécois literary tradition of the manifesto, and more specifically the manifesto on the 'language question.'[12] Micone launches his critique by rewriting that tradition's paradigmatic text: Michèle Lalonde's 1968 manifesto-poem, 'Speak White' (1979). Where Lalonde's poem famously casts English as a colonial language and marks it as racially white, Micone's palimpsestic rejoinder frames French as the new colonial language in Quebec vis-à-vis the languages of allophone *néo-Québécois*.

Transcultural analysis of Micone's dramatic trilogy has by and large established the through-lines of interpretation for 'Speak What' as well. Micone's poem, like his plays, was taken as a sign of the changing face of Québécois culture and an entrée into the Québécois literary institution. Here again Micone expressly engaged with a Québécois 'classic,' updating it for a more ethnically diverse and self-confident society. Micone explains, '"Speak What" illustrated my will to appropriate for myself Quebec's symbols and myths in order to compose a poetic-political text better attached to our era and to my vision of Québécois society twenty years after Michèle Lalonde's cry of revolt' (1996b, 21). As with the plays, critics of the poem focus on its treatment of the language question. Certainly, the poems' respective contexts point one towards careful readings of their language politics. Lalonde wrote 'Speak White' during a period charged with conflict over language that had become tied to ethnicity. The issue of the educational system's role in assimilating immigrant children into French had come to a head in the Montreal suburb of Saint-Léonard the year before the poem's first public performance. The population of Saint-Léonard in the late 1960s was approximately 40 per cent immigrant, the majority of whom were Italian. In 1967, when the local school board proposed eliminating bilingual (French and English) education for immigrant children in favour of unilingual French education in the name of more effectively and completely integrating the allophones, the immigrant community protested in court and, in some cases, in violent encounters with their francophone neighbours (Woolfson 1984). Quebec's steep decline in birthrate since the Quiet

Revolution combined with allophone immigrants' massive preference for English-language education – according to statistics cited by Ines Molinaro, in 1971 90 per cent of allophone children attended English schools (1999, 119) – made the *francisation* of allophones imperative for the vitality of *le fait français*. Without it, the neo-Québécois would literally become the site and vehicle of French's muting within Quebec. As early as 1969, a contributor to *Action Nationale* writes of the 'harsh lesson that the immigration problem in Quebec is teaching us,' namely that without encouraging immigrants to integrate into the majority, francophone society instead of the minority, anglophone one, 'we will disappear little by little from history' (Arès 1969, 227). As Quebec's birthrate falls to a low of 1.36 per woman in 1986, the concern with French's disappearance persists in the 1990s; Jean-Michel Lacroix writes that 'the collapse of the percentage of unilingual francophones compared to allophones justifies in itself concern for the future and the extreme importance of new minority-focussed *francisation* programs' (1996, 175).[13] In this context, 'Speak White' – a rallying cry for the protection of *le fait français* and the language of collective identity – swiftly entered popular political consciousness.[14] As Lise Gauvin – the most assiduous interpreter of 'Speak What'– documents, some perceived it as a response to the recently passed Bill 22, a precursor to the Charter of the French Language. Although Bill 22 made French the official language of Quebec, it was criticised by *indépendantistes* for countenancing too many exceptions (and by federalists for infringing on individual liberties) (1995, 21–2).

'Speak What' was written at another linguistically/ethnically fraught juncture in Quebec's history; Bill 178, which mandated French-only exterior, commercial signage and provided for bilingual indoor signs only so long as French predominated, had just been passed by the government of then-Premier Robert Bourassa. The bill was intended as a measure of protection against French's muting and potential extinction within Quebec's own borders. However, many business owners of Montreal's 'communautés culturelles' (cultural communities) protested the bill's binary logic. They argued that bilingual signage in French and Hebrew, Italian, Portuguese, or Vietnamese, for example, did not risk the assimilation or the dilution of *le fait français*. Rather, the bill was directed at eliminating English-predominant signage. 'Speak What,' one of Micone's responses to Bill 178 from the point of view of immigrant communities, self-consciously rearticulates the terms of Lalonde's celebrated poem by turning command into question and exploding the two solitudes into a hundred.

My reading departs from a critical norm whose analysis concludes with noting Micone's triangulating moves, consistent with other Italo-Québécois writers and intellectuals of the 1980s and 1990s who articulated a politics and poetics of 'transculturalism.' In this de-ethnicized cultural poetics, Italo-Québécois are positioned as intermediary figures between franco- and anglo-Québécois poles, figures whose very appearance clarifies the terms on which language and identity debates take place. Poet Lamberto Tassinari, a key instigator of the transcultural movement, describes transculturalism as follows: 'Transculture implies a vision of displacement, of nomadism, the possibility of setting up one's territory anywhere. That's the force we can set against the dictatorial force of territory' (Caccia 1998, 218).[15] This work is important and has been hugely influential in the Quebec academy and beyond. Nevertheless, I choose instead to tarry over the two poems' deployments of binary relationships – 'nous' and 'vous,' French and English, Black and White – in an effort to uncover something of their force. In an interview with *Le Jour* on the occasion of the initial publication of 'Speak White' in 1974, Lalonde explains her goals in writing the piece: 'I had a very clear trajectory: to bring to the surface again all the implications contained in this kind of slogan [the command "speak white"]' (quoted in Dostie 1974, V3). Critics have addressed aspects of the insult's implications, especially their linguistic and class overtones, which I also will revisit below. Curiously unremarked, however, has been the Black-White binary that founds the insult that founds the poem that founds Micone's pastiche. I contend that it is precisely in this unremarked founding condition that the real 'danger' of Micone's 'Speak What' lies. In his un-founding engagement with the 'essence' of 'Speak White,' 'Speak What' marks the limits of metaphor's national mimesis.

Lalonde's 'Speak White' was written to be recited at the first of a series of *manifestations-spectacles* (political demonstration-shows) called 'Poèmes et chants de la résistance' (Poems and songs of the resistance); these evenings were organised to raise money for the legal defence of nationalist activists jailed for violent activities.[16] Informed by the political context in which it was born, this 'texte de combat' indicted colonial forces that blocked Quebec's political independence and claimed *le fait français* for Quebec (Dostie 1974, V3). Through her significant uses of French and English, of *nous* (us) and *vous* (you-plural/formal), Lalonde's 'Speak White' enacts a vexed dialogue between English/anglophones ('vous') as the locus of power and French/francophones ('nous') as that of resistance. 'Speak White' utilises the manifesto's typical rhetorical figure, the opposition of centre and periphery, in order to advocate for their inversion. Lise Gauvin traces the reversal through the poem's five-act structure. In the first act a '*vous* of culture opposes an "uncultivated and stuttering" *nous*'; the second act 'accentuates the ironic distance between *vous*'s supposed grandeur and *nous*'s also supposed baseness'; and the third 'poses the linguistic relationship as a class relationship.' The fourth act generalises the *vous*'s 'speak white,' 'which becomes the language – no matter what the language – of the coloniser' (1995, 20–1). Or, as Lalonde recounts in the *Le Jour* interview mentioned above, 'The English also said ["speak white"] in Africa, I think. By extension, the French said it to Algerians to get them to speak French. All colonised have an experience of this kind.' In the last act of 'Speak White,' *vous*'s language is appropriated by *nous* to say in the booming voice of united workers worldwide, 'we're doing all right / we're doing fine / we / are not alone' (Lalonde 1979, 40).[17]

But let us go back to the hiccup in act 4, where the French-English binary that has been operative through the poem's first three acts expands to include any language that, in its context, is the language of authority. Thus, Lalonde enjoins *vous*, 'parlez un français pur et atrocement blanc / comme au Viet-Nam au Congo / parlez un allemand impeccable / une étoile jaune entre les dents / parlez russe parlez rappel à l'ordre parlez répression / speak white' (39). (speak a pure and atrociously white French / as in Vietnam and the Congo / speak an impeccable German / a yellow star between your teeth / speak Russian speak call to order speak repression / speak white.) In this transmutation of the colonial English-French binary into a Hegelian master-slave relation, we see that the unifying essence of 'Speak White' is not to be found in the first word of its title, but rather in its second: not in speech but rather in race. The invective appears sixteen times in the poem, endowing it with its rhythm and structure (Gauvin 1995, 20). Centre-periphery relations are emblematised in a racial metaphor common during the period by which francophone Québécois are symbolically 'Black' and their colonial oppressors are symbolically 'White.' In the metaphor 'Québécois-are-black,' 'Québécois' is what I.A. Richards names the 'tenor' or the subject to which the metaphoric word is applied; it forms the metaphor's centre or point of reference. 'Black' is the 'vehicle'; this 'metaphoric word' is applied to the tenor 'in the form of an identity instead of comparison,' as M.H. Abrams puts it (Richards 1950, 96; Abrams 1981, 63).

To 'speak white' meant to speak English; it is a colloquialism that demands the francophone interlocutor speak in the language of power, which is associated with 'civilization' and, in the Quebec context of 1969, is English. The colonizing role of English is referenced via English literature's major figures (Shakespeare, Keats, Milton) and finds its contemporary, extraliterary equivalent in the language of bosses. French's subjugation, however, is raced. It is a language darkened by menial and physical labours (Lalonde 1979, 39), whereas English is a 'rich' language that allows speaking of the good life (38). The anticolonial struggle of the franco-Québécois, on the other hand, is aligned with those of insurgent Algerians and African-Americans: 'nous savons que la liberté est un mot noir / comme la misère est nègre / et comme le sang se mêle à la poussière des rues d'Alger ou de Little Rock' (we know that liberty is a black word / like poverty is Black / and like blood mixes with the dust on the streets of Algiers and Little Rock) (40).

There is much to say on this questionable if galvanizing metaphor, and George Elliott Clarke's article 'Liberalism and its Discontents: Reading Black and White in Contemporary Québécois Texts,' admirably begins that task (Clarke 2002).[18] Suffice it to say for the moment that it came out of a kind of sympathetic identification with African-Americans during the civil rights era on the part of leftist Québécois intellectuals inspired by African-Americans' increasing self-possession, their rights-based activism, and its political momentum. Pierre Vallières's 1968 book entitled *Les nègres blancs d'Amérique* (The White Niggers of America, 1971) is probably the best-known expression of this cross-racial metaphor. In fact, Vallières and Charles Gagnon were to be the beneficiaries of the 1968 'Poèmes et chants de la résistance.' While they were jailed in New York for involvement in *indépendantiste*-related violence in Montreal, Vallières wrote his political autobiography, which makes common cause between Quebec's francophone working classes and the United States's Black population. He states that both are exploited under capitalism as reservoirs of cheap and expendable labour. Consistent with the *partipriste* outlook that informs his analysis (he was one of its founding members), Vallières also concerns himself with the degradation of the person that attends exploitation and that renders him or her 'sub-human.' Significantly, he attributes his coinage of 'white nigger' to his antiracist stance:

Even the poor whites consider the nigger their inferior ... Very often they do not even suspect that they too are niggers, slaves, 'white niggers.' White racism hides the reality from them by giving them the opportunity to despise an inferior, to crush him mentally or to pity him. But the poor whites who despise the black man are doubly niggers, for they are victims of one

more form of alienation – racism – which far from liberating them, impris-
ons them in a net of hate or paralyzes them in fear of one day having to
confront the black man in a civil war. (1971, 21)

Following Vallières, politically engaged, leftist writers and intellectuals sometimes availed themselves of his forceful metaphor in this same
spirit (however naïve) of solidarity and common struggle. Lalonde has
reprised Vallières and flags metaphor's identity work: '"Speak White" is
the protest of the white Negroes of America. Here, language is equivalent to skin-colour for the black American. The French language is our
black colour' (quoted in Dostie 1974, V3). As was the case with Québécois 'womanliness,' Québécois 'blackness' was a matter of condition, of
shared oppression; however, the 'blackness' metaphor would encounter
fewer 'real life' claimants to the category than did 'woman.' As Vallières
makes clear, this application of the standard usage of 'Black' and 'Nigger' to 'Québécois' circulated more widely in Quebec than it might have
in another sociocultural environment precisely because it moved largely
(although not entirely) in the absence of people of African descent.
Montreal historian Dorothy W. Williams estimates the total number of
anglophone blacks in Montreal by the end of the 1960s at about 15,000
(1997, 109). Vallières writes that 'in Quebec there is no "black problem"'
(1971, 21). (To be clear, the relatively small black population is in part
the result of Canada's racist immigration policy, which stated a preference for 'white' immigrants and was in effect until its amendment in
1962.)

By 1989, Quebec's spaces of exiguity, formerly outside the province's
borders, had been internalized. The Vietnamese and Congolese, who
learned an 'atrocement pur' French under colonialism in 1969, had installed themselves in Quebec's major urban centre, Montreal, by 1989.[19]
With 'Speak What,' Micone implies that the peripheral Québécois culture of the 1960s had become the hegemonic culture by the late 1980s.
Quebec's 'marginals' are no longer working-class francophone Québécois; Micone asks in 'Speak What,' 'vous souvenez-vous du vacarme
des usines' (do you remember the noise of the factories) (2001, 85).[20]
Rather, neo-Québécois now populate Quebec's periphery. The situation
of French had also changed significantly in the twenty years between
poems. Lalonde's 'us' struggles with a French language all-too-perfectly
suited to telling 'you' of 'l'éternité d'un jour de grève / pour raconter /
une vie de peuple-concierge' (the eternity of a strike day / to tell / the
life of a concierge-people) (1979, 39). Micone's 'us' uses the French lan-

guage imposed upon them by provincial legislation to tell 'you' of their
experiences of conflict and privation (1989, 85). In a statement on language politics, Lalonde's *nous* speak a French riven with English expressions. 'Gracious living' and 'big shots' significantly do not have French
equivalents in the poem. In what is equally a statement on the politics of
language, Micone's *nous* use English only once – 'and of the voices des
contremaîtres / you sound like them more and more' – and that when
referring directly to the *contremaîtres* of 'Speak White,' whose loud voices
can be heard from Montreal's Saint-Henri quartier to Santo Domingo
in the Dominican Republic. In 'Speak What,' English is no longer required. The poem's opening stanza articulates this shift in orientation
in its explicit rewriting of the opening lines of 'Speak White.' Micone
recapitulates almost exactly Lalonde's scansion and diction but replaces
her references to English 'classics' with references to the Québécois literary canon and cultural history. For Lalonde's reference to *Paradise Lost*
Micone substitutes 'La Romance du Vin,' a poem by late nineteenth-
century Romantic and symbolist poet, Émile Nelligan, who has become
a mythic figure of Québécois poetry; for 'les sonnets de Shakespeare' he
inserts Gaston Miron's *l'Homme rapaillé*, a collection of his *poésie du pays*
and a touchstone of Québécois literature and identity.

Employing the same manifesto rhetorical figures as did Lalonde, Micone turns her use of 'nous' and 'vous.' Where 'Speak White' establishes
'nous' as a symbolically blackened, francophone, colonized proletariat,
'Speak What' speaks from the position of a 'nous' that does not repose
on blackness, nor indeed on any single vehicle: 'nous avions les mots /
de Montale et de Neruda / le souffle de l'Oural / le rythme des haïku'
(we had the words / of Montale and Neruda / the winds of the Urals /
the rhythm of haikus) (84). 'Speak What,' like *Trilogia*, expands Québécois literature's linguistic repertoire and cultural references. And again
like *Trilogia*, the invocation in 'Speak What' of a Québécois source-text
has the effect of reinforcing that source-text's originality, which is to say
its foundational place in Québécois literature. But in this case, Micone
removes the source-text's vehicle of authenticity. In *Trilogia*, even as his
contact language revealed joual's constructed nature, the plays retained
the spirit of joual as a means for conjuring identity through speech. In
'Speak What' – a pastiche-homage that takes up practically every element of its source-text (scansion, theme, geographical references, etc.)
– Micone explicitly avoids Lalonde's preferred vehicle of 'blackness.' By
this notable absence, this non-repetition, 'Speak What' highlights the vehicle's anchoring function in 'Speak White.' As we have seen, in 'Speak

White' a sympathetic but imagined relationship to blackness, not a nationalized French language, anchors the poem's imagery, rhythm, and structure. In other words, the metaphor's vehicle acquires the function of the tenor, becoming the metaphor's pivot point.

In addition to exposing the vehicle's usurpation of the tenor in 'Speak White,' 'Speak What' also grants that usurping vehicle a tenor's historical density in his recast 'nous.' We saw above that Lalonde's poem ends with an invocation of international working-class solidarity in her blackened 'nous' expressed in English: 'we're doing all right / we're doing fine / we / are not alone // we know / that we are not alone' (1979, 40). Micone's closes with *nous* and *vous*'s linguistic interpenetration:

> imposez-nous votre langue
> nous vous raconterons
> la guerre, la torture et la misère
> nous dirons notre trépas avec vos mots
> pour que vous ne mouriez pas
> ...
> speak what
> nous sommes cent peuples venus de loin
> pour vous dire que vous n'êtes pas seuls (1989, 85)

> [force your language on us
> we will tell you
> war, torture and poverty
> we will confess our sins with your words
> so that you will not die
> ...
> speak what
> we are one hundred people come from afar
> to tell you that you are not alone.]

In 'Speak What,' the immigrant 'nous,' the vehicle of the 'white nigger' metaphor – the person of African descent – is granted historical density by being surrounded by other 'others.' The presence of national and ethnic 'others' in the 'nous' denies the 'Québécois-are-black' metaphor; the connection between the two terms can no longer be one of identity, as in metaphor, but must instead be one of comparison. This intrusion of 'others' into Lalonde's poem and Québécois society establishes 'black' as its own tenor, not someone else's vehicle.

Micone has indicated that 'Speak What' signals his immersion in Québécois cultural referents: 'There is no greater proof of integration for an immigrant writer than to rewrite a classic of the host culture' (1996b, 22). Nevertheless, some mistook his public declaration of cultural enfranchisement for a lack of originality, an inability to speak with his own authentic – and distinct – voice. Instead, the implied argument ran, he needed to ventriloquize Lalonde's, bastardizing it in the process. Micone's upsetting of tenor-vehicle relations in a founding metaphor of modern *québécité* begets concerns about the unregulated proliferation of vehicles in 'Speak White's uptake. In the face of Micone's exposure of the material limits of racial metaphor, some critics worry about the possibility of adequate and fruitful figural relations. In 1993 Micone was accused of plagiarizing 'Speak White' in letters to the editor of *Le Devoir*, the Montreal daily associated with Quebec's intelligentsia, sparking another controversy regarding national language, identity's authenticity, and artistic originality. Instead of being seen (at least partially) as a sign of his Quebec-ness and his integration into majority Québécois culture, 'Speak What' was misrecognised as (only) a sign of his foreignness.

The context of the controversy is significant, as it erupted in the midst of a heated and extended public debate over the meaning and limits of Québécois literature. Nancy Huston, a native speaker of English fluent in French, Alberta-born, Paris-based author who publishes in French and English had just won Canada's Governor General's Award for best fiction of the year in French for her novel, *Cantique des plaines*. Her win outraged some of Quebec's most prominent literary editors, who publicly objected to the award committee's decision because she had written *Cantique des plaines* first in her native tongue, English, and published it under the title *Plainsong* simultaneously with its award-winning French version. They argued in *La Presse*'s editorial pages that *Cantique des plaines* should have been considered under either the rubric of translation or that of English-language novel, instead of that of the French-language novel (Gauthier et al. 1993). This volley provoked widespread commentary in the pages of *La Presse* and *Le Devoir* on the subjects of authorship and language in Québécois literature. *La Presse*'s outspoken columnist Nathalie Petrowski worried about what the win of 'an Anglophone outside of Quebec and a Canadian outside of Canada' would mean for the future of 'Québécois literature.' She wrote, 'Henceforth, it seems we are told, there will no longer be Québécois literature, no more symbiosis with the territory, no longer a mother tongue that sticks. Henceforth, the French-language writer will be a hybrid who lives in Bangkok or Bora

Bora, an exile, an itinerant, an uprooted person, someone who not only doesn't write in his language, but also no longer maintains any tie to the territory' (1993, D3). In *La Presse*'s Books section, Pierre Vennat argues the case for a more flexible border policy with regard to Québécois literature and suggests that Québécois immigrant authors might 'bring new blood to our literature' (1994, B4; see Hurley 2009b for more on the Huston controversy).

Micone appears in this debate as an example of an immigrant Québécois author's contributions to Québécois literature in Vennat's piece and figures quite prominently in Governor General's Awards jury member Marie José Thériault's response to the editors' calls to strip Huston of the prize. Thériault's letter to *Le Devoir* complicates ideas of literary originals and counterfeits *chez* multilingual writers: 'What can one say of a Marco Micone, who writes *Babel* [a one-act play published in *Vice versa*] in four languages? How can we know, without leaning over his shoulder while he works, if a passage in French was not first started in Molisan patois, in English, in normative Italian, or in *italese*? His "original" could very well have been a patchwork of translations!' (1993, A11). In response, Jacques Lanctôt of VLB Éditeur and a signatory to the letter opposing Huston's victory, asks about the nature of Micone's 'Speak What.' He wonders if Thériault can tell him 'whether it is a question of translation, borrowing, pastiche, plagiarism, etc., when the same Marco Micone publishes a long poem called "Speak What," traced in every respect from the famous "Speak White" of the writer Michèle Lalonde, without having consulted her – nor, moreover, the publisher?' (Lanctôt 1993, A9). Micone defends his poem as 'inspired' by Lalonde's and appends 'Speak What' to the end of his short letter to the editor of *La Presse*, which catalyzes another round of accusations of plagiarism.

In the plagiarism charge, Micone was accused of inappropriate and inauthentic figural relations. First, he repeated a referent (Lalonde's poem) without expressly acknowledging the original. He cites exactly and in quotation marks four words of 'Speak White'; for the rest, he relies on his Québécois readership's familiarity with Lalonde's poem to enrich and make resonate his own 'Speak What.' Second, he repeated the referent without a legitimated claim to surrogation; as a 'néo-Québécois' writer in the 1980s, he is neither a direct descendant of nor an inheritor to the Québécois literary institution. Rather, he helps found another branch of literature in Quebec, 'écriture migrante.' And third, he repeated a referent without taking up its racialized 'essence.' Micone did not produce a true copy of the original, as in metaphor. Rather, his illegitimate surrogation produced a simulacrum, or a copy without an original. In 'The Simulacrum and Ancient Philosophy,' Gilles Deleuze distinguishes copy-icons from simulacra-phantasms, or true pretenders from false, as follows: '*Copies* are secondary possessors. They are well-founded pretenders, guaranteed by resemblance [to the Idea or essence of the model]; *simulacra* are like false pretenders, built upon a dissimilarity, implying an essential perversion or deviation' (1990, 256). In other words, the original possesses certain qualities; the copy possesses those qualities in a secondary way by resembling the Idea of the original. Simulations do not possess any percentage of the original's essential qualities; they do not participate in the essence of the original, just reproduce its external appearance. Thus, in her letter to *Le Devoir*'s editor, Theodora Vassaramva counts the number of words the two poems have in common and remarks on their similar style, typographical arrangement, and rhythm, while maintaining that Micone 'twists the meaning of the original while appropriating its merits' (1994, A9). Another reader seconds Vassaramva's interpretation, writing, 'Not only does he borrow the form of Michèle Lalonde's famous poem, but worse, he minimizes its argument in order to better exalt his own' (Juneau-Garneau 1994, A6). 'Speak What' evinces all the signs of *québécité* – linguistically, institutionally – yet lacks the 'substance' that would guarantee an uncontested Quebec-ness; it bypasses what I have located as the unifying 'essence' of 'Speak White': its racial metaphor. In this separation of sign from essence, Micone exposes the sometimes nativist, ethnocultural lineaments of the national guarantor. Positioned outside of the Québécois poetic tradition of manifestos, a fundamentally dissimilar, *néo-Québécois* Micone can only repeat its surface features. According to this schema, 'Speak What,' the poem of an *indépendantiste*, francophone *néo-Québécois*, is a plagiarised simulacrum of Lalonde's. At the same time, and more crucially, by exposing this origin-guarantor as unnecessary to convincing – if short-lived – representations of *québécité*, his simulations unfound metaphor as the preferred and predominant mode of national mimesis.[21]

The danger of simulacra – these copies without originals – is that they can pass as true copies, as copies made through the original. Thus, these exiguous allophones could be mistaken for secondary possessors of *québécité* instead of as false pretenders. Purveyors of false-consciousness, simulations substitute 'signs of the real for the real itself.' Like the cave-dwellers in Plato's 'Allegory of the Cave,' witnesses to simulacra – to the shadows dancing on the cave wall – may believe in their reality. As Plato worried, when people are cut off from the world of True Forms (outside of the cave, in the light), they have no way of distinguishing false images from true. Hence, as simulations, neo-Québécois are even more dangerous to the symbolic order of a restrictive, ethnicity-based *québécité*.[22] They might mute the French fact in Quebec with their 'other' tongues and, of greater concern, prefer English to French as their vehicular language. More insidiously, if the false pretenders are taken for the real thing, they might effectively extinguish it. Simulacra-images, Baudrillard tells us, murder 'the real' and eliminate the possibility of truthful and direct communication (1983, 10). In a nation aspiring to statehood on the basis of its cultural-linguistic distinctiveness from the rest of Canada, false pretenders are particularly threatening. If they can pass as copies of Québécois, as true pretenders, then they could hinder the recognition of Quebec's 'essential' (historical, francophone) distinctiveness. What would be recognized is not the distinctive *québécité* of *les Québécois*, but the multivalent and differential *québécité* of the neo-Québécois. This is not to say that *québécité* as performed by *Québécois de souche* cannot be differential; indeed, our previous case-studies prove the opposite – that *québécité* varies over time, in response to changing conditions of possibility and the needs and composition of its people. However, the status of *néo-Québécois* – a category, we should be reminded, without referential ballast – is such that their embodiment of *québécité* is, by definition and in their appellation, differential. Hence their destabilizing position.

Another danger of simulacra is that they signal the failure of representational contracts premised on an Idealist affinity between originals and copies. 'Faithful' model-copy relations of the kind desired by anticolonial critics are no longer required in order to be 'fruitful.' Indeed, Pierre Nepveu contends that Micone creates from origins that are 'almost fictional'; because Micone left Italy as a child, his memory of his country of origin is substantially informed by fantasy even as it is 'haunted by the original and the authentic' (quoted in Mathis 1996, 279). Despite, or perhaps because of their fantastical status, these compromised origins animate Micone's prolific work as a writer, activist, and teacher.

Further, simulation eclipses metaphor's vertically organised figural relations. Simulacra are self-serving vehicles unmoored from tenors. In the example Micone's palimpsest provides, the politics of metaphor are again clarified. In the reception of *Les belles-sœurs*, metaphor's tendency to collapse difference into sameness was striking. In 'Speak What,' metaphor's politics of servility are particularly salient.[23] Micone's poem makes conspicuous the privilege of being the dominant term, or the tenor, of metaphors like 'Quebec-is-a-woman' and 'Québécois-are-black.' These metaphors' hierarchical relations, whereby 'woman' and 'black' serve 'Québécois,' translate actual social relations rather baldly and uncomfortably. This particular instance of metaphor as primary figure for national mimesis seems to touch the limit of metaphor's efficacy, not to mention its desirability. Its efficacy is blocked by others for whom 'black' is a tenor and identity in its own right. Micone's introduction of 'cent peuples venus de loin' into the heart of Québécois literature reminds that *as* neo-Québécois, these 'others' are no longer vehicles for a metaphor of Québécois identity; they live their own Québécois identities.

Simon Harel suggests in a recent article that the enunciative pact characterised by flux and hybridity, which was new to Québécois cultural discourse in the 1980s when Micone's plays were being produced, attained the status of critical reflex by the late 1990s, a critical reflex to which his *Voleur de parcours* (1989) has substantially contributed. Harel argues for a renewed critical focus on attachment, ties, stasis, and location within the context of nomadism in the hope of continuing to shake up received wisdoms about Québécois literature in the 2000s, in the way that *écriture migrante* (writing in movement) did in the 1980s and 1990s (2002). His more recent project, an extension of his thinking about a durable tie to place and outlined in a series of four articles in *Liberté*, argues that the appeal of the 'foreign' other has led us away from the internal others who are neither recent arrivals nor likely to depart. One might argue that Micone's plays, in their explicit focus on problems of affiliation with Quebec society, fulfill this updated mandate as well. One brief example: in *Le figuier enchanté*, Micone introduces the neologism 'amigré.' This combination of 'ami' and 'immigré' speaks in a word the possibility of affiliation in the context of nomadism. Importantly, Harel places these differences not simply *within* Quebec, as is also the case with the immigrant, but also at Quebec's very *origin*.

Marco Micone and the *Vice versa* transculturalists fruitfully and critically triangulated French with English *and* Italian in Montreal's urban matrix, proposing their new admixture as harbinger of a pluralist future. Of transculturalism's sociocultural project, Alessandra Ferraro writes, 'the birth of *Vice versa* in 1983 is emblematic: the choice to publish a revue in three languages (French, English, Italian), while having the merit of displacing and playing down the English-French tensions that had always run through Québécois society, aims to introduce the Italian community as an active partner in the culture of Quebec' (1999, 144). Immigrants and Québécois would find common cause in their common marginalization. As Micone's own critical work makes clear, the immigrant/ated condition is not unique to the immigrant. Indeed, its general contours line up nicely with those of the Québécois condition. In 'La culture immigrée réduite au silence' (Immigrant culture reduced to silence), for instance, Micone advocates a political rapprochement between working-class Québécois and immigrants, on the basis of their shared histories and often difficult living conditions (1981); this is not unlike the Québécois spirit of comradeship with U.S. Blacks evinced in the 'white nigger' identification (see also Micone 1990b, 159–60). Italo-Québécois poet Fulvio Caccia makes a similar argument in his introduction to his volume of interviews with Italo-Québécois writers, *Interviews with the Phoenix*, when he writes, 'Dual identity is what immigrants and the colonized share in common' (1998a, 11).

Harel, on the other hand, sidesteps binary, analogy, and metaphor, however well-intentioned or persuasive. Instead he sketches three contiguous nuclei of *québécité* – in anglophone, First Nations, and francophone versions (2006).[24] These three origins for *québécité* are fractiously united in their centrality. Harel posits a kind of 'big bang' theory of *québécité*, whereby Quebec's origin is in an explosion. Nuclei are multiplied and tenors proliferated, complicating metaphor's representational labour.

In a felicitous coincidence, Carbone 14, an image-theatre troupe whose major works were created between 1981 and 2000, performs a similar deconstructive labour using the nuclear metaphor. Carbon-14, an unstable, radioactive isotope, is formed when cosmic rays add two neutrons to carbon-12, the stable isotope of carbon, a common element found in all living things. As carbon-14 undergoes beta decay, it transforms into a stable isotope of another element, nitrogen-14. Both Harel and Carbone 14 seem to understand as problematic the metaphoric vehicle's evanescence, its invisible subjugation to the tenor. Yet, where Harel's nuclear theory highlights the Québécois nucleus's productive expansion, Carbone 14's work emphasises its spectacular decomposition into durable parts. Their hybrid performance form features the metonymic part in the arresting scenic images and plastic dancing bodies for which their devised performances are internationally known. The affective impact and singularity of those often incongruous parts eclipse the whole of which they are elements, thereby highlighting the necessary partialness of any performance-nation reference. Because they do not come to rest comfortably within any unified semantic orbit, the parts exhibit a certain restlessness; they keep moving into different domains of usage, forging temporary, if piercing, bonds across contiguous semantic fields.

chapter six

National Metonymy: Arresting Images in the Devised Works of Carbone 14

'L'art sert à changer les yeux des gens.' [The purpose of art is to change people's eyes]

Gilles Maheu (quoted in Pavlovic 1992, 16)

If the 1980s in Quebec were the years of 'transculture' and the discovery that Quebec's self-created *Terre des hommes* was also a *terre des autres* (land of others), the decade was also experienced as cultural production's relatively apolitical interlude. Following on the political and cultural effervescence of the 1960s and 1970s marked by the establishment of a Quebec literary institution and specifically Québécois genres (*la chanson québécoise, le nouveau théâtre québécois*), and attempts to build and sustain *québécité* via the performing arts, the 1980s were distinguished by a noticeable retreat from *québécité*'s dominant mode – spoken and written language – to be supplanted by the visual image (Vigeant 1991). The political malaise some detect in the move toward non-text-based theatre, a corollary emphasis on the body in performance, and a thematic interest in highly personal stories is often attributed to the disappointing results of the 1980 referendum on sovereignty for *indépendantistes*.[1] Politics having abandoned the artists who campaigned for sovereignty, artists abandon explicitly political discourse – and its signs in joual and realism. Disaffected with a political reality that kept Quebec a province, many artists searched for another reality, finding it in corporeal experience and oniric landscapes. It is also the case that many felt that the previous decade's crucial experiments with joual had reached their limits, and that new aesthetic and critical strategies needed to be found to reinvigorate the theatre. New forms of writing made their way to centre stage: a poetic writing style among a new generation of playwrights and scenic writing or devised, movement-based performance.

In the performance of national allegory, one character stands in for a national many; thus Tremblay's Rose gives vent to the frustrations of those *nés pour un petit pain* (born for a small loaf). In much of the image-based theatrical performance with which this chapter will be primarily concerned, however, the one was often simply, idiosyncratically one. Indeed, this focus is a feature common to both strands of theatrical activity of the decade (the poetic dramas and the devised performances); theatrical production of all kinds in the 1980s seemed to abound in idiosyncratic 'ones.' This is the decade that supports the rise of solo performance as a distinct genre in Quebec, building on the venerable monologue tradition whose locutionary power Tremblay also marshalled (see Aird 2008 on the monologue; see Badir 1992 on solo performance).[2] It witnesses the demise, although not quite the extinction, of collective performance as well; for instance, two foundational collective troupes, the Théâtre expérimental des femmes and the Grand cirque ordinaire, disbanded in 1985 and 1978 respectively. Even beyond these generic and institutional shifts, the themes and preoccupations of the plays that define the decade's dramatic style attune themselves to the singular. A spate of plays about the figure of the author, creator, or actress make an impression (Moss 1998); among them are Michel Tremblay's *Le vrai monde?* (1987), René Daniel Dubois's *Ne blâmez jamais les Bédouins* (1984), Jovette Marchessault's *La terre est trop courte, Violette Leduc* (1982), Normand Chaurette's *Provincetown Playhouse, juillet 1919, j'avais 19 ans* (1981), and Michel Marc Bouchard's *Les Feluettes ou la répétition d'un drame romantique* (1985–86; published 1987). Two of these plays' hallmarks, autoreferentiality and autorepresentation, direct attention once again to the one, in this case to the single and singular creator; a third feature – intertextuality (see, for instance, Lise Vaillancourt's *Ballade pour trois baleines*, 1982) – signals a literary universe of referentiality (Godin 2001, 58). Mariel O'Neill-Karch observes of these plays, '[They] propose a new construction of reality where the text, with its explicit literary qualities, its intertextuality, its frequent use of *mise en abyme* (play within a play), dominates the multiple stage languages' (1997, 327).

Carbone 14, a dance-theatre troupe founded in 1980 by its artistic director Gilles Maheu (b. 1948), built its international reputation during this decade of relative political quiet. Its productions, which, contra the poetic drama outlined above, emphasize performance text over written text, are part of a generation of theatrical experimentation that moved

the generic location of 'exemplary' *québécité* in the theatre from popular
realism to avant-garde mixed-genre performance. In the 1980s, Carbone
14 and Robert Lepage come to national and international prominence
with their image-theatre productions. Certainly, this estrangement from
spoken and written language in devised, movement-based performance
cannot be merely an aesthetic choice in Quebec, given the area's history of linguistic conflict as well as the frequency and charge with which
the language question was and is broached in cultural production. And
yet, this shift in the cultural discourse defining *québécité* from linguistic
style – the point of Tremblay's intervention and of Micone's critique –
to physical style does not necessarily entail political disengagement. Indeed, to presume that national allegory's absence betokens the absence
of 'politics' is to fall once again for metaphor's national mimesis. If Gilles
Maheu's 'scenic writing' lacks the explicit national-political commentary
on *québécité* that defines Micone's dramatic writing, it does not lack for
politics. Carbone 14 performs its own kind of carbon-dating of *québécité*,
tracing its half-life across four hundred years. Yet it eschews the idea that
art's social value lies in its documentary effects. The challenge it mounts,
rather, is to uncover the representational modes at work in the devised
productions of image-based theatre companies like Carbone 14. How
might its indirect, often obtuse relations to *le fait national* 'change our
eyes' regarding the work of performance to produce and reproduce the
nation? Moreover, what might the singularity of the idiosyncratic 'one'
reveal? To invoke Michael Taussig's work on mimesis, I wonder whether
the 'resistance of the concrete particular to abstraction' could preserve a
non-devalued place for difference in a national project (1993, 2).

  In this chapter, I examine several of Carbone 14's devised works –
predominantly *Le Rail* (The Rail, 1983–84), *Le Dortoir* (The Dormitory,
1988), *La Fôret* (The Forest, 1994), *Les Âmes morts* (Dead Souls, 1996),
and *L'Hiver-Winterland* (1998) – for the interventions their hybrid forms
make in national discourse. I argue that in their linking of theatre and
dance, Carbone 14 shows issue invitations to meaning on which they
then foreclose, prompting a kind of bifocal vision which focuses the
eye alternately on signification and effect/affect, a kind of biological
ground of difference. Carbone 14's hyphenated artistic practice holds
distinct formal attributes and relations to meaning in productive tension, summoning a peculiar way of seeing the work of art. On the one
hand, the theatrical framework with its narrative impulse – though often
fragmented – and its emphasis on representation invites spectators to
make associations beyond the stage frame. On the other, the dance and

visual images that carry the show often deny the fulfilment of meaning, focusing us instead on how the form makes itself up. They write a visible grammar of the stage that draws into prominence the make-up of the 'really made up.'[3] Taken together, I argue, theatre and dance enact a metonymic structure that challenges metaphor, whose Idealist cast is supplanted by a materialist, historicist consciousness and whose assimilating, vertical relations get reoriented along a more horizontal axis.

You will remark a shift in approach and emphasis in this chapter, consonant with the changed figure of national mimesis summoned by Carbone 14's image theatre. Because metonymy demands that one pay attention to the singularity of the part which will stand in, however briefly, for the whole, I bring a kind of formalist attention to the composition of Carbone 14 pieces and the affective reality of their effects. I enlist theatre and dance phenomenology in my reading of the particularity of Carbone 14's image-theatre and its relation to national discourses for a similar reason: because Carbone 14's visible grammar of the stage enjoins us to look as much at the work of the art – how it is put together – as the work of art itself. Finally, my own 'changed eyes' in this chapter, eyes that attempt to clarify the bifocal vision required by Carbone 14 productions, can be attributed to the fact that I spy in the image's resistance to set narratives, its refusal to compromise its singularity, a generative means of accounting for difference in national performance historiography. This would be a historiography that safeguards the integrity of the one within a national imaginary by reading that one as a tenor in its own right and tracing its own dense historicity of associations.

Since its founding in 1980, Carbone 14 has produced a hybridized performance form that might well be considered an unstable isotope to the *nouveau théâtre québécois* and *néo-Québécois* drama. Incorporating the neutrons of dance and music (and to a lesser extent mime, architecture, and electronic media) into theatre, Gilles Maheu, the troupe's *concepteur* and *metteur en scène*, devises thematically organized, image-based spectacles using shifting combinations of movement, light, environmental design, and music. These multiple origins for the performance text pose definitional problems. Many have proposed *le théâtre de l'image* (image-theatre), a category that would include the work of director-scenographers like Maheu, Denis Marleau and, most famously, Robert Lepage. For Chantal Hébert and Irène Perelli-Contos, authors of *La face cachée du théâtre de l'image*, the appellation 'image-theatre' indicates the 'primacy accorded to the scenic image, which finds itself elevated to the level where the occidental theatrical tradition had placed the dramatic text, by a generation of artists active beginning in the eighties' (Hébert and Perelli-Contos 2001, 11). Diane Pavlovic, who assisted Maheu on *Rivage à l'abandon* (1990, after Heiner Müller's *Paysage sous surveillance*) and *Titanic* (1985, after a play of the same name by Québécois playwright and director Jean-Pierre Ronfard), invokes sculpture in her description of Maheu's image-theatre: 'These productions are highly choreographed and visually impeccable: the bodies of the actors are molded like sculptures or plastic elements – shaped, moved around, synchronized and integrated into carefully created spaces' (Pavlovic 1987, 27). Writing about processional productions outside of Quebec, Sarah Hood defines image-theatre as 'the technique of "sculpting" a human body to create an image expressing a state or situation' (1995, 51). This is not so distant from Maheu's own penchant for describing his theatre as photography or painting, in order to capture the import and impact of the visual image to his art. Maheu says in an interview, 'At base, I feel more like a failed painter than a man of the theatre,' and in conversation with Irène Perelli-Contos and Chantal Hébert, he compares his scenic writing 'which happens directly on the physical material of the actor, to the work of a sculptor' (quoted in Beaunoyer 1988, D5; quoted in Perelli-Contos and Hébert 1994, 68).

These definitions of image-theatre second Maheu's statement of his artistic goals, first printed in the quarterly Quebec theatre journal *Jeu* in 1978, when he headed a company of mimes and acrobats (that he founded in 1975) called 'Les Enfants du paradis': 'To recreate a theatre where movement, dynamics, and form would have predominance over literature. A theatre of mimes, acrobats, jugglers where action would have predominance over acting. To create a naïve theatrical language which would address itself equally well to children and adults' (G. Maheu 1978, 80). During its 'Les Enfants du paradis' period, the troupe performed at festivals and fairs, in public buildings, and in the street for varied crowds of passers-by. In 1980, the troupe was reconstituted as 'Carbone 14,' quit public venues, and began experimenting with theatrical apparatuses at the Espace Libre performance space in Montreal, which Carbone 14 shared with Jean-Pierre Ronfard's Nouveau théâtre expérimental and the Omnibus mime troupe (Gendron 2008). Despite the new venue, their mission of researching a physical theatrical grammar for revealing the meanings of the body and its senses remained unchanged; in a 1985 article, co-founder Danièle de Fontenay articulates a similar set of goals: 'to create a theatre where the language of the body occupies the primary place' (Fontenay 1985, 111).[4]

For his image-theatre, Maheu has developed a visual dramaturgy called 'écriture scénique' (scenic writing) whose primary syntactical components are actor-dancers' bodies and evocative physical environments that are often of his own design. *Écriture scénique* describes a creative process in which the performance is composed in the scenic space. Hébert and Perelli-Contos outline its principles:

> Scenic writing consists of an assemblage, a mixing, or a *bricolage* of objects, words, music, sounds, lighting techniques, texts, gestures, movements, technological apparatuses, screens, etc. – in brief, of disparate and heterogeneous elements used as sensitive resources that may be exploited to advantage throughout the theatrical creation process. The combination, recombination, displacement, and play of these elements permits the constitution of the visual material or text, which is held together precisely by the intimate relationship that these materials or *scenic elements* establish among themselves and with the theatrical space. (2001, 9)

Maheu's devised works are generally constructed around a set of visual images, drawn from specific yet generous themes inspired by Maheu's eclectic reading list. (For example, *Le Rail* was inspired by his reading of D.M. Thomas's *L'hôtel blanc* and Jack Henry Abbott's *In the Belly of the Beast*; Maheu's one-man show, *L'Homme rouge* (1983), drew on clinical descriptions of physical pain for its movement vocabulary.) Based on his fairly complete idea of the show worked out in advance of the rehearsal process, Maheu directs the company in improvisatory movement based on their responses to the chosen images. Maheu says of their creative process, 'Ordinarily the work happens in collaboration with the actors, during the process of the show's creation. I submit my proposals/suggestions to them, I eliminate things, I keep others ... I work the actors around the core [of the idea]. I may say, "No, that's not it. Stop." Then we start again until I feel the image, the speech, the gesture, or the movement of which I had an intuition appear before my eyes' (quoted in Perelli-Contos and Hébert 1994, 69). He emphasizes that while he is influenced by the actors and their work with the images presented to them, he already has a vision of the show 'in his head.'

Importantly, the 'meaningfulness' to which Maheu refers is more sensory or affective than discursive. Contra Expo, Tremblay, and Micone's outward-facing disposition to the world – Expo will construct it, Tremblay will reflect it, Micone will simulate it – Maheu's disposition is rather more inward-facing and somewhat less grand in its gesture. He seeks less to recreate reality than to reanimate its parts and activate its human elements. In his review of Carbone 14's *Le Rail* (1984), influential *Devoir* theatre critic Robert Lévesque underscores image-theatre's wary relationship to referential signification: 'We see in it the first evident signs of a new theatrical aesthetic which, in Pina Bausch's generation, rediscovers the *sense of the sign*, keeps its distance from rational discourse, finds a modern sensibility at the heart of the space's magic' (R. Lévesque 1984a, 8; emphasis mine).[5] Louise Vigeant contends that *le théâtre de l'image* triggers 'cathartic "effects," rather than effects of "sense" resembling logos or rational discourse' (1991, 7). In keeping with these observations, Maheu's productions dramatize states of being or un/subconscious elements of human existence that escape or exceed language. Thus, 'Carbone 14 productions are articulated around the critique of contemporary social archetypes,' including consumer society in *Pain blanc* (White bread, 1981); solitude in *L'Homme rouge* (The Red Man); physical and moral brutality in *Le Rail*; dream and childhood in *Le Dortoir*; generational and sexual divides in *La Forêt*; comfort and escape in *Les Âmes mortes*; and dualities in *L'Hiver-Winterland* (Carbone 14's web-page, 'Usine C: Carbone 14'). In Maheu's words, they try to 'meet up with the irrational via movement,' colouring his work with a neo-expressionist quality (quoted in M.-C. Lortie 1989, D4). Moreover, Carbone 14's stage environments appear as dream-products: they open suddenly in the dark either with encompassing music or in complete silence. *Le Rail* begins with a piercing train whistle; *La Forêt* opens in the dark with the ripples of children's laughter. In *Les Âmes mortes* and *L'Hiver-Winterland*, the audience enters a fog-filled auditorium. In the former, a lone trumpeter sounds sustained, trailing notes and a single, exposed lightbulb hanging from the ceiling is illuminated; the latter begins almost imperceptibly, in silence. These dream-like opening effects are reinforced by the appearance and disappearance of the stage's inhabitants from and into blackouts. For the most part, the dancer-actors do not make visible entrances or exits through doorways or curtain-openings, for instance; instead, they appear out of the darkness of the stage, discovered *in medias res* – in place and often already moving – by the lights.[6] It is as if they exist only in performance's vanishing present; their movements do not point to an off-stage life.

Let me draw out two points about Maheu's encryption of the irrational in movement that contribute to a renovated, non-metaphorical national mimesis. First, it attempts to capture that which most thoroughly challenges representation; the irrational – presented in Maheu's pieces as autonomic nervous-system-like 'impulses,' 'urges,' or, more elaborately, 'desires,' – is deemed effectively unrepresentable because of its profound interiority. These impulses are what David Graver, in his taxonomic analysis of the actor's body, calls the body of 'sensation': 'The most secretive of the actor's bodies and, yet, arguably, the most ontologically primary ... is the body of private sensation that constitutes itself for each of us just below the skin ... The interior of this body is the nervous system and the sensations of pain, pleasure, numbness, and sensitivity that it brings to mind.' Even if one can display the effects of those sensations – in the form of contracting mid-sections, primal screams, or tears, for instance – the sensations themselves are nonetheless not exteriorized. They maintain their 'invisible reality' (2005, 169; 170). In the face of this obstacle, Maheu searches for ways of releasing the internal histories of the sensate body with their subterranean significance.[7] To this end, he puts objects in the actor-body's way, forcing deviations from familiar patterns and the relearning of certain movements in altered conditions; thus, dancers navigate fifty trees planted in dirt and moss during *La Forêt* or wade through several centimetres of water in *Opium* (1987), directed by Maheu's long-time artistic associate Lorne Brass. Carbone 14 choreography also requires actor-bodies to do things to which they are not accustomed or to perform actions that are not overlaid with a particular training or physical culture – again to take their bodies out of their *habitus* such that they may access differently, and thence more profoundly, their sensate experience. Thus, in *L'Hiver-Winterland*, Lin Snelling, Carbone 14's *interprète en residence* (actor in residence) at the time, breaks up ice on stage; and Louis Robitaille, a former principal dancer with Les Grands Ballets Canadiens, performs a dance suggestive of First Nations dance styles.

Although sensation is resolutely idiosyncratic inasmuch as it cannot escape its individual corporal envelope, it is also, Graver insists, ontologically primary and, hence, shared. One does not experience another's impulse, however suggestively its effects are displayed. However, in that display, which signals the presence of, say, suffering or sexual pleasure, the spectator may recognize a similar but non-identical affective experience of her own. In other words, sensation forms a primary point of connection between stage and auditorium without reducing them to identity. Graver writes of sensational performance, 'An atmosphere of concern and reverence is built up between performers and spectators because there is so much that does not meet the eye in the event, so much that remains locked in the body of the performer. The performers stand between two worlds: the one in the spectators' eyes and the one

inside their own bodies' (2005, 170). They shimmer at the threshold
of representation. Reinforcing this shared affective terrain are Maheu's
encompassing environments, where the stage atmosphere permeates the
auditorium sonically and, in the case of the fog, also physically. Further,
his establishing technique of deploying suddenness and extremes of volume prepare the ground for reception by waking up the spectator's nervous system, shocking it into a more alert state.

The affective bridge Carbone 14 builds is valuable to a renovated, non-
metaphorical national mimesis inasmuch as it disallows even the illusion
of full commensurability between different subject positions. The impulse's internment within the body guarantees its idiosyncracy. Contra
metaphor's collapse of its two components – tenor and vehicle – into
one, their difference into (the tenor's) sameness, Carbone 14's sensational effects preserve each component's distinction. In fact, the display
of sensation by the actor-body and its effects on the audience, while
linked, are not assimilable to metaphor's tenor and vehicle. The effect
on the audience is not the copy of or substitute for the actor's (display
of) sensation. Rather, their connection is causal to the extent that the
actor's display prompts an effect in the audience.

The causal and proxemic links between sensation and effect lead us
to the nonrational's second contribution to a non-metaphorical national
mimesis. Maheu's *écriture scénique* tends to reach for the nondiscursive via
metonymy. As theatre phenomenologist Bert O. States defines it, metonymy is a device 'for reducing states, or qualities, or attributes, or whole
entities like societies, to visible things in which they somehow inhere'
(1985, 65). The connection between signifier and signified – using tears
for 'grief,' for instance – is typically causal and/or proxemic, and often
stems from a physical relationship between the part that comes to stand
in for the whole and the whole itself (Lakoff and Johnson 1980, 40).
Although the signifier is an aspect of the signified, it cannot be reduced
to the signified's vehicle. For 'tears' are not presented in metonymic relations as coextensive with 'grief'; they may index grief, certainly, but
they are also their own tenors with their own sets of references. Thus,
they may also connote joy or relief or sympathy. In this sense, tears loan
themselves in a particular domain of use for a limited duration to act as
an index for grief, allowing for a more horizontal figural relation than
what we've seen in metaphor. As we saw in the last chapter, metaphor's
vehicles, too, are enmeshed within referential networks other than those
of the tenors to which they are attached. However, metaphor occults
its figural operations, hiding the vehicle's provenance and the costs of

its loan. Metaphor requires a suspension of disbelief with regard to the vehicle's networks, a suspension facilitated by tenor and vehicle's arbitrary relationship. Micone's simulations of *québécité* show the suspension of disbelief to be fragile grounds for figural relations.[8] Metonymy, on the other hand, requires illuminated networks since it functions courtesy of agreed-upon associations. Thus, metonymy displays its grammar as it yokes parts or aspects to wholes.[9] Importantly, that display reveals the operations by which parts come to surrogate wholes such that *Québécois de souche* come to stand in for *Québécois*, for instance. As important, however, is metonymy's revelation of the part's independence from the whole. When metonymy codifies links between parts and wholes, it also highlights the part's phenomenological weight, that is to say, its heaviness with itself. Carbone 14's *écriture scénique* capitalizes on metonymy's stubborn partiality and maximizes metonymy's semantic displacements in its productions' syntactic narrative structure, reflexive choreography, and associative deployment of images.

Let us examine, then, how parts fit into wholes in Carbone 14's œuvre. We'll first investigate how the 'resistant particulars' of Carbone' 14 metonymy articulate with theatrical (and national) narratives that would incorporate them into a whole. Then, we'll look at how the metonymic part retains its independence by capitalizing on its own phenomenological weight; this requires an analysis of dance as form and system of representation.

The primary narrative frame for each Carbone 14 creation is the performance environment. All of the performance environments of the devised works at issue here index flash-points in Quebec's national narrative, from a territory of France, to its incarnation as 'Lower Canada' under British colonial rule, through Confederation as a province, to modern clashes with the federal government. In their representations of material locations strongly associated with particular moments and/or events in Quebec's history, Carbone 14's performance environments perform representational labour for (or about) the nation. *Le Rail, La Forêt,* and *L'Hiver-Winterland* situate themselves in unspecified but culturally meaningful outdoor locations. Its costuming identifies *Le Rail*'s male dancers as Second World War–era soldiers, evoking a fraught period when the Canadian federal government conscripted French-Canadian men into service, against the will of the Quebec provincial government and the Quebec people, as evidenced in the 1942 nationwide plebiscite on conscription.[10] Its exploration of physical and moral brutality transpires in a no-man's-land with a single, *Godot*-like tree – an unclaimed territory where social norms and convention do not apply. *La Forêt's* woods are a space of transformation where 'everything is possible, everything is permitted, anything could happen' (Program from *La Forêt*). Again, it is the costumes that encourage extrapolation to Québécois referents; *coureurs de bois canayens* (French-Canadian foresters) with their red shirts, deer-skin pants and moccasins, and fur hats share the stage with somnambulists and characters out of Grimm's fairy-tales. *L'Hiver-Winterland* is Maheu's most direct and extended representation of what I have been calling *québécité*. It opens with a dedication to Quebec, as dismissively described by Voltaire, projected in script on a downstage scrim: 'Pour quelques arpents de neige' (For several acres of snow). Journalist Marie Labreque writes, '*L'Hiver* is interested in our national mythology, in our deeply-rooted collective symbols: religious education, *cabane à sucre*, referendum' (1998).[11] Crisscrossed by *habitants* (French settlers), Catholic *curés* (rural priests), Santa Clauses, Inuit shamans, New Wave–styled youth, and 1980s break-dancers, *L'Hiver's* landscape exhibits some of the more densely layered temporalities of Carbone 14's environments.

In the interior spaces of *Le Dortoir* and *Les Âmes mortes*, the sets likewise establish national referential frameworks. *Le Dortoir* is performed in the imaginative recreation of the Marieville convent school Maheu attended for several years during the early 1960s (Program for *Le Dortoir*). Symbol of the power of the Catholic Church, its stranglehold on provincial education, and its personal and sexual repression, the dorm hosts its political and social opposites as well: revolt in Algeria, student demonstrations, sexual experimentation, and the assassination of John F. Kennedy, among others. The social space of the dorm, both a symbol and an experience for many Québécois, compresses in its layers the paradigm shift from *canayennité* to *québécité*, as discussed in chapter 2. *Les Âmes mortes* unfolds in an unfurnished house with a bare lightbulb hanging from a long wire centre-stage. The set's major feature is its three, double-height walls, whose spatial configuration harkens back to the 'fourth wall' sets of domestic realism, but whose permeability aligns it with farce: the two side walls are lined with doors, two high and three deep, through which one set of characters makes frequent, often frantic, entrances and exits. A wooden, rectangular kitchen table and two chairs are brought centre-stage, placed beneath the bulb. At this table sit a silent, turn-of-the-century *paysan* couple who pray before eating their soup; then an anglophone couple from the mid-century with a chattering wife interested in her new cookware; then a young, urban, francophone couple from the 1990s dressed in black, drinking wine and arguing about their relationship; and finally an old man and a young girl.

Within these already partial imitative narrative frames – whereby a house stands in for homeliness or a dorm for a people's awakening – stories are told in pieces; they are broken into short sequences – scenes, images, tableaux – arranged in nonlinear fashion, and disrupted by blackouts or other indications of changed perspective or place. The 'narrativity' of Carbone 14 performances might be best understood as what Patrice Pavis calls 'gestural narrativity' with respect to mime. That is to say, it is 'organized syntactically rather than semantically – for example, by systems of thematic or meaningful oppositions' (1982, 58). For instance, *La Forêt* concerns itself with the passage of time, its vagaries, and humanity's responses to it – looking forward, looking backward. Its scenes are organized non-sequentially around the stages of a lifespan: childhood, youth, maturity, and old age. In the life-stage scenes, each of life's stages is represented by a person: childhood by a rebellious boy in his tree-house; youth and maturity by two (generally naked) young men and two (frequently topless) women; and old age by a thin, elderly man. Often representatives appear in the same sequences, foreshadowing future actions, reenacting past ones. Even on the level of staging, Brigitte Purkhardt writes in *Jeu* that *La Forêt* is organized like a 'game of mirrors': 'Sometimes the action is repeated. What is performed stage right seems to be the perfect reply to what is transpiring stage left. Or, it is upstage and downstage which are projected in each other' (1994, 164). What unites the scenes, despite the blackouts that separate them and their nonsequential order, is not plot-line but their mutual, if varied, reflections on the production's theme. This theme-and-variations approach to organizing movement, called 'parataxis,' generally forms the superstructure of Carbone 14 shows. If the series of sequences gesture to a larger story, or a meta-narrative, they do not fully enact it.

In terms of choreography, Maheu's is generally organized in abbreviated, even abrupt, phrases. Movement sequences do not accumulate force via their duration, leading some critics to accuse him of deploying *l'effet vidéoclip* (the videoclip effect) of the closely related '*nouveau bouger montréalais*' (new Montreal groove) (Tembeck 1992, 216). For instance, *Dance Magazine* critic Sally Sommer counts the costs of abrupt narrative and foreshortened choreographic phrasing in her 1991 review of *Le Dortoir*, which played in the company of two other Québécois dance companies – O Vertigo danse and Margie Gillis with Christopher Gillis – at the Brooklyn Academy of Music: 'While this gave the pieces smart pacing and us the illusion that a lot was happening, it stopped the sustained flow of phrases. The intent, I think, was to land a fast, hard jab at the heart, but more often the work merely pummeled you with too much energy and too little substance' (1991, 90). Even the quality of the actor-dancers' movements seems to eschew metaphor's vertical reach, as the movements tend to be grounded and their flow more horizontal than vertical. Group movement patterns in *Le Dortoir* and *L'Hiver-Winterland*, for example, are laterally organized; dancer-actors move across the stage (from stage left to stage right, or vice-versa) in profile. In addition, Maheu's choreography places little emphasis on replicating idealized geometric patterns in the manner of Balanchine's ballets or some of Merce Cunningham's postmodern dances. For instance, in the contemplative, lyric sequences on the tundra of *L'Hiver-Winterland*, full body extension is common; however, Maheu does little with 'line' in the balletic sense of the term.

Instead, the movement sequences tend to replicate systems – power relations, emotional pendulum swings, societal organization. Dance scholar Susan L. Foster isolates replication as one of dance's four key modes for representing the world; in replication, the world is perceived as a systemic whole. Replication isolates the system's signal constitutive elements in order to show the relation between its parts (Foster 1986, 66). The emphasis, then, is not placed on apprehending a single, summary quality of the represented – as in metaphor – but rather on the functionality of the system. For instance, the movement vocabularies of *L'Hiver-Winterland* contrast Quebec's agrarian past with an urban present, sketching a developing society in terms similar to Expo 67's Quebec Pavilion. The generalized First Nations dance vocabulary which opens the piece demonstrates a light quality: dancers turn, bouncing on the balls of their feet, arms outstretched and palms turned up, their focus skyward. Two scenes later, after an explicit reference to the 1995 failed referendum on sovereignty, four dancer-actors dance, all jagged edges and broken line, moving to another actor's chanting/rapping of 'Les Corbeaux,' (The Crows), a poem by the emblematic Romantic, French-Canadian poet Émile Nelligan (1879–1941). The poem's portents of disaster – in which the lyric narrator's soul is devoured, Prometheus-like, by flocks of crows – translate into New Wave dancing style. The quality of the movement is frenetic and thrashing, recursive in its leaps and crashes, and staccato in its rhythm (Fig. 6.1). Following a similar pattern, the next sequence of scenes opens with three self-mortifying *curés* (parish priests) illuminated by top-spots, who turn their gently swinging,

6.1 New Wave styled dancers in *L'Hiver-Winterland.*
Photo: Yves Dubé. Courtesy Usine C.

encircling arms against their torsos. Following another reference to the referendum, stylized self-mortification transmutes into percussive jabs directed away from the body but still held well within its perimeter across three dancing bodies.

In *Le Dortoir*, Maheu depicts the tensions of the Quiet Revolution, torn between a *repli sur soi* mentality and the socio-political awakening of a generation of young Québécois. In the first half of the piece – its dreamy, night-time component – the quality of the choreography is light, innocent, fluid. For example, two girls play a relaxed game of catch, tossing the ball underhand in easy arcs to each other. Their central torsos lift and open in the toss, contract and stoop in the catch. In the second half of the piece – its harsh, daytime exposure of the power-relations informing those games – the play-like movements distort into those of violent conflict. The girls extend and contract their mid-sections in response to torture, their tossing hands tied to the top of an up-ended bed. The boys appear behind them, slightly elevated; their bodies open and close in response to self-flagellation.

Concerned with systemic wholes, replication reduces them, in States's sense of concentration, to their salient elements, which are then put into motion. As a result, each element carries with it an extra semantic charge – it is both itself and the surrogate for a larger system of which it is a part. However, in being themselves, the particulars to which systems are boiled down in Carbone 14's metonymy are also particularly resistant to abstraction. For instance, if in *La Forêt* differently aged bodies index different life-stages, those bodies nonetheless attract – even demand – the audience's sustained, focused attention. I should note that most of Maheu's devised works reveal the naked or nearly naked body at one point or another.[12] However, in *La Forêt* dancers spent more time naked or nearly naked than in any of his other shows, and an unusually pronounced aesthetic emphasis was placed on the dancers' naked bodies. The lighting threw into relief their sculpted contours, and the men in particular were arranged in tableaux, draped across mounds of moss for extended periods. One had the sense of the body here 'consent[ing] to be the grounds of a possible expressiveness,' as States puts it in *Great Reckonings* (1985, 26). The naked body's phenomenal charge – its thingness – hedges against its being digested into abstraction. As in the case of Carbone 14's shows' syntactical narrative organization, in Maheu's choreography and in the troupe's deployment of images, metonymic relations place an unusually strong emphasis on parts, both in their singularity and in their associative and usage networks.

Carbone 14's use of dance urges close attention to movement's singularity, to movement *qua* movement, first by privileging performance text (or physical signs) and second in sequences of reflective movement or display. Carbone 14 performances capitalize on the difficulties dance as form poses to interpretation by privileging physical signs over more readily accessible verbal signs. Carbone 14's theatre is one in which 'the spoken word is unimportant; body language creates what is essential to the work' (Laplante 1982, 108). In her analysis of 'theatres of creation,' Hélène Beauchamp (with Yves Raymond) qualifies Carbone 14's work as a 'choreographed theatre' that 'cedes to the evocative force of images, to the expressivity of the actor-dancer's body which moves in a ludic space' (2005, 225). Verbal expression, when present, is employed more for its sonic effect or emotive appeal than for its discursive sense. In *Les Âmes mortes*, for instance, there is practically no spoken text at all. The longest spoken sequences are delivered by Molnar in Hungarian, a language equally unintelligible to francophone and anglophone audiences, as it does not belong to the Indo-European language group. In *Le Rail*, an aria from *La Traviata* is sung neither to forward the plot, nor to delineate character. Excerpted from its original context, the aria punctuates with its lyric sadness the menacing atmosphere of violent encounters between Second World War soldiers and female travelers along the lonely stretch of railroad track. *L'Hiver-Winterland* also makes use of sung text in its investigation of the binary codes that have largely composed the story of Quebec, this land of winter, including French/English, female/male, languor/speed, traditionalism/modernity, Quebec/Canada. In the first instance, a woman sings to French techno-pop. The music assaults the ear, her delivery likewise. Both sacrifice melody for volume and pace. Furthermore, the singer is engulfed by increasingly quickly moving images of crows and fetuses projected on scrims that cover the entire proscenium opening both in front of and behind her. Upstage right and left, two company members dance to her song in an angular club style. In the second instance, the text itself is rendered almost incomprehensible in its vocal performance. Two *danseuses* rap a found text, the poem, 'Soir d'hiver' (Winter evening), again by Nelligan. It is set to a throbbing bass beat and sung in French and English by the two dancers into microphones that amplify their vocal production. Their songs overlap one another and are accompanied by three top-lit dancers moving according to its rhythms. The combination of vocal and musical sound, shadow-puppet projections, and isolated dancers whose movements do not stray outside the tight border of the follow-spot creates a net effect of noisy urban isolation pierced by shards of bleak imagery drawn from an encounter with an unyielding nature: 'Tous les étangs gisent gelés, / Mon âme est noire! Où-vis-je? où vais-je? / Tous ses espoirs gisent gelés: / Je suis la nouvelle Norvège / D'où les blonds ciels s'en sont allés' (Nelligan 1952, 82–3). (All the pools around lie icy. / My heart is dark. Where go? Where stay? / All the hopes around lie icy. / Now I am the new Norway / Its fair skies are gone from me (1983, 21).)

Employing a similar overlapping technique in *Le Dortoir*, three students recount the history of the nation, again into a microphone, again using found texts. The first is the story of Canada, recited in English. Shortly after it is begun, a second history lesson, the story of Quebec, is introduced in French. As the English and French students increase the volume of their recitations, a third student tells the story of 'America' in Spanish. The history lessons are interrupted by the radio announcement of U.S. President Kennedy's assassination. Following a brief silence, the

students form two lines centre-stage, parallel with chalkboard, perpen-
dicular to audience; each mixed-gender line of six dancers takes turns
running to the board to scrawl semantically loaded words naming conflicting ideologies, political figures, and social movements on its surface,
only to be increasingly violently torn away from the board by the other
line of six students. The groups use each others' bodies as erasers, hold-
ing their partner's back to the chalkboard and moving them up and
down, back and forth. The girls' black jumpers and the boys' black pants
are whitened with chalk; the blackboard is one large, grey smear. The
pace, intensity, and volume of the sequence picks up; the Middle-Eastern
vocal music (of Chaba Quarda Aghira) is encompassing, pulsing as the
students yell at the top of their lungs. They rush to the blackboard now
only to vault off of it in a kind of pure, because excessive, expenditure
of physical energy (Fig. 6.2). The physical activity of vocal production,
and finally just physical activity, overwhelms spoken and sung text as the
body's drives and emotions take over the stage. About such moments,
dance scholar Michèle Febvre writes, 'Meaning is diluted, floats, is lost
when that which is given to be seen, to be felt, is the abruptness or the
sensuality of a contact, the flight of a jump, the irreversibility of a plunge,
the sweetness of a sliding of one body over another, the ecstasy of an un-
balancing' (Febvre 1987a, 78).

    In sequences like the one just described, Carbone 14's performance
texts enjoin audiences to notice singular physicality in its spectacular
presence, in its stealing the focus from the spoken word. They also draw
attention to dance's essence or the way in which it makes itself up in
sequences of what Susan L. Foster calls 'reflexive' movement, by which
she means movement that 'makes exclusive reference to the performance of movement' (1986, 66).[13] 'Reflexion' is another of dance's modes
for representing the world, as schematized in Foster's *Reading Dancing*,
and is one of the hallmarks of postmodern dance, the tradition in which
Maheu largely choreographs. Much postmodern dance, as defined by
Sally Banes in *Terpsichore in Sneakers*, took as its object programmatic in-
vestigations of dance's form and fundaments. U.S. choreographers like
Yvonne Rainer, Steve Paxton, and Lucinda Childs asked, What makes
dance 'dance'? and When is dance no longer dance? Their answers –
and those of their compatriots – took many different forms, but were
united in their search for 'new ways to foreground the medium of dance
rather than its meaning,' as against historical modern dance's 'bloated
... dramatic, literary, and emotional significance' (Banes 1987, xvi). (As
Banes points out, in this, its formalist mode, postmodern dance was not

6.2 The chalkboard war in *Le Dortoir*.
Photo: Yves Dubé. Courtesy Usine C.

'post-modernist.' Rather, it was more closely related to the modernist experiments of action-painter Jackson Pollack and composer John Cage, for instance, who sought to uncover the essence or ground of their arts.) Similarly, for its phenomenological research into corporal thea-tre's generic limits, Carbone 14 has been called 'action-theatre' (David 1983, 95) allying it with the mid-century Pollack and Willem de Koon-ing, whose heavy drip-canvases emphasized painting's medium (paint) and the artistic act (painting) itself. Consistent with this self-referential strain of postmodern dance, Carbone 14 movements generate meaning from within the context of the dance itself more frequently than they cleave to an external grid of reference. For example, approximately half-way through *L'Hiver-Winterland*, an inter-scenic blackout is filled with the sound of shovels against ice. The lights come up on two kneeling *danseuses* – one mid-stage right, one mid-stage left – breaking up ice in rain barrels by jabbing at it in short, hard strokes with the tips of their shovels. Their sole point of concentration is the ice in the bucket. Shortly, the stage-right *danseuse* lays down her shovel to pick up the bits of ice in the bucket, letting them fall through her fingers and against the bucket's tin sides. The bucket is miked, sending metallic echoes around the theatre. This series of movements – breaking up ice, picking up ice, dropping ice – is reflexive. The *danseuses* are doing an action, to which they devote their whole attention, thereby highlighting the movement as just that. Consistent with what Norbert Servos identifies as paradigmatic of *la nouvelle danse-théâtre* (the new dance-theatre) – a danced theatre whose model is Pina Bausch's Tanztheater and with which Maheu has expressed his affinity – this scene is a situation, an event, as much or more than it is a representation of an event or situation (Servos 1987).[14] The dancers' movements do not *represent* 'women breaking ice up in a bucket,' they *are* dancers breaking up ice in a bucket.

Le Rail furnishes another example of reflexive movement, one that is less an aestheticization of everyday movement, as in the ice-breaking sequence, than a dangerous encounter with the actors' bodies' physical limitations. The soldiers and travelers perform complicated, fast-moving *pas de deux* on the train track bisecting the performance space; the soldiers hurtle themselves through the air, and, on command, throw themselves headfirst against the walls of the dimly lit, smoke-filled scenic environment whose floor is covered with thirty tons of moist earth. And then there's the fire: fire on torches carried by the actors; fire that exceeds its on-stage hearth; fire that creeps up the soldiers' pant legs. Nor are the spectators completely removed from the danger-zone; they line the walls of the space, encircling the action and forming a kind of human barricade keeping the performers inside. Robert Lévesque underscores these movements' reflexivity, calling *Le Rail* 'a form of panic-theatre or emergency-theatre (that is to say, one of felt necessity) born of the show itself, of the actor put into a performance situation, and not of any story' (R. Lévesque 1984b, 28). If the actor is in a performance situation, the spectator is, presumably, in a state of heightened affect. As dance critic Isabelle Villeneuve points out, the danger of the performance situation also fuels its pleasure. She writes, 'Performance is a pleasure: it is immediately visible, in the quality and precision of the lovingly perfected physical movement, which tames its violence. The armed and hand-to-hand combat, the training, the submission, the stupidity and hatred of the soldiers, the whole universe of war is danced with the help of the danger, not in spite of it' (1984, 13). Her observation links the dancers' dangerous reflexive movements with the virtuosic reflexive movements more common to ballet. Those are 'moments of dancing for the sake of sheer formal accomplishment and beauty,' often in 'display sequences' that showcase a dancer's formal mastery (Foster 1986, 69). Beautiful dancing among on-stage obstacles (not to mention while being on fire) focuses spectator attention on the skill of the dancing body. More than anything, display sequences index the performer's exceptional capacity for physical articulation. Nothing in *Le Rail*'s 'story,' such as it is, of an encounter between male soldiers and female travelers in a no-man's-land requires characters of extraordinary physical skills. It is 'just' dance.

While postmodern dance has privileged reflexive movement as part of its allergy to being representational, dance as a form – modern, postmodern, classical – poses its own problems to meaning-making – or, as Taussig would have it, its own resistance to abstraction – of which Carbone 14 also takes advantage. Dances are transmitted through what Ellen W. Goellner and Jacqueline Shea Murphy call 'a kind of oral-and-bodily tradition' in the 'personal transmission of dances from generation to generation' (1995, 5). Because dance's existence lies in the passing moment of the dance, its perpetuation relies on other dancers imprinting its choreographies into their neuromusculature and (re)performing them. Clearly, visual recording technologies and notation systems like Rudolf von Laban's give this transfer a second impress and enable those outside of choreography's golden circle to analyze and appreciate dance as cultural artefact. Nonetheless, strictly speaking the dance itself is lost in the moment it appears, prompting many dance critics, including most famously Marcia B. Siegel, to argue that dance is the most ephemeral of the arts.[15] Siegel writes, 'Dancing exists at a perpetual vanishing point. At the moment of its creation it is gone ... No other art is so hard to catch, so impossible to hold' (1972, 1). Protected in disappearance, dance defers its entry into meaning. It holds out the possibility of unreproducibility, of just being itself. This is not to say that dance does not 'mean' or 'signify'; on the contrary, dance – especially the dance employed in and as dance-theatre in the work of Carbone 14 – is embedded within systems of reference despite its best efforts to extricate itself from sclerotic convention. Nor is my statement that dance holds out the possibility of unreproducibility to mean that dance's resistance to reproduction does not in itself spawn 'systems and performances of high reproducibility,' as enumerated by André Lepecki in his important re-evaluation of dance's essence. Among those systems are dance techniques that model bodies, disciplines of physical culture including dieting and surgery, brand merchandizing (e.g., 'Mark Morris's "The Hard Nut"'), and dance studies' own efforts at recuperation via archival research (Lepecki 2006, 129). In a final clarification, I do not intend that dance's 'just being itself' is not already a hugely complex endeavour.

What I wish to point out in this rehearsal of what has become a given of dance and performance studies is that dance perhaps offers its 'just being' most pointedly as a challenge to interpretation. Dance challenges in its slipperiness, yes, in much the same way that Peggy Phelan has posed performance's ontology of disappearance as a challenge to reproduction (1993). And its slipperiness is tied to the presumption of dance as movement; not only does dance disappear, but it won't stay still in the brief moment of its appearance. (Lepecki's reconceptualization of dance, to which I will return shortly, overturns this supposition as well.) But dance also challenges in the conceptual and historical thickness of that very brief moment in which it appears. Siegel writes of this moment at the vanishing point, 'All of a dancer's years of training in the studio, all the choreographer's planning, the rehearsals, the coordination of designers, composers, and technicians, the raising of money and the gathering together of an audience, all these are only a preparation for an event that disappears in the very act of materializing' (1972, 1). Lepecki spies in Siegel's melancholic relation to dance's disappearance a definition of the present as punctual, as a series of 'irreversible and unique instants performed by a series of "nows"' (2006, 129). Via Bergson and Deleuze, Lepecki proposes expanding 'the present' beyond the fleeting now to simultaneous 'presents' composed of acts whose effects are ongoing. However, while Siegel clearly mourns dance's alacritous passing from the 'now' to the 'then,' she also points to the fullness and durable materiality of its conditions for being, for its appearance in the first place: for instance, the dancer's physical conditioning that has moulded her musculature and, often, worn thin her joints; the working relationships forged between theatre professionals; and the gathering of the audience members in whose memory the dance extends its existence. These conditions have duration in the way Lepecki seems to intend, for all that goes into that fleeting moment of performance is also what allows for its perpetuation.

Unattainable as integral presence, dance de-composes in Carbone 14's image-theatre. It breaks into pieces, into images that, in their piercing quality, arrest perception and that, in their thing-ness, refuse being folded wholly into a sign. They detain the spectator, inciting in her an experience of wrappedness in the stage image. These pieces also lead the spectator along a chain of contiguous associations, deferring and defying meaning. Thus, grasping this 'hard to catch' form requires a mode of perception that registers at once the singularity of the act as well as its density and extension.

If the phenomenologically inflected reading I performed above on the part's singularity risks idealism, accounting for its density and extension through metonymy, as I do below, returns to it its historicity. In its images and objects, Carbone 14's action-theatre foregrounds the creative process, the way by which image-theatre makes itself up. The associative networks their images stitch draw attention to national mimesis's operations; that is, they spotlight the work of culture to produce and reproduce the nation.

L'Hiver-Winterland provides the clearest example of Carbone 14's multivalent use of images and its reflection on national history. This 'visual poem' employs familiar, even stereotypical, images symbolizing Quebec. Following on the projected dedication to 'quelques arpents de neige' are a series of projections that explode this image of Quebec as an undifferentiated blanket of white. As reindeer shadow-puppets frolic across the scrims and *habitantes* (female settlers) work the land and pulverize grain with mortar and pestle, dozens of Inuktitut words for 'snow' are projected onto the front scrims.[16] Each is translated into French: 'light snow,' 'sticky snow.' Invoking the oft-overlooked precolonial 'first nations' of Canada's indigenous peoples, and projecting the many ways of specifying that difference is inherent in that which is most familiar, *L'Hiver-Winterland* begins its excavation of the many layers of *québécité*. The remainder of the performance explores the variety of beings, attitudes, and expressions housed in and buried under those several acres of snow.

Following the Inuktitut renderings of 'snow,' a series of shadow-puppets representing indigenous Canadian animals float over the scrims – whales, fish, otters, rabbits, foxes, bison, polar bears, beavers, owls. The beaver, Canada's official national animal, is paired with a maple leaf, Canada's national symbol, on the stage-left scrim. A snowy owl is paired with the *fleur-de-lys*, a French heraldic emblem adapted as the symbol of Quebec and used on the Quebec flag, on the stage-right scrim. (In 1948, Quebec Premier Maurice Duplessis decreed by Order in Council that the fleur-de-lys would be the Quebec flag.) From this point on,

symbols associated with Canada will be assigned to stage-left; those with
Quebec, to stage-right. This scenographic and choreographic dissection
of the stage spatializes the land of winter's dualities as outlined by Maheu in the program, 'country of snow and of ice, country of yes and of
no, country of north/south oppositions, country of "shamans" and of
priests, of whales and of moose, of solitude and of flags, of gold-diggers
and of homeless people, of poetry and of lottery' (Program for *L'Hiver-
Winterland*). For instance, a *danseuse*, stage-left, and a *danseur*, stage-right,
engage in a conversation. He asks questions in French about whether
she likes different things: winter, ice, sand, the sea. She responds, alternating affirmative and negative responses in English. (Note the inversion of the more usual gender associations of the two solitudes and
the heterosexualized love-story of French with female and English with
male.) To his final question, '*Aimes-tu mon pays?*' (Do you love my country?), she responds 'No.' Reinforcing the divide, the image of a whale is
projected on the stage-right scrim; that of a crow is projected stage-left.
Under the whale is the percentage of 'oui' votes in the 1995 referendum
(49.4%); under the crow is that of the 'non' votes (50.6%). These projections fade and are replaced by two more divisive images: a *patriote* hold-
ing a rifle, symbol of nineteenth-century French-Canadian nationalism,
and the acronym 'FLQ' (*Front de libération du Québec*) are drawn on the
stage-right scrim; a Mountie and the acronym 'RCMP' (Royal Canadian
Mounted Police) is drawn on the stage-left scrim. However, the binary
story of Quebec/Canada is interrupted by images referencing Inuit or
First Nations peoples and activities. Unclassified, they extend over the
full stage and their movement vocabularies are distributed across the
whole corps of dancers.

The familiarity of the enacted and projected images elicits audience
laughter. The images are easily recognizable for their immediate identification with different moments in Quebec's history. That the images
of *québécité* are multiple and form a series indicates that identity symbols
change over time and with the needs of the community. Lest the sequences be interpreted as solely an attempt to establish continuity among the
different ways of representing Winterland, Carbone 14 introduces a
parallel theme. The symbols' easy classification as either Québécois or
Canadian, right or left, French or English, liberationist or colonialist is
undermined by their exploration of illusion as it relates to identity. This
theme is manifested in the text that scores the web of images and in the
use of projections on scrim. The text, recited in French at various points
throughout the show, is drawn from the cautionary tale about the attrac-

tions and dangers of illusions: *La petite sirène* (The Little Mermaid). In the classic story, countless sailors succumb to the mermaids' siren-songs, which they follow to their watery deaths. Not only are the mermaids' songs misleading, but so is their appearance. They look like women to the waist, below which they have fish-bodies. Significantly, an actor-dancer begins reciting the story right after the beaver/maple leaf and snowy owl/*fleur-de-lys* projections bisect the stage into Canadian and Québécois territories. Moreover, that these familiar identity images are projected on scrims underscores their construction and their evanescence; images made of light and shadow, they appear and disappear without warning. The audience can see the shadow-puppets being manipulated by human hands. The *patriote* and the Mountie that appear on the scrim are drawn live on a backstage overhead projector. The audience sees their creation and, eventually, their erasure. The successive presentations of different images signifying Quebec leave open the possibility that more images will present themselves in the future, that the repertoire of *québécité* will not be limited to that for which we already have codified meanings.

Carbone 14 productions model this creative mixture between familiar images and their new counterparts in the manipulation of culturally significant objects on stage. Each Carbone 14 production employs a single object that is displaced into often contrasting semantic fields via metonymic labour in performance. (It is often the object which spurred the troupe's early improvisations.) Thrust into variable use environments, the object's meaning mutates. For example, in *Le Rail*, the railroad track on stage is first used as a means of transportation for railroad cars and their passengers. Later, it becomes a footpath to the travelers and, in the hands of the soldiers, a weapon. On a symbolic level, the railroad is a symbol of Canada's conquest of its own vast space through modern technology (see Berton 1970 and Francis 1997). In *Le Rail*, it represents unresolved conflict and division. The single, exposed lightbulb which hangs from the ceiling in *Les Âmes mortes* functions literally as a light source and symbolically as a symbol of desire, constantly chased after by the *paysan* couples. For the little girl, it serves as a toy that she drags across the empty stage; she fashions its cord into a leash for the old man who crawls after her. To the young man in the throes of heroin detoxification, it is a swinging pendulum above his head, ticking away the passing seconds. From illumination to time-piece, the lightbulb acquires different meanings through its different functions in the play.

Along with its central object's manifold and shifting significations across time, each Carbone 14 piece must wrestle with the object's stubborn reality. For example, at the same time that the rail indexes a time-period and conflict-laden relationships (between women and men, desire and violence), it is also just an obstacle around which Maheu and his troupe must find choreographic solutions. The dancers' movements in relation to the rail underscore its hardness and slipperiness. If its impressive size and central place on stage signal its thematic importance, they also make of the intransigent rail a focus of attention in its own right. It is perhaps *Le Dortoir*'s iron beds that enact most eloquently this tension between thing-ness and meaningfulness. First and most strongly identified with the dormitory environment, they are institutional twin beds of utilitarian design, placed on casters. Only big enough for one person, they are to be slept in and rolled to the side during the day. In the opening scene, the bed is indeed used as a place to rest: a man enters a disused dormitory, turns on the lights, walks to the stage-right blackboard and writes, 'Léa a avalé la pillule amère' (Lea swallowed the bitter pill). Sitting on a bed, he recounts the story of his wife's suicide and then withdraws a handgun from his pocket. He lies down on the bed and is engulfed in a blackout.[17] Henceforth, however, the bed is used in 'inappropriate' ways, accruing divergent meanings in its various use-contexts. (The following description of the various uses of the bed is mine and is based on my notes from the original 1988 production, the February 1996 revival, and my viewing of the televised version of *Le Dortoir* [1991].)

Twelve actor-dancers dance in unison around their beds; the quality of the movement is light, dreamy, almost somnambulist. They leap from one side to the other in slow-motion split-jumps, slide delicately under it, and suspend their bodies in a parallel line with the bed while gripping the headboard.

Six beds are rolled into a horizontal line upstage and up-ended so that their under-sides are presented to the audience. Six students are forced up against the bedboards, their bodies outlined in chalk, as if corpses at a crime scene. Beds form a vertical sidewalk.

A danseur rolls one bed to centre-stage and spins it in a circle around him. Other students take turns jumping over it, sliding under it, riding on its end as it spins with increasing speed and force. The bed is a playground roundabout, displaced into the field of dangerous childhood play (Fig. 6.3).

Upstage centre, women stand in front of the remaining up-ended beds, one arm raised as if attached to the bed's foot. Increasingly lifeless, they twitch and moan against the

6.3 The spinning bed as dangerous ride in *Le Dortoir*.
Photo: Yves Dubé. Courtesy Usine C.

bed as torture-chamber, now operating in the field of political violence. The transparent bed boards reveal men self-flagellating.

The men wander the stage in a group, throwing coins at women behind beds – their up-ended undersides transparent – now connoting red-light district viewing windows and moving the bed into the semantic field of sexual trafficking.

Women fire handguns repeatedly and methodically toward the audience from behind firing range windows, again formed by the beds' undersides.

Downstage left, a boy and a girl are stretched out together on the same twin bed. Dusted with flour falling from the grid, they perform Act III, scene v of Roméo et Juliette, *awakening after their wedding night.*

Playground and frame, window and grave, the bed and its meanings are increasingly divorced from their first environment. Subsequent use-contexts supplement the metonymic bed's initial symbolic impact. Each time the bed as stage object is recycled, its trail of significances grows longer.[18] Deployed and redeployed, the bed never really comes to rest – on stage or in the viewer's perception. As Sandra Bermann writes, metonymy's effect on the viewer can be similarly propelling. 'Never resting in a fully viewed image,' Bermann writes, 'the reader's mind journeys forward, itself desirous of the next, contiguous word, restlessly seeking something, someone stable to contemplate ... Instead of an end and a fullness of meaning, the reader finds postponement, deferral, and desire, the semantic complements of the involuted metonymical visible grammar' (1988, 23). The metonymic part illuminates but one bond at a time, a bond already figured as temporary and incomplete, hence its restlessness.

And yet, these sequences in *Le Dortoir* also smack of a kind of phenomenological experimentation; they could be the results of exercises in 'things to do with a bed.' The opening scene may be a response to the question, How might a bed be a dance partner? Perceived from different angles, the bed presents different possibilities for movement and display. Up-ended and immobile, it frames bodies; on casters it can be spun madly. If the bed sequences don't add up to one thing exactly, they are nonetheless reducible (phenomenologically) to iterations of bed-ness. What remains in the semantic shifting, in the proliferation of meanings, is the durable reality of a twin-sized iron bed. Indeed, it is as though the bed is stripped to its phenomenal essence, paradoxically in its accretion of meanings. States comments on the dynamic between thing-ness and meaningfulness, writing that 'there is a playful tug-of-war in the image between the useful and the delightful. Usefulness implies the image's transitivity, its sign-ness, or convertability into social, moral, or educational energy; delight implies its "corporeality" and the immediate absorption of the images by the senses. So the sign/image is a Janus-faced thing: it wants to say something about something, to be a sign, and it wants to be something, a thing in itself, a site of beauty' (1985, 10). Carbone 14's devised works encourage apprehension of the shimmer between phenomenal thing and semiotic sign, between real and really made up, between the delight of corporal sensation and the utility of a sign. Its images waver on these boundaries, falling alternately to one side or another, cultivating ambiguity of meaning in the very precision of their effects. It is important to remember, however, that the phenomenological thing's loans to meaning are on its own terms. It keeps returning us to the resistance of its own concrete particularity – in this instance, to 'iterations of bed-ness' – offering a model of difference in national collectives.

Paradoxically perhaps, Carbone 14's type of image-theatre has become a hallmark for Québécois cultural production's difference vis-à-vis the rest of Canada. That it is the result of research in creative process points to Quebec's more generous cultural funding, which allows for longer play-development and rehearsal periods; the primacy of the image differentiates image-theatre from a more text-based modern dramatic tradition in English Canada; its metaphysical emphasis, too, marks it as 'French' and 'Québécois.' But its metonymic cast makes it peculiarly resistant to playing the part of national ambassador. Its powers for forming a recognizably 'national' assembly, such as they are, are limited to glimpses – and deconstructions – of iconic images of *québécité*. And yet, the sensational impact of their images may 'change our eyes,' focusing them once again on affect. In the next chapter, the mimetic figure of affect takes centre-stage in my analysis of Céline Dion, herself an icon for *québécité* similar to those circulating through *L'Hiver-Winterland*.

chapter seven

National Affection: Céline Dion

I argued earlier that Expo 67 exemplifies the 'construction' pole of performance's representational labours; its *productive* national labours are credited with building a Québécois national imaginary and styling it as male, modern, urban, and sexy. At the other end of the production-reproduction spectrum, pop diva Céline Dion (b. 1968) emblematizes the arts' *reproductive* labours. As such, Expo 67 and Céline Dion comprise the limit-cases of my analysis of the performing arts' mimetic labours vis-à-vis the nation. Dion is generally deemed to naively yet opportunistically mirror trends in national, musical, commercial, and biological spheres. Neither a composer nor an instrumental musician, she interprets and performs other people's songs. She is a vocal chameleon whose song stylings cover the spectrum of contemporary popular music genres: from Mariah Carey–like power anthems ('Power of Love'), to Meatloaf's Broadway-rock theatrics ('It's All Coming Back to Me'), to the Back Street Boys' upbeat harmonics ('That's the Way It Is'), to Barbra Streisand's adult contemporary easy-listening ('Tell Him'), to Euro-pop's synthesizer-heavy romanticism ('Je danse dans ma tête'), to *chanson*'s close word-music pairings ('S'il suffisait d'aimer'). Moreover, she specializes in pop, the genre of music that has laboured longest under the labels of 'inauthentic' and 'derivative,' due to its hyper-commercialization, its lack of political edge, and its capacity to fabricate stars regardless of their musical ability.[1]

Dion's public image is equally pliable, a perfect screen upon which any national fantasy might be projected. In a book that charts her changing aspects of *québécité* from her first recorded notes in 1981 through the mid-1990s, sociologist Frédéric Demers describes her national representational labours: 'In her modest origins, through her numerous reminders of her Quebec-ness, Céline Dion has stayed loyal to the land, to family, to a more traditional definition of identity. She also actively participates in the redefinition of Québécois identity by personifying the archetype of the modern Self – capable, entrepreneurial, profitable, hardworking, productive' (1999, 15). On the one hand, her public image resonates with that of a *mère de famille à la québécoise* with its strong emphasis on family values and intergenerational cultural continuities. In guarding her Québécois accent even while on tour in France, referring to her poor but happy childhood in a small town with thirteen brothers and sisters, and expressing her current baby mania in which her young son, René-Charles (b. 2001), is the point of all reference, Dion's story reprises the narrative contours of a traditional notion of *canayenété* rooted in *la survivance*'s cultural and biological reproductions.

At the same time, however, her public image is informed by other national discourses. For instance, David Young uncovers a tendency in the English-language Canadian press to frame her 1991–92 cross-country tour as a symbol of Canadian national unity, or as a potential national unifier (Young 2001). (Her tour followed the collapse of the Meech Lake Accord, an effort to enfold Quebec into the Canadian constitution, which had been patriated from the United Kingdom in 1982 without Quebec's signature. This helped pave the way to the 1995 Quebec referendum on sovereignty.) Since then, because the bulk of her work now happens in English, Dion is often characterized as a 'vendue' to anglophone/U.S. interests. In many ways, she is a model United States immigrant who is willingly assimilated, joyously participating in the American Dream, and spreading its consumerist gospel of hope and happiness through her ever-expanding repertoire of branded products. With her living example of overcoming adversity through the power of love and an indefatigable positive attitude, she was a favourite Oprah Winfrey guest in the late 1990s. At once a corporate icon and a small town girl who values traditional gender roles – she took a two-year hiatus from her career starting in 2000 to care for her husband, René Angélil (b. 1942), who was recovering from cancer treatment, and to have a baby – Dion is a VH-1 'diva' with a pronounced Québécois accent.

Her image likewise intersects persuasively with a revivified notion of Quebecness called 'américanité.' *Américanité* is a conscious sense of continental attachment and identification rooted in a francophone identity that is 'sufficiently strong to be open to the continent (to economic free trade), without succumbing to the values of the United States' (Lesemann 2000, 43). Referencing shared historical and cultural formations of North and South American non-indigenous peoples, derived from their transplantation to the New World, *américanité* contributes to the articulations of Québécois identity in the contemporary context of continental economic integration – and its history as *canadienne-française* and, earlier still as of New France. The definition of Québécois, associated explicitly with the territory of Quebec since the Quiet Revolution, is extended in its reimagining as 'American' and in its affiliation with performers like Céline Dion. Quebec once again extends its geographical reach into international commercial and cultural networks and enlarges its ideological parameters to include being pluralist, modern, and open to the world (Ministère de la Culture et des Communications, 1996).[2] In this respect, Dion, like the Quebec Pavilion hostesses and Tremblay's sisters-in-law, serves as a useful and internationally visible national allegory for Quebec in Fredric Jameson's sense of the term: '*the story of the private individual destiny is always an allegory of the embattled situation of the public third-world culture and society*' (Jameson 1986, 69; emphasis in original). Unlike Carbone 14 pieces that cleave to the partial and its particular resistance to that kind of abstraction, Dion is peculiarly *un*resistant to the national service of representational labour. The story of her humble beginnings and subsequent ascent to global pop domination recapitulates Quebec's narrative of national maturation and international expansion. Her refashioned 'American' identity, product of the New World and its unique affordances for self-fashioning, is consonant with Quebec's refashioned self-image. And her service is not limited to a Quebec nation; rather, she loans herself / her image out to any number of discourses – national, international, corporate, etc.

That Dion participates in a range of national imaginaries – French-Canadian, cultural nationalist, and global, to name but a few – is without doubt an advance in how female figures function in and for national discourses since 1967, the year before Dion's birth. No longer, it seems, does the woman-as-nation metaphor signify only negatively as *revanchist*, marginal, and colonized, as in the modernizing national discourses of the Quiet Revolutionaries and the anticolonial national discourses of *Parti pris*. At the same time, however, that the mimetic figure by which Dion generally enters national discourses as outlined above – namely, metaphor – remains unchanged invites us to examine the whys and wherefores of its persistence across a half-century of Quebec's history. The repetition of woman-as-metaphor-for-nation (or national allegory) across the performing arts points not only to that figure's continuing, however lamentable, power. Its insistent recurrence also draws attention to two related phenomena. First, it flags the perpetual need for national groundwork, the nation's vulnerability to erosion, and its constant need of symbolic labour's backfilling. Second, the woman-as-nation metaphor's durability signals a continued misrecognition of the intertwined gender-nation and performance-nation figural relations that are at the centre of this study; interpretations of these relations (especially where images of women are concerned) are stalled in a realist mode that deploys metaphor as its primary figure.

In many respects, Dion-the-reproducer is a perfect object for iconic analysis. She reproduces with facility the panoply of national discourses that have circulated through Québécois sociopolitical landscape since the Quiet Revolution. And yet, her availability to any number of national, corporate, or musical meanings troubles the fairly neat lines of influence on which metaphorical readings rely. More troubling, perhaps, is the fact that despite being a reproducer par excellence, what emerges out of her is never really hers; she is a vehicle, not a tenor. Instead, Dion's polysemy and plasticity make her a kind of reproductive machine, a conduit for musical styles, national narratives, and goods (including compact discs, calendars, photographs of babies, perfumes, T-shirts, tote bags, and shot glasses available online and, formerly, in her eponymous store at Caesars Palace in Las Vegas) that are not of her own creation. She is her own brand. Even Céline Dion works for 'Céline Dion,' or, I should say, 'Celine Dion,' no accent.[3] To account for this, communications scholar Line Grenier calls her 'the Dion phenomenon,' a designation that includes the person, the voice, the icon, and the brand (2001a, 37). But, like any machine, 'the Dion phenomenon' is someone else's (re)production. Dion – the person and the product – is reputedly her husband and manager's 'creation'; all business and artistic decisions are widely attributed to René Angélil, making her a stereotypical 'diva,' 'a product produced by men as a vessel for men's voices' (Leonardi and Pope 1996, 12). He has guided her career since its inception when she was twelve, and has overseen its global expansion as well as her physical and linguistic transformations. (At Angélil's urging, Dion took a year off at seventeen to learn English and re-emerged with a more grown-up look, straightened and capped teeth, and a sexier wardrobe.) Consistent with Susan J. Leonardi and Rebecca A. Pope's wide-ranging analysis of representations of 'divas' as gender-disordered, Dion's attempts at biological reproduction required medical intervention in the form of in-vitro fertilization. To press the point, even in the space of 'nature,' Dion is again vessel or point of passage for someone else's creation.

Micone's conscious simulations of an ethnic model of *québécité* under-mined metaphor's truth model; by producing Deleuze's 'wholly external likenesses,' Micone's simulations posited an illegitimate or false relation to the original, thereby demonstrating the deconstructive value of a simulated relation to the nation which might allow for a visible re-orig-ination as Québécois for those whose origins are not found in Quebec. 'The Dion phenomenon' takes this move one step further. In the terms of simulation theory, Céline Dion personifies the simulacrum, a star who is 'commodified and transformed into [her] own image' (Jameson 1984, 61). Céline Dion seems to be a copy of an unreal real; she reproduces the unreal real of 'the Dion phenomenon' – the forged (in its doubled sense of to make and to fake) persona and the brand – to which I will now simply refer as 'Céline' or 'the phenomenon.' This renders Dion what Umberto Eco calls 'hyperreal' – the reproduction of an image or fantasy (1983, 6), estranged from the positions of referent and original. With 'the phenomenon' the copy takes the original's place. Surrogate is origin; surface trumps depth. That she lived and worked in the faux-natural environment of Las Vegas from March 2003 to December 2007 performing in her '"one of a kind" theatrical musical spectacular,' is the icing on the proverbial cake ('Céline Dion'). To many people's minds, Dion's public image of cultivated genuineness or manufactured authen-ticity make the union of Dion and Vegas *un mariage rêvé* (a match made in heaven) (Hurley 2009a).

In this chapter, I return to the pole of reproduction to draw out an alternative point of entry into thinking the national of performance. However, this time the reproductions have taken the place of originals and, as such, our previous methods of analysis and evaluation no longer have sufficient explanatory power. Reference's indications and meta-phor's truth criterion are foiled by Dion's 'fake' national surrogations. With 'the Dion phenomenon' as hyper-real – a simulation of something that never really existed, a copy of a copy without an original – we must instead develop the potentials of the surface over depth for a revised national performance historiography. This will require attention to the real effects of the really made up, especially its impacts on the sensate body in the form of affect. We began this work in the last chapter on Carbone 14, where I highlighted the bodily effects and sensations image-theatre stimulates. In the unassimilable idiosyncracy of the body of sen-sation, the untranslatability of sensate experience, I located a renovated national mimesis that would preserve distinction within the collective (of audience, of nation). Each part maintained its integrity while still being part of the group. In the case before us now of a hyper-real pop music diva-brand, a turn to 'Céline''s preferred medium – music – may assist us in scratching the surface once again.

Music clogs the dominant representational contract between performance and nation in which performance re-presents nation. Nietzsche tells us in *The Birth of Tragedy* that music is non-representational, *non-mimetic* (Nietzsche 2000).[4] What kind of national mimesis then might music perform? How might it labour in service of a national project? Music's apparent resistance to representational labour – the fact that it cannot stand in for Quebec – challenges most baldly the referential basis (and depth-model) of common understandings of *québécité* in the performing arts. While I do not agree with Nietzsche that music is non-mimetic, I do believe that semiotic readings of music fall well short of explaining its national mimesis. This shortcoming combined with music's resistance to depth-models of interpretation suggests another perspective for reading *québécité*: the figure of 'affection.'

But first a note on vocabulary. By 'affect' I intend modes of 'mattering' dispositions. Affects are ways of paying attention to the world, relational modes by which subject and object are put into contact, a means of letting the world impress itself upon you and of putting yourself in the world. Deleuzian communications scholar Brian Massumi, whose *Parables for the Virtual* theorizes the political potentials of thinking affect, defines affect as 'intensity,' where intensity is one side of a doubled response to image reception, the other side of which is 'qualification.' Aligned with sensation and feeling, affect captures the 'strength and duration of the image's effect,' the intensity of response to the impact of an image (2002, 24). Affect – an immediate, skin-level registration of relation that in the last chapter we called 'the body of sensation' after David Graver's work – gives us an immediate sense for what matters to us, for what moves or, indeed affects us. But the basis of that being moved lies not, in this first instance of intensity, in a fully cognitive understanding or interpretation of what the image is 'saying,' nor is it an identificatory or empathetic response (which would require recognition, for instance). Rather, affect makes itself known through autonomic reactions like sexual arousal or sweating. (The autonomic nervous system helps bodies adapt to changes in their environment; active at all times, it regulates automatic, compensatory reactions – like blood vessels expanding [say, into a blush] or the adrenal medulla excreting greater amounts of adrenaline ([to sharpen our concentration]) – without our control and generally without us noticing.) Indeed, of the difference between affect and interpretation Massumi writes, 'the primacy of the affective [over 'qualification'] is marked by a gap between *content* and *effect*: it would appear that the strength or duration on an image's effect is not logically connected to the content in any straightforward way' (24). It is in the processing of the image's content or 'qualification,' its 'indexing to conventional meanings in an intersubjective context,' that emotion arises. Affect, then, precedes not only interpretation or 'qualification,' but also emotion, where emotion is understood as an expression of or name for (hence, a conventionaliza-tion) of affective experience. Thus, for instance, on catching Dion hold-ing a long, high note on a televised variety show while flipping channels, one's skin may crawl or raise goosebumps, and this before one thinks, 'I love Céline Dion' or 'I hate Céline Dion.'[5] The signs of 'affection' are unruly; they happen to you in spite of yourself.

Affect becomes interesting in considerations of how hyper-real celeb-rities like Dion and how music produce and/or reproduce the nation for two reasons: one, because affect, like music, exceeds semiosis; and two, because affect presumes a different kind of relation than any of the figures seen thus far. In her recent book *Touching Feeling*, Eve Kosofsky Sedgwick turns to affect-theory to clarify dispositions to the world that are not (solely or primarily) semiotically organized. Critical literature on the affects in cognitive science, psychology, and philosophy often ap-praises them for their indications of value, determinations of salience, and motivations towards future action. Affects are linked to cognition as barometers for reflective judgment and as contributors to attitudes and beliefs which, in turn, inflect action; they are indicative.[6] In this way, affects' dispositions to the world are routed through reference. Pity and fear for Oedipus's predicament, for instance, may indicate an evaluation of his situation as tragic. Joy at hearing a Céline Dion power-ballad may point to how one rates a particular kind of melodic line or vocal range. One of the central merits of this work on affect is that it has convincingly enmeshed body in mind against an Enlightenment aesthetic tradition that rendered them distinct and rigidly hierarchically related. Neverthe-less, as Charles Altieri argues, this reinsertion of affective response into cognitive process by suturing affects to meaning may still be at affects' expense, subordinating affect once again to cognition inasmuch as its value is determined by its 'reasonable' labours (2004).

Contra these approaches that tie affect's value to its cognitive outcomes – and consonant with though not identical to Massumi's approach[7] – both Sedgwick and Altieri highlight affects' autotelic functions, their self-satisfactions and reinforcements, that are not reducible to their instrumentality to a rational process. Sedgwick cites mid-century U.S. psychologist Silvan Tomkins, whose three-volume work *Affect Imagery Consciousness* Sedgwick uses to build her sense of affect: 'Affect is self-validating with or without any further referent'; and 'Affect arousal and reward are identical in the case of positive affects; what activates positive affects "satisfies"' (2003, 100 and 19). So, potentially in addition to joy's indications of value or discernment, 'joy' is simply self-fulfilling; we seek joy because that experience is joyful.

In other words, affect means more than one can discern from its signs; one can feel joy or despair for no apparent reason, for instance. Affect is also unpredictable – it attaches itself to unlikely things and moves in unanticipated directions; it can move you to love the wrong person, for example, or feel part of a national collectivity that excludes you by defini-tion (if you are an illegal immigrant, for instance). In short, affects are ways of interfacing with the world that are not necessarily semiotically organized and whose outcomes are not predetermined. For this reason, Massumi calls affect 'incipience, incipient action and expression' (2002, 30); it affords any number of potential results. From this perspective, af-fect is a supplement to meaning that also undoes meaning.

Capitalizing on affect's excess to meaning, its primacy over qualifica-tion, I suggest in what follows that the category of 'affection' provides performance scholars with an alternate point of departure for perceiv-ing the national. 'Affection' can be built up and incorporated (which I mean literally: made corporeal, taken into the body) through emotional labours, such as those of the Expo hostesses, where the manipulation of mood and emotion weave shared emotional repertoires (e.g., visitors are guided to feel at ease in the Quebec Pavilion or proud of Quebec's ac-complishments). You'll see below 'Céline''s own hosting role. But 'affec-tion' also names the impress this particular image makes in Quebec and the contributions of that impress to articulating in and through Québé-cois a shared sensibility, or sensitization to the range of 'Céline''s effects.

Céline Dion is a particularly affecting hyperreal image and hence a signal locus for affective response in Quebec: 99.3 per cent of Québécois know who she is and most have a strong reaction to her (Grescoe 2001, 140). Those reactions are generally codified as love and hate; a mark of affect in her reception is that 'Céline' (most frequently and colloquially 'notre Céline,' already a sign of her intimate impress on Québécois) is dismissed with an enthusiasm effectively equal to that with which she is loved and hated. For the strong and strongly opposed receptions of 'the phenomenon,' witness, for instance, the crowd waiting outside Notre

Dame Basilica at her 1994 wedding on the one hand, and, on the other, the *de rigueur* drag acts that mercilessly lacerate her public image as perfect daughter, wife, and mother. I conducted a small online poll from 8 October 2005 to 8 January 2006 in which I asked Québécois to answer questions about their emotional responses to Céline Dion.[8] Here too, the pool is fairly clearly divided into those who really admire or even love her and those who cannot abide her or her music. Of the 151 responses, only seventeen said they were 'indifferent' to Dion; the rest picked a side, some with more nuance than others.

Again, it is not simply that people identify with her ('she has a family just like I do'), or recognize in her performances significations of *québécité* (she rolls her *r*s and loves Florida like any good Québécois) – although that is also true for some. Rather, she summons intensities like few others in the territory (possibly excepting the Canadiens hockey team). This affective investment – which, according to many respondents, happens in spite of or against their will – takes place quite regardless of whether people read her as signifying Québécois. This bears out again that there is no conformity between effect (or 'intensity') and content (or 'qualification'). Indeed, many commentators understand her as 'American,' particularly since she opened the 1996 Atlanta Olympic Games with a performance of 'The Power of the Dream' and her participation in September 11, 2001 fundraising endeavours, including the television special *America: A Tribute to Heroes* and the Sony album on which she reprised her performance of 'God Bless America.' In this expenditure of energy, people are drawn together by the intensity of their responses to common performances. By 'drawn together' I do not mean that they resemble each other or agree or become united somehow in a utopian public space. Affective alliances such as those afforded by Dion's impacts on people's environments (sonic, intimate, public, etc.) are striated by difference: difference that might be grasped socioculturally (i.e., differences in race, sex, gender, and class coordinates); cognitively (i.e., differences of opinion and interpretation); and affectively (differences in the particular affect summoned, like love, hate, shame, joy). Rather, I intend that in their disposition towards Dion, Québécois locate themselves within a geography whose coordinates correspond with varied responses to Céline Dion, who is the geography's *point de repère* or landmark. Popular culture scholar Lawrence Grossberg calls this kind of virtually produced, really experienced geography a 'mattering map,' 'which direct[s] our investments in and into the world.' He continues, 'These maps tell us where and how we can become absorbed – not into the self but into the world – as potential locations for our self-identifications, and with what intensities. This "absorption" or investment constructs the places and events which are, or can become, significant to us. They are the places at which we can construct our own identity as something to be invested in, as something that matters' (1992a, 57).

Both positive and negative intensities require investment. In *The Cultural Politics of Emotion*, Sara Ahmed ties investment to affect, writing, 'investment [in the object, in this case in Dion] involves the time and labour that is "spent" on something, which allows that thing to acquire an affective quality.' In other words, the object itself is devoid of inherent affective quality. Rather, the object is rendered affecting by virtue of the generation of what Ahmed calls an 'affective economy' around it. In a definition that highlights her analysis's debts to both psychoanalytic and Marxist criticism, Ahmed offers 'a theory of emotions as economy, *as involving relationships of difference and displacement without positive value.* That is, emotions work as a form of capital: affect does not reside positively in the sign or commodity, but is produced as an effect of its circulation' (2004, 57; emphasis in original). Mattering maps, then, might be sketched by the circulation of particularly affecting commodities.

Collectors, of course, emblematize this investment in their acquisitions of all things 'Céline,' linking emotional investment to financial expenditure. 'For a collector,' wrote Walter Benjamin, 'ownership is the most intimate relationship that one can have to objects' (1968, 67). A recent authorized biography, *Céline Dion: Pour Toujours* performs this collecting labour for you; interleaving the biographical narrative are reproduction scrapbook items: the draft score of 'Ce n'était qu'un rêve,' her first recorded song penned by her mother; a personal letter from Barbra Streisand; the ultrasound photo of her son, René-Charles (Glatzer 2005). The relationship enabled by the confluence of ownership (financial expenditure) and experiences of intimacy (emotional investment) is crucial when considering the affective economies of pop music, given not only its domination by economic interests but also its machinery for commodity circulation. There is a seemingly endless supply of 'Céline' paraphernalia, both as a result of the brand's constant innovations (new perfumes, the most recent photos) and through a kind of 'Disney-vault' operation in which previously unreleased effects are made available to consumers. The cache's constant renewal incites recurrent investment.

Collectors are likewise emblematic of fandom's generation of alternate spaces of identity in the form of listening communities. In their circulation of collectors' objects – by trading bootleg concert tapes or show posters – and in the ways they join together people, products, places, and activities – by attending concerts, lurking in 'Céline'-devoted cyberspace, purchasing records – fans forge connective webs that complement, and sometimes supplant official networks structured by corporate distribution. (Almost all Dion-related sites have a section or board devoted to trade in ephemera. John Connell and Chris Gibson would call the resultant webs 'cartographies of music' [2003].) For instance, the Montreal record store Francophonies boasts 'La Célinothèque,' a permanent, rotating display of 'Céline' paraphernalia from a collection of over 10,000 items amassed by two fans (one in Montreal, the other in Paris) and with the contributions of about fifteen others. While Francophonies sells print and musical materials related to Dion, it also offers itself for free to the public as a kind of museum, a place to learn more about her career (Fig. 7.1). 'The Dion phenomenon' holds the focus, then, of what Will Straw calls in another musical context 'a sociologically complex "scene," whose participants built effective links between a wide range of institutions and activities' (2005, 189).[9] In this respect, the love-response to Dion uncovers pop music's generation of affective alliances with and through its performers; put differently, love-respondents' mattering maps conjoin at key nodes. Importantly, the affective economy 'Céline' anchors emphasizes 'economy' – as in the circulation and exchange of material goods – as much as it emphasizes 'affect.' In a very real sense, one 'buys into' a Céline Dion–centred affective alliance.

If these official and subcultural circulations of 'Céline' commodities heighten the affective power of 'the phenomenon,' Dion's performances up the ante again. She expressly and insistently solicits affective expenditure like few other performers. The musical structure of her songs, their lyrical content, her performance of them, and her image combine such that they demand engagement of some kind. These elements provide qualifications to the affective experience of 'the phenomenon' in performance; they construct narrative frameworks for the intensity her music and persona elicit. True to affect's power for overriding will, it is difficult to *not* have a disposition vis-à-vis Dion; it happens in spite of yourself. As Doris Sommer writes about similarly affecting engagements in a different context, affective engagement with the performance – getting caught up in a melody, affected by a rhythm, absorbed in a voice, for instance – 'is already to become a partisan' (1994, 191).

In its catchy rhythmic and melodic qualities, pop music is a particularly powerful partisan-producing medium. Music has what feminist musicologist Susan McClary calls 'an uncanny ability to make us experience

7.1 The Célinothèque at Francophonies on St Denis Blvd in Montreal.
Photo: Laura Fisher.

our bodies in accordance with *its* gestures and rhythms' (McClary 2002, 23). For instance, the power ballad – the genre with which Dion is probably most strongly associated – evokes consistent, predictable patterns of tension and relaxation in its AABA structure. It adheres to the dominant or 'tonic' key in the A sections, departs from the tonic in the B section (often called the 'bridge'), and usually returns to the tonic at the end. (The tonic note forms the basis for the key. So a song in the key of C major has C as its tonic note.) Departure from the tonic is marked by a key change (usually a step up and sometimes a shift from major to minor); by fuller sound (often through the addition of accompanying instruments, denser orchestration, and/or full-throated singing of the

kind that seems to revel in the sound itself); and by increased volume
and sustained notes. One need only recall Dion's mega-hit, 'My Heart
Will Go On,' the theme-song from the movie *Titanic* (1999) for a clear
example of how these technical manipulations conspire to generate affect. Approximately two-thirds of the way through the song, following a
thundering musical introduction, her voice lifts off in the bridge to pro-
nounce, 'We'll stay forever this way. And I know that my heart will go on.'

Lest we assign this affection exclusively to her English-language songs,
where it is indeed prominent, let me encourage a close listening to her
2003 French-language album, *1 fille + 4 types* on which the slots often
assigned to songs with the greatest 'hit' potential (at the beginning, middle and end) are occupied by songs with a clear AABA structure. (Not insignificantly, pop albums are often organized according to this standard
form where the middle songs – usually numbers six to eight – stand out
from the rest, forming a kind of B section of their own. A hang-over from
the vinyl era, these numbers used to close an album's A-side and open
the B-side.) Or, for an early-career example, note the dramatic departure
from the tonic in 'Le blues du businessman,' written in 1978 by Quebec's
most illustrious pop songwriter Luc Plamondon and recorded on *Dion
chante Plamondon* in 1991. The return to the tonic at the end of a pop-
song imparts a sense of completion or appropriate ending. This strict
and ultimately containing structure allows for a dynamic sonic build
through the B section, which then settles back to A. Within this centrifu-
gal musical structure organized around a keynote, affective intensity can
be as strong as it is fleeting. They aren't called 'power ballads' for nothing. Their power lies at once in the force of the vocal instrument used to
sing them and in their generation of response. (Not inconsequentially,
the affective power of sound swells is also tapped in national anthems
and other 'stirring' musical styles like marches and theme songs.[10])

This heightened visceral response to musical structure, while ephemeral in any given instance, can be more long-lasting in its effects. In *Having a Good Cry: Effeminate Feelings and Pop Culture Forms*, Robyn Warhol
argues that 'certain genres invoke ... physical responses in predictable,
formulaic patterns.' Warhol contends that narratives mark readers' bodies with their sensational effects that, in their repetition, provide what
she calls, after Raymond Williams, a 'structure of feeling in the daily lives
of their devotees.' Patterns of tension and relaxation across her œuvre;
repeated listening to her songs by her fans; singing and/or playing along
to them by amateurs – each of these repetitions, structural and practical,
're-engrave the genre's affective patterns on [listeners'] bodies while re-

experiencing its conventional narrative moves' (2003, 7–8). Shared affective repertoires result from this musical conditioning, activating that out-of-body experience of responding to a song you don't know or don't like according to its musical cues – so the *Titanic* theme-song gives you goosebumps despite your mental preparedness for its manipulations.

Repertoires of feeling are further consolidated in musical practice. Pop music remains what Roland Barthes calls '*musica practica,*' music that moves amateurs to want to play it – think sing-alongs, garage bands, karaoke nights, and auditions for *Canadian Idol* or Quebec's pop-idol star-search equivalent, *Star Académie*. Quebec has a significant, family-based amateur musical tradition of which the Dion family is emblematic. Dion's parents, Adhémar and Thérèse Dion each played an instrument, as do many of her brothers and sisters, some of whom formed bands of their own and/or have gone on to independent musical careers. In her autobiography, Dion fondly recalls Sunday nights spent singing at home and credits her early and frequent exposure to music by her family as the foundation of her career (Dion 2000). Line Grenier has described the collective import of *Jeunesse d'aujourd'hui,* a hugely popular *American Bandstand*–like television show broadcast on Saturday afternoons from 1962 until 1972, and along with which many a Québécois teenager danced in her living-room (2001b). And since 2003, TVA, broadcaster of *Jeunesse d'aujourd'hui,* has taken back Sunday night for its *Star Académie,* a televised amateur night that highlights the contestants' regional origins. It has been lauded as a return to a Québécois tradition of family musical entertainment and, in a similar vein, called 'un grand party de famille' (a big family party) enjoyed by the vast majority of Quebec households (quoted in de Billy 2004; Desaulniers 2004; Baribeau 2003). At another party, the 2006 version of 'Mascara: La nuit des drags,' the open-air drag show held the night before Montreal's Divers/Cité pride parade, Montreal's preeminent drag queen, 'Mado,' orchestrated a living tribute to Céline Dion: twelve drag queens portrayed Dion at a different stage in her career (Schwartzwald, personal communication). As practised music – sung with, danced to, performed on instruments, imitated – pop songs' affects are incorporated manually into the viscera of articulate fingers, vocal folds, lung capacity, and comportment (Barthes 1977).

And in instances where listeners do not actively participate in the making of music, pop's dominant storing technology will involve them at a level just as intimate as that of *musica practica*. Take the example of the mp3, a digital file for recorded sound. The crux of mp3 technology is its capacity for compressing the information of digital recordings into

ever smaller files. Mp3 encoders perform this reduction by discarding
sounds from the original recording that they anticipate the ear will not
pick up on anyway. Although the human ear 'cannot keep up with sound
as it actually happens,' people still 'get a sense of the detailed rise and
fall of sounds'; we effectively fill in missing sound data, organizing what
makes it through the inner ear's filter into meaningful patterns. Based
on this psychoacoustic model of human hearing, mp3s mimic the sound-
shaping activities of the ear to filter out sounds whose frequency exceeds
hearing capacity, for instance, and sounds that are too close together
in time to be distinguished. Jonathan Sterne, to whose work the above
description is indebted, comes to a remarkable conclusion about the relationship of sound, technology, and the body produced by mp3s. 'The
mp3 *plays* its listener,' he says (2006, 834–5; emphasis mine). Here is a
body's remarkable adaptation to its (sonic) environment! Mp3s capitalize on our necessarily incomplete hearing; they offer less and less sound
information (in the name of more compact storage) and rely more and
more on the listeners' bodies to reconstruct the sound into music. In
other words, our bodies are as much an mp3 player as is an iPod. The
mp3 as recording format conditions listeners' sensory responses not
over time, as musical practice and repeated exposure to a certain musical structure might, but rather even before the sound is 'delivered' to the
listener. In this context, the virtues of an AABA musical structure – not
to mention a recognizable 'sound' such as 'Céline's' – are even more
apparent than they might have been before. Because AABA is a familiar
sound pattern, it is easily filled in by listeners' ears. A near-perfect structure for fast, easy, and widespread distribution and recirculation in mp3
format, the peculiarly affecting musical commodity accrues additional
affect in its promiscuous circulation.

Where the circulation-friendly AABA structure of so many of her songs
induce and incorporate affect, the lyrics of Dion's songs conspire to convey and encourage emotions, those named or conventionalized qualifications of affective sensibility. Lyrics provide an organizational strategy
for emotions raised by the musical properties of structure, tone, rhythm,
and the like (Levinson 1997). So if the tone of 'Ziggy, un garçon pas
comme les autres' elicits a feeling of wistfulness in its final trailing notes,
its lyrics organize that feeling into a narrative of unrequited love. The
theme of love dominates Dion's recording history from early expressions
of familial affection and teenage crushes written by Eddie Marnay (e.g.,
'D'Amour ou d'amitié' [Love or friendship, 1982] and the *C'est pour
toi* album [1985]) to more urgent single-girl desires post-*Unison* ('J'ai

besoin d'un chum' [I need a boyfriend, 1991], 'Le Ballet' [1995]), to her recent paeans to the satisfactions of committed and/or parental love ('Pour que tu m'aimes encore' [1995], 'Je lui dirais' [2003]). 'Love' or 'Amour' figures in 53 of 285 song-titles recorded by Dion between 1981 and 1999; its priority in the title establishes the song's lyrical preoccupation and helps organize its reception.[11]

Lyrical choices also focus song address. On *1 Fille + 4 Types*, all songs but two address a 'tu,' the familiar form of 'you.' This shorthand intimacy can be very seductive as it allows, even encourages, the listener to project herself into the position of the one-sung-to. This individual address reinforces pop music's implied habits of private, individual listening. These habits of listening are embedded in the arrangement of musical sounds behind and around the pop singer's voice, for instance, an arrangement that places the voice front and centre, building the effect of her direct address to the listener (Frith 1996, 188).

The sound technologies by which pop music is now generally delivered and consumed also reinforce the habits of private listening upon which the 'tu' address capitalizes. In the pre-recording past, musical consumption required the listener's physical proximity to musical production (e.g., to hear the guitar, one would have to sit close to it) and often her physical displacement to a genre-specific performance space (e.g., opera could only be enjoyed at the opera) (Stockfelt 1993, 159). John Corbett insists that the contemporary mode of musical exchange is *recording* and he critiques digital recording technology, in particular the compact disc format, for dividing musical production from contexts of performance, for constructing music 'as autonomous sound – production free from the body of the performer; reproduction free from its own noise' (Corbett 1990, 84; 91). Corbett's assessment is especially acute in the case of Dion since she has abandoned touring in order to become a pilgrimage site; from March 2003 to December 2007 she performed *A New Day ...* in a purpose-built theatre at Caesars Palace in Las Vegas. (She toured again to promote her *Taking Chances* album in 2008 and then withdrew from performance in 2009–10 to try to have a second child.) As such, most listeners' contact with her music is via a recorded form that effaces the labours, technologies, and networks required for its making and delivery. The distinct and distant social world of 'the phenomenon' thus obscured, fantasies of her unmediated connection to her listeners – 'she's singing just for me/right to me' – are enabled.

With 'Céline,' however, it is not enough that the structure and lyrics of her music combine with their technologies of recording and distribution to produce affective responses in her listeners. Concert and video performances feature elaborate indications of her own strong emotion, of how fully she embodies the musical message. Sometimes the message is 'playful,' like when she plays air-guitar with a wide-eyed look to 'J'irai où tu iras.' In the power ballads, she punctuates the emotional high points of her songs (generally in the B sections) with her iconic chest thumping, hand clasped over her heart, closed eyes, and head thrown back as if in ecstasy, so completely transported is she. Every performance sign is fully, redundantly interpreted as profoundly moving. For example, during her 1996 concert tour, Dion plays back-up singer to her audience's croonings of 'Because You Loved Me'; the audience sings melody while Dion embellishes with vocal flourishes over top. Symbolically turning the microphone over to the audience to sing hit songs from the performer's repertoire is a concert staple. However, the act of 'singing along' with the audience establishes 'Céline' as the singer of the audiences' songs, as a vehicle for a shared emotional life captured by a song. The lyrical content of 'Because You Loved Me' reprises pop stars' frequent attributions of their success to their fans' fandom, rendering it a particularly apt choice for the fan sing-along. The song's persona sings to her lover, 'You gave me faith 'coz you believed / I'm everything I am / Because you loved me.' And, finally, it reinforces Dion's personal love-story/success-story with Angélil, who is often cast as a Svengali figure controlling her every move. She's everything she is because he loved her.

All these (redundant) displays of emotion and insistent invitations to feeling provoke intense emotional responses – of love and of hatred. Because of the popularity, longevity, and widespread diffusion of 'the phenomenon', it is difficult in Quebec to escape being a participant, however unwilling, in the affective repertoires her music engenders – regardless of one's taste culture. Indeed, we might understand her sound as the keynote, or tonic, if you will, of Québécois pop. Although any number of things draw one's attention to Dion's singing – her three-octave range, the crispness of her articulation – the ubiquity of her sound renders it background. Her sound permeates Quebec: she gives frequent television interviews, often (somewhat surreally) punctuated by song snippets thematically-related to the topic at hand, and makes frequent guest appearances on music-related shows like *Star Académie* and *L'école des fans*, another TVA show in which four- to seven-year-old children pay homage to a singer by interpreting her or his songs in her or his presence. In part due to Canadian content and French language broadcast regulations, Dion's music gets even more radio play in Quebec than in the other parts of North America.[12] *Chanson*, an expansive vocal music tradition in Quebec in which Céline's albums (French and English) participate, dominates the 'Middle of the Road' format that fully half of Quebec's FM radio stations share (Grenier 1993, 139) and to which 80 per cent of Québécois listen frequently (Pronovost 1989).[13] That her songs might also often be qualified as 'ballads' – 'a slow-beat and simple structure (verse and chorus) music having an overall romantic or sentimental tone – identifiable in both instrumentation and lyrics' – again increases the likelihood of her radio play, not only on MOR format radio stations, but also as a transformat music on soft-rock, rock, or even dance music radio stations (Grenier 1990, 224).

Céline Dion's inescapability, her musical groundwork, is a particularly sore point for anti-fans and is often what drives their refusal to be hailed by the phenomenon's address. Again, this refusal is as much a coordinate on a mattering map as is being positively disposed to her address. Over and over in the poll I conducted, those who said 'Céline' provoked in them feelings of disgust, rage, or hatred attributed their response in part to their forced proximity to her repertoire of music and emotions. Many report having to listen to her music in the family car or home. In these accounts, the 'Céline'-lovers who subject 'Céline'-haters to her music or products are inevitably female and a generation older than the respondents; respondents refer to them as 'my mother,' 'my mother-in-law,' or 'my aunt.' In fact, 2005 demographic data on members of Dion's official fan-club, 'TeamCeline' provided by Dion and Angélil's production company, Feeling Productions Inc. (!!!!), reinforce this impression. Women comprise 66 per cent of the total membership; of this, 30 per cent of the female members are between forty-five and fifty-five. (Another 17 per cent are over fifty-five, and 25 per cent are between thirty-five and forty-four.)[14] Although one should in part attribute the preponderance of middle-aged fan-club members to their potentially greater disposable income (it costs US$25/year to become a member), this data also correlates with that gathered by commercial radio stations to which one can listen without cost (after the cost of a radio, of course).

It is not just middle-aged women who perpetrate 'Céline' on Québécois anti-fans, however; it is also managers of public spaces and the Quebec media. Anti-fans are repeatedly subjected to her hit songs by their incorporation into the musical wallpaper of shopping centres, offices, indoor skating rinks, and other public spaces. Dion enjoys fulsome media coverage in Quebec, to say the least. In July and August 2006, the airwaves were inundated with tributes to Dion's twenty-five-year career on every Québécois television station. Any appearance she makes in Quebec merits an above-the-fold mention, obliging a certain attention, presuming a shared and apparently insatiable interest, and underscoring her contribution to circulation numbers and revenues. She is ubiquitous.

The hate-response, while still a part of 'Céline'-generated affective alliances, points more revealingly to the emotional labour the phenomenon performs for others. In this instance, the phenomenon functions as a kind of repository for negative emotion, often a high level of annoyance or irritation, although there is a significant population who 'hate' her. This more violent response registers in the number of hate-sites devoted to 'Céline' and the amount of screed one can find about her in the yellow press and from a Google search, as well as in my survey.[15] People hate her, or more gently, are irritated by her because she is ugly, *kétaine* (kitschy), or vulgar; for singing with a nasal or otherwise grating tone; for being overexposed and too commercial. That said, the dominant reason and unifying thread of the negative affect for which she is the nucleus lies in her presumed 'fakeness' or lack of 'authenticity,' returning us to the phenomenon's lack of origin, her perfect copy nature. For instance, her via-satellite appearance at 2005's Live 8 concert (intended to put pressure on the G8 countries to end African poverty) was loudly booed. Journalists and web-respondents explain the reaction as a comment on her perceived insincerity; Andre Mayer, the CBC's blogger for the Live 8 event writes, 'Celine Dion's taped address from Las Vegas is met with boos from the hard-rock audience in Barrie. Her assurance that she wishes she could be at Live 8 is met with a collective eye-roll' (2005). (Shane Birley corroborates this response on his blog [2005].) Her emotional appearance on 'Larry King Live' in which she denounced the United States government's slow response to Hurricane Katrina's 2005 devastation of the Gulf Coast was likewise met with scepticism.[16] It is as though her promiscuous affiliations with products, national narratives, and musical styles, along with her forceful (or even 'forced') performances of emotion support her lucrative circulations at the same time that they undermine them.

The negative affect often locates its target clearly and specifically in Dion the person. At one extreme, I received three rather disturbing responses to my survey – one in French and two in English – which detailed the respondents' (possibly tongue-in-cheek?) desires to beat, rape, and kill her. (Similarly violent responses are posted in response to antiGUY's 'Top 5 list of uses for Céline Dion CDs' [1999].) A more benign, though still negative, implication with her physical being is revealed in criticisms of her appearance, on the order of this poll response from a young man from Saint-Hyacinthe, Quebec: 'Desfois [sic] le *look* est à discuter ... comme ses cheveux très court et blond :S' (Sometimes the look is questionable ... like her very short, blond hair :S). (The emoticon that closes the comments indicates 'I don't know what to say' or 'That's disgusting.') More often than not, the emotion's object surpasses Dion to target something she is made to stand in for, for example, her annoying fans, those with bad taste, sell-outs, or an outmoded vision of Quebec. A.A. Gill's notoriously cutting *Vanity Fair* article about Las Vegas unflatteringly positions Dion's *A New Day ...* show at the epicentre of Las Vegas's 'great bulimic consuming engine.' The author depicts her as having 'gone Vegas'; 'Dion has succumbed to the Vegas makeover.' However, she is deemed slightly less 'astonishingly and monumentally tasteless' than Vegas visitors, who are the unredeemed object of the author's unbridled scorn (Gill 2003, 206).

Her celebrity is a factor here in this double-barrelled targeting, for she is never just *one*: she is both *la petite fille de Charlemagne* and 'the Dion phenomenon.' This is a paradox of celebrity – that she must be both a stranger and an intimate to the public at one and the same time. On the one hand, Dion's celebrity insulates her from even the most virulent expressions of dislike; among her many employees are a class of workers who protect her physically (e.g., bodyguards) and psychologically (e.g., manager, press representatives), by intervening in potentially abusive situations. (Like many celebrities, Dion insists she does not read her press; Angélil says he reads everything.) On the other, her high level of protection may also expose her to more frequent and more highly charged personal verbal assault. In other words, she is 'safe' to hate vocally and openly because the hatred does not risk deleterious consequences for Dion herself. Her perceived invincibility sets her up for attack at the same time that it foils the attack, creating a circulation of emotion around 'the phenomenon' which in turn generates more affect. Because the emotion (of hatred, say) never hits its target, it just keeps circulating, boomeranging back towards the sender, increasing the affect's velocity and, as Ahmed would have it, its 'stickiness.' As a repository for emotion, as someone easily targeted for emotional displays on the part of both fans and anti-fans, 'Céline' manages emotions; she performs emotional labour. 'Our Céline' is our hostess.

Dion's gender is likewise a factor, for emotional labour is more often expected of women than men. As Arlie Hochschild's investigation of female flight attendants' conditions of work has demonstrated, there are fairly clearly defined and gendered expectations about who can or must, according to their role, 'absorb an expression of displeasure' and who, in turn, may put a stop to it. She writes of the flight attendants, 'females' supposed "higher tolerance for abuse" amounted to a combination of higher exposure to it and less ammunition – in the currency of respect – to use against it' (2003, 178–9). This is not to say that Dion's social position is the same as a flight attendant's; clearly, as I indicated above, Dion's fortune buffers her from abuse. Nonetheless, 'the phenomenon' is singled out as a nucleus for negative affect in a way that male Québécois pop stars are not.[17]

And how might the affective repertoires 'the Dion phenomenon' generates get taken up as *national* labour?

The powers of assembly of 'the phenomenon' across difference in emotion (love and hate), in a way that remains open to practically anyone who comes into contact with her music, products, image, and so on, has occupied my focus to this point. 'Céline' functions as a binding mechanism around which fans and anti-fans coalesce in a shared affective alliance, one in which Céline Dion is 'ours' – ours because we buy in, and ours because we have a relationship to her, even if it is compelled or steeped in cool irony: hence the familiar use of the first name, Céline. This task of connecting her emotional geographies to Québécois imaginaries is complicated by the fact that Dion's international success depends in part on her non-referential mode, on her significations' lack of moorings in specific contexts or locations outside of the brand universe of 'the phenomenon.' Whereas Expo 67 hostesses were enjoined to make the Quebec Pavilion feel more homey and natural to its visitors by providing pertinent information about the area and by presenting themselves as typically Québécois, 'the Dion phenomenon' does not perform the same constructionist, pedagogical function vis-à-vis Quebec. Unlike the hostesses, she does not produce 'national sentiment,' that emotional endowment of *québécité*. Furthermore, since declaring her federalist leanings in 1992 – to a media-storm of criticism – Dion has maintained an entirely apolitical public position vis-à-vis Québécois sovereignty specifically. Robert Schwartzwald suggested to me in October 2006 that her criticism of the United States government's response to Hurricane Katrina provoked the interest it did because it had a clear focus and was, as such, a radical departure from her norm. It seems to have functioned as a kind of B-section to her apolitical 'A' persona, reinforcing her usual, innocuous, liberal humanitarianism precisely in its momentary departure from it. Normally, she attaches herself to causes that have no object to critique. For instance, as National Celebrity Patron of the Cystic Fibrosis Foundation since her niece's death from the disease in 1993, Dion need not point fingers at human perpetrators of the disease, for there is none. (Quebec choreographer Dave St-Pierre's 2009 piece, 'Over my Dead Body,' caustically takes her to task for using Cystic Fibrosis and the strong emotions around loss and early death as another kind of fuel for her career.) Likewise, her 2002–7 'godparent' role for Montreal's Ste Justine Children's Hospital fundraising efforts, and her $1 million contribution to 2004's Asian Tsunami relief do not require a position against anything more specific than childhood illness and devastating natural catastrophes.

In addition, music complicates the issues of reference in a way that the other performing arts *National Performance* engages do not. In theatre, dance, or at an international exposition, one may struggle to fully interpret the multitude of signs presented in décor, language, movement, architecture, etc. With music – and I'm thinking here of the dominant contemporary experience of music, that is, listening to recorded music, not music-in-performance – not only are there fewer signs, but those signs are 'semantically underdetermined,' according to musicologist Lawrence Kramer: 'Music per se is not only nonsemantic, but "unsemanticizable"; even the simplest interpretations of it rapidly exceed anything that might be conceivably encoded in its stylistic and structural gestures ... Because it is semantically underdetermined music renders the inevitable gap between meaning and the object of meaning much more palpable than texts or even images do' (2003, 130; 126). Perhaps Dion's tendency to overinterpret and to channel those meanings back into a brand stems from this musical reality. Certainly, her 1996 sing-along to 'Because You Loved Me' described above collapses reference into so many aspects of 'the phenomenon.' Or perhaps this musical reality renders any interpretation overwrought, even those less redundant than Dion's.

The economy of musical interpretation, like that of affect, is thus one of surplus, of excess; as in the case of the mp3's circulations, musical interpretation's semantic promiscuity promotes affective agglutinations which may then be applied to or get stuck on other nodes on one's mattering map. At the same time that the 'Because You Loved Me' sing-along collapses reference, its themes, structures, and performance modes afford an extensive range of uptakes, functioning again like the virtual incipience of affect. Importantly, these multiple affordances facilitate a wider circulation of her products. Thus, anyone who has experienced 'love' might fill in the lyrics' narrative gaps with her own story.

Anyone familiar with the conceit of concert sing-alongs will recognize
the moment as a non-spontaneous summons to participation and group
feeling. Anyone whose ear picks out musical structure will be able to pre-
dict this high-point of the song in performance. These multiple points
of entry into Dion's performance of 'Because You Loved Me' indicate
that musical meaning is neither inherent in musical structure nor wholly
derived from lyrical or performance-based exegesis. Rather, any sense
gleaned from those sources is nestled within a series of relations whose
conceptualization is offered by music's internal and external geographies. Musicologist Richard Middleton translates musical pattern into
conceptual relationships: 'Musical patterns are saying: as this note is to
that note, as tonic is to dominant, as ascent is to descent, as accent is to
weak beat (and so on), so X is to Y' (1990, 223,). In her study of people's
uses of music in their everyday lives, Tia DeNora reminds, however, that
these analogies are concretized not in musical production but rather in
musical reception: 'it is music's *recipients* who make these connections
manifest, who come to fill in the predicates, X and Y.' Those coordinates
reach outside of musical structure, to articulate relationships 'between
works, and perhaps between these and non-musical structures' (2000,
45). In the example of 'Because You Loved Me,' relationships are forged
with the genre of the love-song and with past associations and contexts
of use, as well as with musical practices of melody (the audience singing
the lead) and embellishment (Dion singing back-up). The intra- and
extra-musical relations activated by 'the phenomenon' particularize the
affective bond to *québécité* by providing some of its fixed coordinates; they
act as qualifications to intensity.

One of these coordinates can be located in the poetic *chanson* tradition, a lyric-oriented, solo performer, singer-songwriter genre in which
Quebec's aural culture is steeped. It acquired nationalist associations in
the 1960s when *chansonniers* (singer-songwriters) like Gilles Vigneault
and Félix Leclerc set their *poésie du pays* to music inflected by folk idi-
oms. While contemporary *chanson* is largely denuded of the explicit
political commentary that characterized its heyday, it is still bound up
with assertions of *québécité* in its lineage, and *le fait français* in its French-
language expression. Grenier explains, 'The intervention of different
consecrating agents, among them media and literary institutions, contributed to the promotion of "la chanson" conceived in this context
as the only authentically Québécois genre (in comparison with other,
U.S.-inspired genres) and, it follows, as the carrier of the only music
that might proclaim itself culturally significant and representative of the

Quebecois people' (1997, 37). In addition to performing some songs that conform with the features of '*chanson*,' Céline also participates in the *chanson* tradition courtesy of the term's semiotic expansion since the 1990s, by which '*chanson*' is attributed 'to all popular music created or produced in Quebec, and this independent of distinctions in genre or style' (1997, 37–8). Having begun her career as an artist produced in Quebec by Québécois, and because of her continued popularity, Dion's songs still count as 'Québécois' both in popular consciousness and for the Quebec music industry.[18] She also draws on the genre's contextual significance through acts of ventriloquism. On her French-language albums, she frequently works with a single songwriter who writes the album's material in her voice.[19] Worthy of note, here, is that Dion is channelling a songwriter who channels her to write the songs in her voice. In effect, there are no ventriloquists here, only dummies, pointing out again that 'the phenomenon' lacks an origin. Naomi Levine has drawn my attention to the fact that 'Céline''s lack of origin, that she is not an original, could also align her more closely with drag queens' performances of her. 'Céline' is as much an impersonator as her impersonators. (Her English-language song selections show no particular loyalty to specific songwriters but rather to producers, who craft her 'sound' into other recognizable patterns.)

The Canadian-content and French-language-content regulations for Québécois radio and television to which Dion owes her ubiquity on the airwaves also substantially inform local listening practices. Jody Berland argues that Canada's aural culture is based less on a coherent grammar of musical difference than on the different soundscapes that Canadian public, commercial, and community radio produce (1998). Dion can sound a lot like Mariah or Barbra because they share a musical grammar and similar vocal ranges. But the mix of a high-brow national radio (the Canadian Broadcasting Company [CBC] and Radio-Canada) with an advertising-heavy, popular commercial radio and the grainy-sounding, musically and ideologically varied community radio, is distinctly Canadian and Québécois, says Berland. It is a soundscape comprised of various music formats, programming sequences, relations to for-profit drivers, and audience addresses (e.g., from the familiar, local address of community radio to the more formal, universal address of Radio-Canada). Within it, 'rough' sound alternates with 'smooth,' and Canadian content (CanCon) with American content (AmCon). CanCon itself is internally variable; often figured as alternative (to AmCon), it is just as frequently global pop (e.g., Céline Dion, Shania Twain, Garou, and Bryan Adams) produced out of financial circumstances and corporate structures in which CanCon must generally prove itself as saleable in external markets (the United States or France) in order to be played on Canadian radio. For instance, 'most records manufactured and sold within Canada (nearly 90%) are made from imported master tapes ... Thus a recording artist usually needs to succeed in the U.S. to be heard in Canada' (Berland 1998, 136). Moreover, Berland points out, government programs supporting Canadian music also tend to privilege commercially viable music and subsidize international music tours, but not domestic ones (137). In Quebec, *chanson* forms the sonic backdrop against which the strong interest in hip-hop, worldbeat, and technopop distinguishes itself. On Radio-Canada, the preferred *chanson* is that of either modern-day singer-songwriters like Pierre Lapointe and Ariane Moffat, or that of the French tradition (*à la* Georges Brassens and Édith Piaf, for instance). On community radio, *la chanson à texte* is more likely to be the politically engaged rap of Loco Locass or the *engagé* rock of Les Cowboys Fringants. On commercial radio, *chanson* is Dion-sung ballads. Like the 'A' sections of pop songs, *chanson* is the point of departure, a kind of musical groundwork against which other musical traditions and distribution networks might distinguish themselves. Québécois ears are thus tuned in accordance with these musical structures.

An ear schooled in Quebec popular radio distribution and performance networks might take up Dion's 'Mon homme' (2003) – a tribute to 'my man' – according to its relationship with *chanson* and/or according to other coordinates on its musical map – for instance, its use of musical materials and/or according to its lyrical content. The relationship of 'Mon homme' with *chanson* could be charted through its thematic similarity to the French torch song of the same name by Maurice Yvain (1920), performed by Fanny Brice in the 1921 Ziegfeld Follies and re-popularized by Barbra Streisand playing Fanny Brice in *Funny Girl* (1967). These thematic and melodic histories of use might lead the listener whose ear is attuned to Broadway, for instance, through a series of Dion-Streisand sound-associations founded in range, diction, clarity of musical expression, and a certain nasal quality. And these associations intensify when one considers Dion's self-orientalizing in some publicity stills and during her 2000 wedding vow renewal ceremony held at Caesars Palace. Listening for lyrical resonances differentiates the songs; unlike Fanny's tragic resignation to keep returning to her man on her knees despite his repeated infidelities, Dion's 'Mon Homme' conveys not only the persona's adoration of her man but also his worthiness. Unlike the French and American versions, Dion's *homme* enjoys a merited devotion by his adoring yet non-deluded partner.

The coordinates afforded by musical relations reach outside of musical structure as well to articulate ties 'between these and non-musical structures' (DeNora 2000, 45). Take, for example, the staging of 'I Wish' in her performances of *A New Day* ... When Dion sings this Stevie Wonder composition, the visibly non-white (African-American and Latino), male dancers in her troupe, distributed more widely across the visual field in previous numbers, come down- and centre-stage to surround her in a glancing blow at an unexplicated musical history. This choice may be explained by the lyrical focus of the song itself, the innocent if rough-and-tumble days of an African-American boy's youth. For a Québécois ear attuned not only to American popular song and social change, but also to its impact on Québécois self-perception, Dion's assumption of a 'black' persona in the song re-forges a Quiet Revolution–era identification of Québécois as North America's 'white niggers.' Her over-the-top usage of 'girlfriend' in interviews, particularly with Oprah Winfrey, performs similar representational labour. More importantly, these instances give form to an affective excess associated in the United States with people of African and Latino descent (Muñoz 2000) and in Canada with Québécois, due to their 'Latin blood' and 'excessive' demands.[20] This, of course, feeds again off of the notion that women are not only 'naturally' emotional (therefore natural emotional labourers) but also naturally emotionally 'excessive' and 'sensitive' (therefore perfect affect machines). Thus, an analogized history of marginality joins with an affective structure, and both are perpetuated in their circulation (Fig. 7.2).

Musical performance tests the limits of the 'aboutness' rationale of nationalization – that 'Céline's' performances are Québécois because they reference Quebec in their lyrical content, musical structure, or in her performance ticks. As we have seen, in a case like Céline Dion's, however, the explanatory grid of reference both largely ignores any identifiably Québécois signifieds apart from her biography, and ultimately short-circuits. She does not sing Quebec, as did the *chansonniers*. Her universe of reference is almost hermetic, as in the case of the 'Because You Loved Me' sing-along, where everything comes back to her, her story, her relationship to her fans. It is also fully capitalized. Ultimately, 'the phenomenon' comes to mean whatever one wants it to, which is to say that it comes to mean nothing. Lacking what Elin Diamond calls, after Irigaray, a 'true referent,' Dion's performances 'unmake' national mimesis, unravelling it from within (1997). All dissembling, 'the phenom-

7.2 Dion with dancers performing Stevie Wonder's 'I Wish' on the opening
night of *A New Day.*
Photo: George Bodnar/Tomasz Rossa. Courtesy CDA Productions, Inc. Las Vegas.

enon' evacuates referential schemes tied to an origin or original. In cases
like this, where reference or 'aboutness' is exhausted or indeterminate,
affect may provide another way into reading performances as national
or as nationalizing *alongside* the referential reading. Affect, in this case,
provides the why of performance, the reason we must attend to it, even
when we don't particularly want to; it endows the performance with
sense and impact – with its mattering and, to that degree, its meaning.

So yes, 'Céline' represents different aspects of *québécité* in her accent,
in her biography, in her very emotionality. A resonant figure for the
analysis of national mimesis, 'the Dion phenomenon' stands at once

as metaphor, as simulation, and as affection. But the affective alliances she enables and the emotional labour she performs furnish the conditions of possibility for that referential reading. The alliances she affords may form the substrate of national performance, inasmuch as they help create the conditions of possibility for reading certain performances as 'ours' (or 'theirs'), and thus, as 'Québécois.' In other words, inspiring an affective territory through the arrangement of dispositions around her allows for the conversion of external cartographies to internal coordinates. Affect in this case answers what political philosopher Etienne Balibar isolates as the nation-form's most necessary and fundamental labour. He writes, 'The fundamental problem [of the nation] is to produce the people. More exactly, it is to make the people produce itself continually as national community' (Balibar 1991, 93). With this, Balibar indicates both the difficulty of securing this transformation of individual self into national other as well as that transformation's necessity for sustaining the nation as a viable social form.

Eve Kosofsky Sedgwick and Adam Frank contrast post-Foucauldian critical theory's 'digital' or binary structure (one is or is not; something is on or off) with a more congenial analog structure (of 'graduated and/or multiply differentiated representational models') that they discover in Silvan Tomkins's affect theory (Sedgwick and Frank 1995). Thinking affect along these (analog) lines allows for what Sedgwick calls the 'middle ranges of agency' that exist somewhere between on and off (or 'national' and 'not-national'), between one and infinity (2003, 13). By beginning somewhere different, with affect instead of semiotics, thinking affect opens the door to seeing how people may produce themselves as national, even in conditions that militate against it; how one may identify with the nation (its values, types, etc.) without identifying as national. Dion's emotional labours both lay the affective groundwork of the nation and re-key common understandings of arts-nation links by shifting the frame of reference from signification to 'affection' with its unpredictable and non-utilitarian effects. Thus, in addition to providing symbolic materials to Quebec in her references, then, 'Céline' also furnishes its connective tissue by performing emotional labour for the populace, and by eliciting affective response that one cannot deny, in spite of oneself.

chapter eight

Conclusion: Feminist (Re)production

[W]riting for the theatre is my way of diverting realism, the kind of realism that only succeeds in expropriating us from our own lives by stifling our voices and our imaginations. In writing [*La saga des poules mouillées*], I tried to speak a forgotten language and to find the words to celebrate women's culture and women's productivity. I also wanted to combat all the forces which from generation to generation continue to consume the fruits of the very thing they denigrate, deny and try to render invisible – *women's work.*

Jovette Marchessault, 'Letter to Michelle Rossignol,' 13 March 1981

We have seen across the preceding chapters a history of Quebec and of the Québécois performing arts largely conceived as being of, by, and for men. Expo 67 and the Quiet Revolutionaries are 'fathers' of a modern, urban, potentially sovereign Quebec; the theatre called 'québécois' was also birthed by a man; and we could argue the same for Québécois music (Félix Leclerc and Gilles Vigneault's *chansons québécoises* of the 1960s and 1970s), for poetry (Gaston Miron's *poésie du pays* dating from the 1950s), and for the novel (Jacques Renaud's *Le Cassé*, 1964). Thus, a kind of mythology of male national self-engenderment installs itself into the history and historiography of Québécois performance, and of performing Quebec – although, again, Quebec is by no means alone in this gendered history and historiography (see Canning 1996, Davis 1991, Jackson 2004 for instance).

My primary concern in this book has been to illuminate the conditions in which national mimesis of any kind – iconic, metonymic, simulated, or affective – becomes possible. Women and women's work have returned again and again as furnishing those conditions of possibility. Their labours are multiform: symbolic (as national icons), actual (as mothers, as politicians, as organizers), and emotional (as generators of and repositories for national sentiment and sensation). And yet, as we have also seen, their 'real lives' – their own emotions, experiences, and work, as well as their contributions to national performances – have been largely occluded by a national historiography that privileges metaphorical figures of reflection and construction. As lesbian feminist author Jovette Marchessault (b. 1938), quoted above, would have it, this historiography of Québécois performance 'consume[s] the fruits of the very thing [it] denigrate[s], den[ies] and tr[ies] to render invisible' (1983a, 22). In *National Performance*, I have striven to illuminate these foundational representational and emotional labours that underlie the 'nation-ness' of a given performance. In so doing, *National Performance* traces a kind of phantom history of women's / Woman's role in Québécois national performance. It is fitting, therefore, to close this book with a reflection on women's performance as such, not as enabling condition, ground, or economy but as another way of producing *québécité*. The multiplicity of performance forms under the umbrella of 'women's performance' prevents the theorization of another figure by means of which nation-ness is ascribed to performance. Taken together, however, their efforts investigate the conditions for national performance. When does background labour move into the foreground? What kinds of authors and authorial practices count as national? Feminist performances during the period of their highest visibility – the 1970s and 1980s – unsettle the commonplace notions of 'new,' 'creation,' and 'authorship' on which repose a number of the figures for national mimesis. As we have seen, their male counterparts' creative efforts focused on the production of new and native cultural forms and modes of expression: Expo 67 constructed new land and with it a new national origin; the use of oral vernacular in plays like Tremblay's *Les belles-sœurs* was a pillar to creating *le nouveau théâtre québécois*; Micone introduced new, immigrant characters to the Quebec stage; Carbone 14 discovered formal and semiotic novelty in its body-based *nouveau bouger*. Women artists were also asking these most fundamental of artistic questions: How does one make the new? What is it to create? And whose voices/works are authorized?

Feminist literary critic Barbara Godard points to the impact on Québécois literary history of the 'Christian creation myth of the fecundating divine Father's Word' in which all creation comes into being at the behest and through the speech of a male god (1985, 11). In historically Catholic Quebec, such a beginning would have significant repercussions; while positioning a male god as father to all, it also reserved an elevated yet purely symbolic status for women: as virgin or as submissive mother. However, 'what won them greater symbolic status also restricted women's social role' (15), especially their roles as wielders of words themselves and as creators of their own symbolic universes, be they theatrical, musical, literary, or what have you. Indeed, no women writers emerged as major literary figures in Quebec until the 1940s when Gabrielle Roy, Germaine Guèvremont, and Anne Hébert made names for themselves. With respect to theatre, Lucie Robert argues that it was not until the 1980s that women playwrights were seen as a group 'rather than as exceptional figures' such as was the case for Françoise Loranger in the 1960s or Yvette Mercier-Gouin in the 1930s (Robert 2004, 61). As one way into authorship, many women artists assumed the (fraught) authority granted them as reproducers (in procreative and artistic senses) and made the production-reproduction or creation-procreation dynamic a focus of their work. In these last pages, then, let me recast somewhat the central problematics of national mimesis with the help of Quebec's first feminist theatre 'hit,' *La nef des sorcières* (1976); Jovette Marchessault's theatrical monologue *Les Vaches de nuit* (1979); and feminist playwright, performer, producer, and teacher Pol Pelletier's collective creations of the 1970s as my guides. Not content with their more traditional casting in the cultural national project as mothers to be rejected, mute natural grounds from which to spring, handmaidens to metaphor, or vehicles of affect, Marchessault, Pelletier (b. 1947), and the writers and performers of *La nef des sorcières*, experimented with creating new theatrical languages, forms, and mythologies from the 1970s onward. By highlighting the conditions that keep women's authorial voices quiet, experimenting with anti-patriarchal writing, and privileging collective creation, their work rearticulates the central terms of this project on national performance in such a way that they are more consonant with and revealing of women's contributions to a Québécois national, artistic project.

Let us begin with the opening scene of *La nef des sorcières* (translated by Linda Gaboriau as *The Clash of Symbols*), which opened at Montreal's institutional theatre,[1] Théâtre du Nouveau Monde, on 5 March 1976, and attracted upwards of 25,000 ticket buyers (Pelletier 1979). Via a set of six successive monologues written by seven different writers – Luce Guilbeault, Marthe Blackburn, France Théoret, Odette Gagnon, Marie-Claire Blais, Pol Pelletier, and Nicole Brossard – the play forcefully demonstrates how the theatre in particular has been a key site for the display of 'woman' emerging from men. *La nef* begins with Luce Guilbeault's 'Mad Actress' playing the marriageable ingénue, Agnès, in Molière's *L'École des femmes* – except that she promptly forgets her lines. The off-stage voice of Arnolphe asks Agnès, 'Quelle nouvelle?' (What's the news? or How are you?). She replies, addressing the audience,

> Excusez-moi, je ne sais plus quoi dire; j'ai un blanc! Ça m'était jamais arrivé. (*Elle relève ses jupes.*) 'Quand je suis partie de chez nous, j'étais en amour par-dessus la tête. Je voyais plus clair.' – Pierrette Guérin, voyons. Ce n'est pas la réplique. – 'Échelle au bas, échelle que le lutin escalade...' Gauvreau, non, je le ferai pas, je ne le ferai pas le *strip-tease*, je ne le ferai pas ... Angéline, Marie-Lou, Carmen, mes petites belles-sœurs, où est-ce que vous êtes? (Guilbeault et al. 1992, 45)

> [Excuse me, I don't know what to say anymore; I've forgotten my lines! It's never happened to me before. (*She picks up her skirts.*) 'When I left our home I was head over heels in love. I couldn't see straight.' – That's Pierrette Guérin. That's not the line. – 'Ladder far below, ladder that elves climb...' Gauvreau, no, I won't do it, I won't do the strip-tease, I won't ... Angéline, Marie-Lou, Carmen, my dear Belles-Sœurs, where are you? (Blackburn et al. 2006, 290).]

In response to Arnolphe's question, 'What's new?' Agnès can only come up with old lines from other plays, notably those by canonical Québécois playwrights Michel Tremblay and Claude Gauvreau.[2] Significantly, Agnès is citing the performance history of the actress who portrayed her, Luce Guilbeault (1935–91). Guilbeault, a major force in feminist theatre of the 1970s and 1980s, also directed *La nef des sorciéres* in addition to writing and performing the part of the 'Mad Actress.' As her lines in *La nef* suggest, she had previously originated the roles of Pierrette Guérin in *Les belles-sœurs* and Carmen, daughter of Léopold and Marie-Lou (also cited in Guilbeault's monologue) in *À toi, pour toujours, ta Marie-Lou* (1971). Pierrette, you'll recall, is the estranged sister of Rose Ouimet and Germaine Lauzon whose paramour, Johnny, has ruined her reputation and left her penniless. Carmen is another 'fallen' sister, this time to Manon in Tremblay's *À toi, pour toujours, ta Marie-Lou* (1971), the fourth instalment in the 'cycle des belles-sœurs.' Carmen, too, is a creature of 'the Main,'[3] a country music singer in a bar on Montreal's fabled Boulevard Saint-Laurent, which bisects the city's east (historically francophone) and west (historically anglophone) sides and functions in Tremblay's oeuvre as a zone of social, sexual, and personal liberation (David and Lavoie 1993). Guilbeault /the Mad Actress thereby invokes and refuses the roles assigned her in 'seminal' Québécois plays, plays that would fecundate an expressly 'Québécois' theatre. In so doing she breaks two mimetic ties that restrict actresses to passive reflections of male imaginaries: 'the woman / mimesis of man (Agnès) and the actress /mimesis of text' (Hajdukowski-Ahmed 1984, 264).

As important, however, is the nature and national resonance of the roles she is rejecting, since Pierrette and Carmen are not only similar character types, they are also similarly interpreted in the national allegory of Tremblay's drama. Pierrette, victim of blind love for a man with an English name, comes to stand in for a certain vision of a colonized Quebec, betrayed by its more powerful 'husband.' Her unannounced arrival at Germaine's stamp-pasting party is an effort at reintegration into her family of origin, a revalorization of her roots, however degraded. If she was deluded when she left her parents' home to be with 'le maudit Johnny,' she is clear-headed now about their exploitative rapport and its underlying power dynamics. Her experience translates into transferable wisdom as she counsels the young women in the play, especially Lise, who tells Pierrette of her unexpected pregnancy. This moment is significant not only for its rejection of involuntary motherhood and reproduction (Pierrette provides information on how to procure an abortion). It is also significant because it 'constitutes the only moment when someone is heard and recognized in her desire' (Greffard 1993, 38); Pierrette is able to see and respond to who Lise is and wants to become. Carmen and Pierrette share the plot point of leaving their family home in disgrace. However, while Pierrette is not a recuperated figure, national or familial, in *Les belles-sœurs* (for her sisters reject her to play's end), Carmen is taken up by the influential early interpreter of Tremblay's national allegory, Michel Bélair, as the sign of hope and national futurity for Quebec. Carmen, he writes, 'incarnates a primary truth: that of revolt. Revolt against the milieu, revolt from the bottom of her heart against passivity and resignation ... Having given herself every opportunity to be happy, she forges the way and wants to help Manon follow the same path' (Bélair 1971, 21). Contrasting Carmen's revolutionary act of leaving the family home to pursue what makes her happy with the suffocating universe of *Les belles-sœurs*, Bélair writes, 'The world of Germain Lauzon is already a generation old: Carmen's world may be a sign of the fact that we are finally starting to live and that we accept ourselves just as we are' (29). Having thrown off the static victim-mentality of her parents and younger sister, accepted her own desires, and forged her own way, Carmen lights the way not only for Manon but also for 'nous.'[4]

So, to be clear, the Tremblay roles Guilbeault originated on the stage were not those of the backwards-looking good sisters, dupes of consumerism and the Church. Rather, Pierrette and Carmen were visionaries, harbingers of an independent (from abusive authority figures) and authentic (true to themselves) future consistent with anticolonial visions of Quebec's future. They were (or were on their way to becoming) Chamberland's self-possessed 'hommes québécois' who had been 'demystified' with respect to the values of the dominant class (1963). In their *revanchist* sisters, Pierrette and Carmen confronted the representatives of an unready populace whose false consciousness kept them from seeing their own way to liberation. Near the play's end Carmen exhorts Manon, 'Révolte-toi, Manon, c'est tout c'qu'y te reste! ... Vide-toé la tête! Mets tes souvenirs à' porte! Sors de ton esclavage! Reste pas assis là, à rien faire. FAIS QUEQU'CHOSE!' (Tremblay 1971, 92). (Fight back, Manon, it's all you've got left! ... Empty your mind! Throw your memories away! Put an end to this slavery! Don't sit here doing nothing. DO SOMETHING! [1994, 77].) Guilbeault's rejection of even such positive, hopeful, and national female characters is, therefore, especially telling. By including references to those roles in her opening monologue, Guilbeault condemns them as products of a male imagination, even when the particular male imagination in question is among the most sympathetic and astute observers of women's place in society and their familial (and familiar) roles (see Forsyth 1979; Piccione 1983). 'Bam, bam, bam dans la tête,' says the Mad Actress whose name we learn is Désirée Désire, 'les mots / Avec le grand marteau pénis.' (Bang, bang, bang. The words were hammered into my head with a big penis hammer) (Guilbeault et al. 1992, 47; Blackburn et al. 2006, 290). The roles may be 'positive' depictions of women, but they remain metaphor for men's 'desired desire' and, as such, cannot predicate an agential future for women.

As Louise Forsyth argues so convincingly, the Mad Actress's forgetting 'cleared the stage for those who come after her in *The Clash of Symbols*' (2006b, iv). (See Fig. 8.1 for all the characters of *La nef.*) No longer subject to speaking lines written by someone else, subsequent monologists take full advantage of that emptied space to reveal women's bodies, emotions, and experiences without disguise; they describe menopause and lesbian love, rail against worker-oppression, revise dominant scripts of seduction, and advocate self-fulfilment in part through public speech. Indeed, *La nef des sorcières* privileges the act of enunciation, making it

8.1 Cast of *La nef des sorcières* at the Théâtre du Nouveau Monde, 1976. Seated in the middle is Françoise Berd ('La ménopausée'), seated on the floor is Michèle Magny ('L'Écrivain'), then clockwise, Michèle Craig ('L'Échantillon'), Pol Pelletier ('Marcelle'), Luce Guilbeault ('Une Actrice en folie'), and Louisette Dussault ('la Fille').
Photo: André Le Coz. Fonds André Le Coz (P29), Université de Sherbrooke.

both the central formal element of the show and a clear thematic across the monologues. One by one the women find a voice; each monologue is a journey of self-discovery, emergence, and rejection of imposed words, images, activities. Put differently, each embarks on a process of self-authorship; they find their own fecundating words that would create a new reality. In her introduction to the printed version, Lori Saint-Martin reprises suggestively the Christian origin story: 'In the beginning, seven women wrote' (1992, 21). In the end, 'The Writer' speaks – 'Je parle' (I am speaking), Michèle Magny says, to close *La nef des sorcières* (Guilbeault et al. 1992, 139; Blackburn et al. 2006, 329). At the instigation of the Mad Actress, the six characters leave behind their status as vessel to emerge as author; they move from reproduction to production, articulate witnesses to their present circumstances, undammed desires, and burgeoning hopes.

As a precondition to speaking her own words, however, not only must the Mad Actress clear the stage of her previous incarnations, she must also lay claim to her own physicality; she must reclaim her body from its (theatrical and societal) condition of that-to-be-looked-on (the 'desired' object of her first name). She addresses her audience, 'Vous regardez mon visage. / Vous voyez cent visages collés l'un devant l'autre. / Mon visage? / Non. / Je vous donne un visage-trou. / Vous regardez mon corps. / Mon corps? / Non, un corps déguisé, corseté, creusé à la taille, allongé ou ramassé suivant l'emploi' (Guilbeault et al. 1992, 48-9). (You look at my face. You see a hundred faces, one on top of the other. My face? No. My face is blank for you to fill ... You look at my body. My body? No, it's a body in disguise. Corseted, curved, stretched or bent for the part [Blackburn et al. 2006, 291].) Against this distorted image of Woman, the 'witches' of *La nef* propose images drawn from the physical site of their difference to men – their sex. About half-way through her opening monologue, Agnès / Mad Actress / Guilbeault squats on a toilet: 'Je prends un miroir, / Je le mets entre mes jambs, / Je regarde mon sexe' (I take a mirror, I put it between my legs, I look at my sex) (Guilbeault et al. 1992, 47-8; Blackburn et al. 2006, 291). The promise of the Actress's turning inward, her close attention to her sexual difference, will be realised in the ecstatic words of Nicole Brossard's monologue, 'The Writer,' which closes the play. At its conclusion, the writer's sex births a text. 'Petites contractions. Détente. Petites contractions. J'ai la langue sèche. Fait chaud. Je suis humide. Ça coule. Poussez. Poussez. Respirez bien. Détends-toi. Fait chaud. Encore. Jouis. Jouis. Poussez. Poussez. C'est une fille ... Les pages se décollent. Les mots affluent autour

du clitoris' (Guilbeault et al. 1993, 136-7). (Little contractions. Release.
Little contractions. My tongue is dry. It's hot. I am damp. It starts to
flow. Push. Push. Breathe deeply. Relax. It's hot. Again. Enjoy it. Enjoy it.
Push. Push. It's a girl ... Pages are coming out. Words gather around the
clitoris' [Blackburn et al. 2006, 328]). Those body parts that have been
the means of reproduction will henceforth be the source of her fellow
witches' pleasure and writing. To counter the Father's fecundating word,
they will write the body; as symbolic and actual culture-bearers and biological reproducers, they know well it too produces the new.

We hear here the articulation of a feminist poetics, one consistent with
the French feminist project of *écriture féminine* galvanized by the playful
theories of the likes of Luce Irigaray and Hélène Cixous and adapted
by Québécois feminist writers like Brossard, Louky Bersianik, France
Théoret, and Madeleine Gagnon. In brief, they encourage writing 'otherwise,' writing from and of the difference that Woman represents with
respect to Man, particularly in the discourses of Freudian and Lacanian
psychology that are the joint object of Cixous and Irigaray's post-structuralist critique, in which 'she' is body, nature, and domestic interior to
'his' mind, culture, and public sphere. This hierarchical binary influences all manner of discourse, which, in turn, structures one's sense of
'reality.' How, then, can a woman express her reality on the losing end
of that binary so as to overturn it? How might she find her public voice
if, as Alvina Ruprecht asks, 'the feminine voice is obliged to use a speech
structured and imposed by man' (1985, 171)? A line in Brossard's 'The
Writer' monologue stands as response: 'Il faut ravir le sens, du sens. /
Sur toute la surface du corps et dedans' (We must seize the sense and the
senses. All over the body and inside) (Guilbeault et al. 1992, 137; Blackburn et al. 2006, 329). Writing in the feminine would locate women's
enunciative power precisely in the break from language rules shaped
predominantly by men. This idea of seizing 'sense' to make new meanings for women by acknowledging the senses, by following their indications, is taken up with some gusto by the witches of *La nef des sorcières*, as
well as by Jovette Marchessault and Pol Pelletier. These writers and performers emphasized the materiality of the text – its corporeality, if you
will, that highlights its continual unfolding. This corporeal inscription
takes the form not only of references to the female-sexed body, bodily
processes and sexuality, but also to textual strategies that, in the words
of Karen Gould, 'have brought forth new forms of corporeal imagery,
increasingly transgressive thematics centering on the insurgent libidinal
desires and creative power of women's bodies, and fluctuating poetic

structures suggestive of the body's alternating rhythms and of the fluidity of language itself' (1990, 46).[5] We've already seen an example in Brossard's text for *La nef*. The language used in the birthing scene refers to the actions of childbirth in which one has contractions, pushes, and relaxes. But the passage's organization – with its repetitions, its stops and starts, its summons to breath between each word – also mimics childbirth's physical reality.

In her solo show, *Joie* (Joy, 1990–93), which casts a retrospective glance over her then twenty-year career in Quebec theatre, Pelletier jokes (lovingly) about these new forms of corporeal imagery so dear to early feminist theatrical experiments. 'C'est remarquable, au début du théâtre de femmes, le nombre de spectacles où on retrouve / des boules, / des sacs / et des cordes avec des nœuds' (In the early days of women's theatre, it's amazing the number of shows that featured: / moons / mounds / and ropes with knots) (Pelletier 1995, 21; 2008, 133). She also usefully details early work where bodily writing trumps linguistic symbolization. In *Essai en trois mouvements pour trois voix de femmes* (Experiment in three movements for three women's voices, 1976), 'qui explore un univers exclusivement féminin' (an exploration of an exclusively female world) featuring 'un énorme tas de coussins en forme d'étrons ou d'intestins, très longs et bruns et entortillés' (an enormous pile of very long, fat, brown cushions all coiled up like turds or intestines), the three women squirming underneath them emitted only gurgles and other 'sons étranges' (strange sounds) (1995, 19–20; 2008, 132). Neither was a word spoken in *Finalement* (Finally, 1976); 'que des sons. Des sons de poules et d'oiseaux entre autres' (just sounds. Chicken and bird sounds, among others) (1995, 20; 2008, 132). This kind of theatrical communication without spoken language undertook to present the pre- or non-verbal experiences of women that lay outside of what could be put into words. If such a strategy risks essentialism, relying as it does on a presumably common female experience and the incommunicability of intense physical sensation (like childbirth, for instance), we would do well to remember the strategy's historicity. For at the same time that this wariness around words, of naming women's experience in speech is another approach to 'seizing sense,' it is also a response to a history of theatrical, national, and specular service in Québécois theatre in which the word, written by others, determines – and deforms – women's being on stage, such as was forcefully verbalized in *La nef*.

Jovette Marchessault's *Les Vaches de nuit* (Night Cows) is an exuberant and oniric text that dares to surpass sounds in order to put into

words women's bodily experience precisely in order to grant to women
a future in which they are actual and self-actualized, instead of metaphor. Performed as a monologue by Pol Pelletier in a production called
'Célébrations' in honour of International Woman's Day (5 March 1979)
again at the Théâtre du Nouveau Monde, *Les Vaches de nuit* is the second
text in Marchessault's *Tryptique lesbien* (Lesbian Triptych, published in
1980). In it, a young female cow narrates the nightly transformation of
herself and her mother into sexually awakened and colourful creatures,
liberated from their quotidian servitude as they join a communion of
exclusively female creatures. In their company, crows recall for the assembled a pre-patriarchal era, '*le temps des mères*' (Mother Age) (1980,
93; 1985, 79), in which women were whole, unified, 'moissenneuses,
douceurs, ivresses' (gentle, rapturous and kind) (1980, 93; 1985, 79).
At the end of each night the cows return to their kitchens. But they
do so renewed and certain of a similarly transformed future. 'De tant
s'aimer, de tant espérer, de tant s'enseigner la conscience et la fierté
chaque nuit, chaque vache de nuit, je sais qu'on se rapproche du moment où cette terre promise nous sera rendue' (Because every night,
each cow of night loves herself so well and hopes so hard, and teaches
herself so much consciousness and pride, that I know we approach the
moment when we will redeem the promised land) (1980, 94; 1985, 80).
The female history related nightly by the crows to a rapturous audience
of mammals is situated as both anterior and posterior to the moment of
its enunciation. While in the myth it clearly precedes the current epoch
of 'castration,' it is also the very image of a utopic future. Reborn themselves, the cows will bring into being a new society, for *Les Vaches de nuit*
locates in women's bodies an origin to rival that of the Christian, male,
creator god. This alternate origin will spawn a transformed society. 'Je
le sais! Je le dit!' (I know and will say it), pronounces the daughter cow,
'Le monde vivant ne dérive pas du songe. Le monde vivant ne dérive pas
de la colère. Le monde vivant dérive du cerveau mammalien des mères.
Ouias! Ouais! Ouais! La blanche matière cervicale est un lait de gloire
en partance dans le temps de la célébration' (1980, 88). (The living
world does not derive from dream! The living world does not arise from
wrath! The living world springs from the mothers' mammalian brains.
Oh yes, oh yes! Their white brain matter is yet another glorious milk
which starts to flow in times of celebration [1985, 76].)

Embracing Brossard's summons to 'seize the sense and the senses.
All over the body and inside,' *Les Vaches de nuit* 'plays with the confu-
sion between the literal and figurative meanings of the word "cow."

Mother and daughter are "really" (which is to say physically) cows; but they are also "symbolically" cows, they are breeders' (Saint-Martin 1991, 247). Beyond this twisting of meaning – important more for its feminist revalorization of an insult than for its aesthetic strategy of language-play, which in any case Marchessault has insisted is not a crucial part of her creative process (Potvin 1991, 221) – *Les Vaches de nuit* illuminates the internal, spiritual experience in which the female body is not a limit, but rather a vehicle to transcendence and to a renewed worldly creation. We are given to know immediately the enforced limits of the female body by the young narrator. All the cows of her herd have been neutered young, forcibly distanced from their sex and sexuality in order to make them more serviceable to Man. The daughter cow explains, 'Les avantages pécuniers de la castration sont indéniables car, paraît-il, c'est le meilleur moyen de tirer un profit maximum pour la boucherie … La découverte, la mutilation miracle, qui d'une vache nymphomane, fait une bête qu'on peut spécialiser dans la production de la viande, du lait, du beurre et du travail' (1980, 83–4). (The monetary advantages of castration are undeniable because, it seems, this is the best method of maximizing the profits to the butcher … The discovery of the miracle of mutilation transforms a nymphomaniac cow into a beast which can be specialized to produce meat, milk, butter, and labour [1985, 73].) Here, then, Marchessault makes literal the exploitative service model she lambastes above in which men 'consume the fruits of the very thing they denigrate.' If the day cow is 'a docile merchandise, deprived of a sexuality and a will of her own' (Saint-Martin 1991, 247-8), the night cow, by contrast, is a resplendent figure who revels in her sexuality, which also forms a basis for an expansive community of female mammals and birds. Their libidinal energy unleashed, the mother-daughter dyad is renewed, after which the cows join with each other and sister 'breasted creatures' of the animal world: 'Entre les dames corneilles et les mammifères, à chaque fois c'est la fête, la joie des retrouvailles, tous les embrassements possibles du corps et de la mémoire' (It is a celebration for the sister crows and the mammals; a time of rediscovered joys, of all possible embraces in body and in memory) (1980, 91; 1985, 78). The cows' nocturnal liberation is matched by Marchessault's vigorous language: 'thoughts and emotions succeed each other so swiftly that the words, liberated from the restrictions of pause and period, go beyond the traditional sentence with its main and subordinate clauses, its finished character, its closed appearance' (Rosenberg 1985, 231). In *Les Vaches de nuit*, the transcendence of the body, like the liberation of language, lies in the surpassing of barriers, in its promiscuous and pleasuring points of contact with others.

In an interview with Claudine Potvin, Marchessault discusses her narrative and linguistic strategies, saying that it is by 'opening narration to the flux of life that lifts us, all the while remaining faithful to the mysterious plan that inhabits us' that her writing might reconnect readers to the 'limitless plenitude' of their interior, spiritual life (Potvin 1991, 228; 227). And so it does, perhaps. Yet writing in the feminine, such as Marchessault attempts in *Les Vaches de nuit*, might also be usefully viewed as a strategy for re-materializing women from national mimesis's abstracted figure of Woman. In the nationalist performance historiography we've charted in this book, a man (or Man) is the ultimate guarantor of meaning for every onstage woman / Woman. In feminist revisions of theatrical *québécité*, women – in their diversity and concrete reality – take the stage. It is not merely that they speak their own words and manifest their own images instead of someone else's, though this too is important; it is also that the words they speak, the situations they describe, and the roles they enact are not given to be interpreted as representative of something else. Where Pierrette's humiliation and Carmen's liberation come to symbolize (male) Québécois oppression and futurity, the physical body of *La nef des sorcière*'s menopausal woman, written by Marthe Blackburn and performed by Françoise Berd, stands in the way of such abstraction, for it describes a passage, liberating for her character, that only female-sexed bodies go through. Her body's sex-specificity thus puts the lie to national allegories built on female figures that disregard women's lives. This is not to say that these feminist performances didn't produce their own allegories or symbolize another kind of collective; indeed, they did – they strove to bring into being collectives of women. However, in a theatrical context invested in national allegory, the gender specificity of *le théâtre femmes* highlights how women's difference constitutes a crucial element of the infrastructure of national mimesis.

Having exposed women's service role in theatrical representation and laid bare the conditions that keep women quiet, *La nef*'s Mad Actress, sitting on the toilet, mirror in hand, literally points to a new source and means for women's artistic production in Quebec. From those 'échancrures roses, ses rondeurs femelles trempées de rosée' (rosy openings, their female roundness moist with dew) (Marchessault 1980, 92; 1985, 78) emerged an era rich with varied feminist theatrical practice and production in Quebec that pointed to different futures marked by personal and political independence, maturity, and authenticity. Indeed, in her article for the first special issue on 'Women' at *Jeu*, Francine Noël singles out *Les Vaches de nuit* as a harbinger of the new in Québécois theatre. She reflects, 'I think *Les Vaches de nuit* marks a turning point of no return in Quebec women's mental landscape: the text not only tosses out traditional images, but it throws the stage wide open to a powerful and ravaging cohort of powerful women, who will be irremediably present from now on. Their expansion will be impossible to contain. When we *see* this ample cohort on stage (shown by the voice and body of a single great actor [Pol Pelletier]), we begin to foresee what that other thing we've been looking for is' (quoted in Forsyth 2006a, 427). Noël's vision, though imperfectly realized, was nonetheless accurate for a certain period which has yet to be fully integrated into Québécois national theatre history:[6] namely, that of feminist production between about 1974 and about 1985. The first date marks the founding of the Marxist-feminist theatre collective, le Théâtre des cuisines (Theatre of Kitchens), which devised '*spectacles*' (the nomenclature is significant in its emphasis on rendering visible) on such subjects as abortion (*Nous aurons les enfants que nous voulons* [We will have the children we want] 1974), domestic labour (*Môman travaille pas, à trop d'ouvrage* [Mum doesn't work, for too much housework] 1975) and the connection of the personal to the political (*As-tu vu ? les maisons s'emportent !* [Did you see? The houses are losing their temper!] 1980).[7] But it is the explosion of feminist theatrical performance clustered around this date that makes it significant. *Le Théâtre des cuisines* was joined by other collectives, les femmes de Thetford Mines (1975), the Commune à Marie (Marie's commune) (1977), Organisation O (1978), 3 et 7 le numéro magique (3 and 7, the magic number) (1979), Théâtre expérimental des femmes (Women's Experimental Theatre) (1979), and Folles Alliées (Allied Crazies) (1980), among others.

When historians of Quebec theatre discuss the ten-year period of ca. 1975 to ca. 1985, they note collective creation and devised shows as the era's distinguishing features; they point to companies like the Théâtre expérimental de Montréal, Omnibus, Eskabel, les Enfants du paradis, le Grand Cirque ordinaire, and le Théâtre Euh.[8] As evidence of the *théâtre femmes*' immersion in the *jeune théâtre*, we might point to the fact that the first *spectacle de femmes* in Quebec emerged out of the *jeune théâtre* troupe, le Grand Cirque ordinaire, whose female members created and played *Un prince, mon jour viendra* (One prince, my day will come) (1974). Moreover, Pol Pelletier, who wrote and performed 'Mar-

celle II' in *La nef des sorcières*, was also a founding member of the hugely
influential Théâtre expérimental de Montréal (TEM) in 1975. It was
within that organisation, but without whose male co-founders, that she
mounted a series of *spectacles de femmes* including those cited above as
well as *À ma mère, à ma mère, à ma mere, à ma voisine* (To my mother, to
my mother, to my mother, to my neighbour) (D. Gagnon et al. 1979),
which put on trial the figure of the self-sacrificing, patriarchal mother.
And yet, their histories have tended to be written separately, with the
male-run or -dominated alternative theatre troupes standing in for the
jeune théâtre while the 'women's theatres' have separate entries. Michel
Vaïs, for instance, in his *L'Accompagnateur: Parcours d'un critique de théâtre*,
offers 'Les femmes et l'institution' its own chapter, following the chapter
that describes 'alternative' theatre; here, the Théâtre expérimental des
femmes is mentioned as a child of the fruitful rupture of the Théâtre
expérimental de Montréal. 'As is often the case in divided families, the
wife keeps the house and the husband puts his building talents to work
to make a new home' (Vaïs 2005, 280). Feminist scholars – notably Lucie
Robert, Louise Forsyth, Jane Moss, and Josette Féral – have striven to fill
the gap in critical literature on women theatre artists, producing col-
lected volumes of essays, introductions to individual plays, and articles in
scholarly journals, many of them quoted in this chapter. The odd effect
seems to be that women theatre artists's contributions are downplayed
in more 'general' histories of the theatre. Féral reminds readers of the
third volume of her *Mise en scène et jeu de l'acteur* series of interviews with
directors and actors from around the globe that 'despite appearances,
contemporary theatre written or produced by women has received little
attention over the years, and studies on the subject are not abundant'
(Féral 2007, 17). Gilbert David's preliminary count of plays from 1920 to
1998 regularly included in the Québécois canon tallies four female playwrights to the eleven male playwrights whose work is canonized. Where
the 'canon' is produced by being listed in only two of the encyclopaedias
or histories in David's corpus, the ratio drops: three female dramatists to
fourteen male dramatists (2008). In a similar vein, a number of notable
women's solo performance works featured the actress as 'a character
to deconstruct and reconstruct differently,' following the example and
capitalizing on the rhetorical power of *La nef des sorcière*'s 'L'actrice en
folie' (Robert 2004, 64). However, it is the plays that thematize and deconstruct the male playwright and/or creator mentioned earlier in the
Carbone 14 chapter – like *Provincetown Playhouse, juillet 1919, j'avais 19
ans* (Provincetown Playhouse, July 1919, I was 19 years old) by Normand

Chaurette (1981), *Les Feluettes* (Lilies) by Michel-Marc Bouchard (1985–6), and *Le vrai monde?* by Tremblay (1987) – that enter the repertoire, receive productions at institutional theatres, and come to stand in for the preoccupations of the decade (see Godin and Lafon 1999; Andrès and Riendeau 1997).

Part of this setting apart of women's experimental theatre work – particularly that of devised collective creation – from more general histories of modern Quebec performance may stem from women's differential relation to the word, specifically the printed word. For many, performance was the preferred mode of making public in both senses of the phrase: publishing and making available publicly one's views. Even taking into account the advances and advantages to women made possible by their revalorization of oral tradition, foregrounding the non-sense of women's experience, and using women's ways of knowing and transmitting their knowledge as alternate dramatic structures, not having a visible publication record cost female theatre artists as well. Robert concludes from her data that in Quebec the path to production – which, to state the obvious is, in the main and certainly among the playwrights in Robert's study, the goal of writing plays – and, with a second production, to inclusion in the repertoire lies in what she designates as a 'literary profile'; this profile privileges publication over theatrical production and is that of writers whose 'dramaturgical practice is accidental or ephemeral in nature, inscribed at the heart of a more significant œuvre which lies in another genre, poetry or the novel' (Robert 2000, 146). 'Whereas the vast majority of plays written by women are aimed at small theatres, playwrights who present a "literary" profile are produced on the "large institutional stages" more than the others' (152).

But part of it, as I hope has become clear, is due to the dynamics and values of dominant notions of national mimesis. Where national discourses of authorship tended to privilege the individual genius/writer, feminist discourses accorded that function to a group; to counter the Father's fecundating word, feminists wrote the body; and to displace myths of origin that positioned women as a second(ary) creation, they sourced and imagined a women's mythology and women's culture. In this respect, the work of *La nef des sorcières*, Jovette Marchessault, and Pol Pelletier is emblematic – but also cautionary. Where *La nef des sorcières* illuminated the means by which women might discover their own authorial power, by a rejection of representational labours in service of other people's stories and a turn to bodily writing, Marchessault's oeuvre tells us that finding one's own fecundating words to create a new, fuller reality

is not enough. Rather, women must find hospitable, all-female contexts
in which to enunciate their desires, tell their stories, recall their myths,
such as the Milky Way of *Les Vaches de nuit*.[9]

You will have recognized the terms I chose for this feminist recasting
of national mimesis through women's theatrical production in Quebec;
they have been recurrent in the preceding text: origin and future; reproduction and production. These sets of terms are linked, of course;
origins are traced to reproductive activity and futures enabled by production. As we have seen, those twinned terms are also gendered, the former set generally designated as 'female/feminine,' the latter as 'male/
masculine.' But these concerns are linked not only causally (as in the
first instance above) and symbolically (the second). They also describe
the cardinal points of national mimesis, where origin-future occupies
the horizontal, east-west axis and reproduction-production the vertical,
north-south axis. Thus, the construction figure at Expo 67 reads southeast as it valorizes futurity (in the form of modern urbanity) and production (of a symbolic universe on created land). On the other hand,
metaphor points northwest, being drawn to reproduction and origins.
With simulation, metonymy, and affection, the compass arm lurches
back and forth between points. These figures do not point to origins so
much as displace them, revise them, explode them; their reproductions
are unreliable, disguised productions; their futures (in terms of progeny
and for the national project) are contested. The geography of national
mimesis is, thus, scrambled. This scramble is more or less where we left
off with 'the Dion phenomenon' in the last chapter. The compass arm
passes through metaphor's northwest position when Dion is taken up as
an icon of *québécité*, swivelling thence to a northeast position when her
ventriloquism renders her a national simulacrum (a reproduction without an original). The affection 'she' affords finally sets the compass arm
spinning, no longer drawn to any one north but instead building velocity
and force in its circular movements. These movements create their own
kind of magnetic field, drawing in even those who would prefer to stay
away.

   As we have seen, feminist production in Quebec has a substantial and
fascinating history of thematizing and theorizing the compass points of
national mimesis. But feminist theatrical and literary production has
taken these poles up in ways that unhinge the compass arm altogether,
using it like an arrow to pierce north, south, east and west. In their attempts to alter the representational contracts struck under the terms of a

facile national mimesis between performance, nation, and woman, they strive toward liberation from national 'service' – as representational and emotional labourers – to become actors in their own right and creators of their own futures. They remind us, once again, that when reading national female figures, so *porteuses de sens* (meaningful, literally bearing meaning), it would be well to be mindful of what and whom else they are carrying.

Notes

2 Marginals, Metaphors, and Mimesis

1 Lepage was artistic director of *théâtre français* at the National Arts Centre, 1989–93; in 1992 he was the first North American to direct a Shakespeare play at the Royal National Theatre; and in 1995 he directed Strindberg's *A Dream Play* at Sweden's Dramaten (Royal Dramatic Theatre).

2 A note on translation practice: here, as in all subsequent cases of French-language secondary (i.e., interpretive) sources that do not have a published English-language translation, I use my own translation. Where an English-language translation exists, I quote from it. Where I quote from French-language primary texts (plays, poems, manifestoes, songs), I quote the original first and then provide an English-language translation. The source of the translation varies: in cases where a published translation exists, I use that (and you will find it in the References); where it does not, I provide my own translation.

3 For instance, during his tenure as Liberal premier of Quebec (1960–66), Jean Lesage developed an increasingly interventionist (provincial) state, consolidating the province's areas of jurisdiction and expanding the public sector. During that period, the Quebec government established a Ministry of Education; nationalized the electricity company, Hydro Québec (1963); founded the Caisse de dépôt et de placement du Québec, which acts as an investor for the Quebec pension fund (1964); and opened offices of federal-provincial relations, cultural affairs, family and social welfare, and national resources (Keating 1996, 68). Since the early 1960s, Quebec broadened its responsibilities in the policy sectors of education, language, immigration, and, to a lesser extent, international relations. It is important to stress, however, that these are not formal amendments to the federal system nor to the

Canadian Constitution, both of which continue to exercise significant control over Quebec (Gagnon 1993, 99).

4 In this appellation, I am following the distinction Létourneau (2006, 159)
makes between the two dominant modes of 'feeling Québécois,' namely,
'québécité' and 'québécitude.' In contrast with *québécité, québécitude* is a
more nostalgic project based in an idea of immutable ethnic essence and
shared cultural memory.

5 On 27 November 2006, the House of Commons passed a motion introduced by the Conservative prime minister acknowledging, while circum-
scribing, the status of the Québécois people as a nation; the motion,
introduced in French, read as follows: 'Que cette Chambre reconnaisse que
les Québécoises et les Québécois forment une nation au sein d'un Canada
uni' (That this House recognize that the Québécois form a nation within
a united Canada) ('House passes'). The motion was made to head off a
similar one intended by the pro-sovereigntist federal party le Bloc québécois, which would have emphasized the transitory nature of Quebec's place
within Canada, thus: 'Que la Chambre reconnaisse que les Québécoises et
les Québécois forment une nation actuellement au sein du Canada' (That
this House recognize that the Québécois form a nation currently within
Canada) ('In Depth' 2006).

6 In 1968, Liberal Premier Daniel Johnson established the Department of
Intergovernmental Affairs to oversee external relations, international co-
operation, and federal-provincial relations; its exclusive mandate is to plan,
coordinate, and implement the Quebec government's international policy.

7 Compilations of performance and publication records document the dominance of foreign plays and playwrights in Quebec during the nineteenth
and early twentieth centuries. With the advent of the Quiet Revolution
and its reorganization of identity came a wave of treatises recovering 'native' plays among the colonial imports and/or documenting the rise of the
Québécois theatre from the mid-twentieth century forward (Hamelin 1961;
Burger 1974; Duval 1978). Complementary statistics demonstrate the rise
in productions by Québécois playwrights on Montreal stages following the
Quiet Revolution (Lavoie 1977; Féral 1985; Nardocchio 1986a).

8 A rapid sampling of books on Québécois theatre suggests that Gélinas's location of nation-ness in the theatre's reflective capacities took firm hold in
Quebec theatre scholarship. The first book to take an explicitly 'Québécois'
theatre for its object, *Théâtre Québécois I*, asserted that 'the theatre, in its particular characteristics, is the most tied (of the literary arts) to the environ-
ment/milieu' (Godin and Mailhot 1970, 20). Although the authors disavow
the necessity of realistic accuracy in the depiction of the milieu on the

national stage, they suggest that what makes the Québécois theatre national is that it 'reflect[s] and identif[ies] our milieu' (23). The only book-length study of Québécois theatre to expressly tackle the theatre's relationship to the nationalist movement, Elaine Nardocchio's monograph, *Theatre and Politics in Modern Quebec* (1986b), likewise reinscribes a low mimetic relationship.

9 Robert Lecker and Frank Davey have both argued that these 'thematic' reading strategies linking narrative content to nation have profoundly shaped Canadian literary criticism and canon formation. Davey writes about this tendency (1983, 6): 'Thematic critics in Canada have been interested in what Canadian literary works "say," especially what they "say" about Canada and Canadians.' Lecker asserts that the value ascribed to Canadian literature and to its criticism is a naively mimetic one that 'attempt[s] to secure a fundamental relation between people and their world and to record the evidence of this relation' (1995, 33).

10 This distinction between identifying *with* and identifying *as* is drawn, of course, from Eve Kosofsky Sedgwick's foundational *Epistemology of the Closet* (1990, 59–63). Scholars of lesbian/gay/queer performance and spectatorship provide important insights into how audiences left unrepresented (in the political and naively mimetic senses) in performance may find their way into those performances. The acts of lesbian/queer/disidentified reading theorized by Stacy Wolf (2002) and José Esteban Muñoz (1999) contribute models for answering how those positioned as marginally national or as non-national by the dominant or emergent terms of national subjectivity may yet assert their place in the nation. Wolf and Muñoz propose resistant reading practices as one way of making place for subjects left otherwise unaddressed by the text. Each draws on a deconstructive interpretive strategy that pinpoints a text's internal contradictions and the contradictions between the text and the spectator. From this dissonance, lesbian/queer/disidentified readers reassemble the text's dominant meanings and use them in the service of minority identity.

3 National Construction: Quebec's Modernity at Expo 67

1 The title, *L'amère patrie* is a play on words: literally, it means 'bitter country,' but it plays on 'la mère patrie,' mother-country.

2 The provinces of Ontario, Manitoba, New Brunswick, Prince Edward Island, and Nova Scotia all have significant francophone populations. The influence and magnitude of the francophone (Acadian) population in New Brunswick is such that the province is officially bilingual (French-English).

3 It is important to note that the continental outlook did not entirely

disappear with the advent of the Quiet Revolution, despite its waning prominence. In fact, chapter 4, 'De l'euphorie à la désenchantement: l'intervention gouvernementale québécoise (1956–1975)' of Martel's *Le deuil d'un pays imaginé* (1997) underscores the commitment of the Lesage government, in particular, to continentalism. Moreover, as we shall have the opportunity to discuss in chapter 6, this outlook is currently experiencing a revival among scholars of Québécois culture and identity in the analysis of 'américanité,' the sense of attachment and belonging to the continent that produces shared characteristics among the Americas – North and South (Cuccioletta 2000; Lamonde 1996; Hurley and Straw 2009).

4 In an exhaustive review article on the sea-change in Québécois historiography since the advent of the Quiet Revolution, Fernand Ouellet (1985) isolates two dominant orientations to the new historiography: first, an orientation to economic history, catalyzed by the work of Maurice Séguin, which traced Quebec's economic retardation to the conquest of New France by Britain in 1760, and to anglophones' superior use of political power and patronage; second, an orientation to intellectual or sociocultural history, which privileges the idea of community. Marcel Fournier (1986) documents a similar 'modernization' in sociological methodology, object, and practice during this period in which Quebec-as-society became the dominant question in the discipline.

5 While the Quiet Revolution still functions as a convenient shorthand for discussing Quebec's entry into modernity, it is understood more and more as exactly that: a convenient shorthand – more the moment of modernity's 'installation, its evidence' than its sudden appearance (Nardout-Lafarge 2004, 289). Recent reflections on Quebec history and Québécois historiographic practices, including those of Létourneau and Michel Gauvreau (2005), are less likely to attribute Quebec's modernity wholesale to the programs and policies of an intelligentsia-led Quiet Revolution. Instead, they establish more of a continuity of modernization and progress between pre– and post–Quiet Revolution eras. For example, they emphasize the gradualism of political, economic, and social change before and after the Quiet Revolution; the revolution's historical antecedents; early settlers' (*les habitants*) moves to the urban centres, and their openness to outside influences; and even Duplessis's modernizing efforts in, for instance, the electrification of the countryside and the introduction of a minimum wage. The feminist historians of the Clio Collective write that women 'began the "quiet" revolution long before it was heard' (1978, 275). See also Rudin (1992).

6 In using the phrase 'refus global,' I mean not only to characterize revolutionary logic but also to conjure associations with the 1948 manifesto by

Québécois artists advocating throwing over Quebec's dominant ideology for a fuller participation in modernism's art movements (Borduas 1977).

7 Aude Hendrick explains the exigencies behind the grouping of largely newly independent African nations in one symbolic and geographical space; among them were the related difficulties of financing and constructing individual pavilions. Fifteen African nations made up Africa Place: Ghana, Niger, Côte d'Ivoire, Cameroon, Chad, Democratic Republic of Congo, Tanzania, Gabon, Senegal, Togo, Kenya, Madagascar, Uganda, Rwanda, and Nigeria. According to Hendrick (2008, 83–4), all gave a 'primordial' place to the tourism sector in their displays and in their promotional literature.

8 Expo's chief architect, Édouard Fiset, described the physical groupings according to aesthetic and marketing principles in 1967, saying (in Chamberlin 1967, 35): 'We tried to locate the large pavilions at the ends of the site, not in the middle, so there are big volumes framing the exhibit ... They act as attractions. You have to pass in front of others to get to them.' So, the pavilions of Canada, the U.S.S.R, and the United States were situated on the ends of the islands, drawing visitors past (and encouraging them to stop into) the smaller national pavilions arranged in the middle. Fiset elaborates the marketing logic in his answer to a follow-up question about how the pavilions should be designed: 'We wanted a diversity of expression. It was desirable that it should excite the visitor all the time, so we must encourage it, even if it meant a clashing of forms, shapes and color elements' (ibid.). His full expression of the intent of the fair's planning can be found in Fiset (1965).

9 A plan for an underground public transport system was first proposed in the 1910s and was finally realized in the form of the metro, with the influx of federal and provincial funds tied to Expo's need for updates to Montreal's infrastructure. Construction began in 1962, the year Montreal was awarded the 1967 World's Fair and Exposition.

10 Expo's Man the Explorer and Man the Producer pavilions, designed by Affleck, Desbarats, Dimakopoulos, Lebensold, and Sise, also used a repeating form – in this case, a truncated tetrahedron.

11 My analysis of the Quebec Pavilion is indebted to the meticulous archival work of Pauline Curien's 2003 doctoral dissertation ('L'identité nationale exposée'), which makes available in its text and copious appendices a range of primary materials concerning the pavilion, including oral histories that she conducted with the major players in its design and functioning.

12 Dupuy writes (1972, 99–100) that he authorized raising the Canadian hostesses' skirts by one inch after having seen the shorter length of the British hostesses' skirts. On girlwatching, see Wallace (2005) and Sauers (2004). In

1967 the Bob Crewe Generation put out an album called 'Music to Watch Girls By'; and the following year, the O'Kaysions had a hit with their beach-pop song 'I'm a Girl-Watcher.' Thanks to Naomi Levine for these references.

13 Hochschild's treatise is centrally concerned with the emotional labourer's alienation from her own emotions. Called upon not only to 'put on' the desired comportment, but rather to 'really feel' the desired emotions associated with that comportment, the emotional labourer risks estrangement from an accurate sense of how she feels. Significantly for our purposes, Hochschild (2003, 35–55) calls the 'put on' or 'seeming' 'surface acting,' and the 'really feeling' 'deep acting,' after Stanislavsky. As but one example of an Expo hostess deploying the 'deep feeling' acting as part of her job, I offer the remarks of Diana Bruno, an Expo hostess interviewed by the *Gazette* on the occasion of the fortieth anniversary of Expo 67. She recalls the most important lesson she learned as a hostess at the fair: 'I may answer the same question 1 million times but for the visitor, it's his first time asking it. And I should treat each person as special. I should be 100-per-cent on and friendly' (Whittaker 2007, n.p.).

14 Pierre Dupuy (1972, 98–9), commissioner general of Expo 67, describes the goals of their training in his memoir of the fair. For hostesses' descriptions of their training, see Anderson (1967a) and *Expo 67: Back to the Future* (2004).

15 Indeed, the hostesses' working conditions were not unlike those of the Delta airlines flight attendants Hochschild describes. For instance, a hostess at the Greece Pavilion, Paula Sperdakos, told me that like other service-sector employees, notably sales staff, hostesses there were not allowed to sit down, even when no visitors were present.

16 My thanks to Kirsty Johnston for pushing me on this point.

4 National Reflection: Michel Tremblay's
Les belles-sœurs and *le nouveau théâtre québécois*

1 In addition to occupying pride of place in Bélair's account of the new Quebec theatre in *Le nouveau théâtre québécois* (1973), *Les belles-sœurs* is singled out in Jacques Cotnam's *Le Théâtre Québécois* (1976) as an expressly political Québécois theatre; similarly, in *Théâtre Québécois I* (1970), Université de Montréal literary scholars and dramatic critics Jean-Cléo Godin and Laurent Mailhot present its opening night as one of the originary dates of Québécois theatre. Tremblay is, moreover, the only playwright to be studied in both volumes of Godin and Mailhot's *Théâtre Québécois* (vol. 2, 1980). English-language studies concerning Québécois theatre tend to emphasize

Tremblay's foundational role even more. For instance, in *French Canadian Theatre* (1989) Jonathan Weiss argues that *Les belles-sœurs*'s 'miroir effrayant' signals the end of colonial theatre and the beginning of Québécois theatre; and Jane Moss ('Quebecois Theatre' 1996b) calls Tremblay 'the spark that ignited the theatrical revolution in Quebec.'

2 All subsequent references to the play are to this edition; the page numbers will be given in the text.

3 A number of critics have parsed this final image of the play and Germaine's 'pulling herself together' to sing the Canadian national anthem as yet another symbol of her false-consciousness with relation to her own best interests. See, e.g., Juéry (1978) and Killick (2006).

4 Articles appeared in all of the daily Montreal newspapers, in Québécois and Canadian theatre and literature reviews (*Études françaises, La Scène au Canada, Canadian Theatre Review, Livres et auteurs canadiens*), cultural journals (*Relations, Perspectives, Voix et images du pays*), popular magazines (*Le Magazine Maclean, Allô Police, Sept Jours*), and activist political reviews including *Action, Action Nationale, Chroniques* (Camerlain and Lavoie 1982, 226ff).

5 This reflection hypothesis infiltrates most critical studies of *Les belles-sœurs*, as evidenced in their homologies of theatre and society via the trope of 'development.' For example, in *French Canadian Theatre*, Jonathan Weiss (1989) recapitulates this history of theatre in Quebec. His progress narrative begins with Jesuit-led troupes of French settlers, educating the artistic tastes of the *habitants*. It continues through the nineteenth- and early twentieth-century tradition of imported theatre, generally from France or the United States. Weiss notes some advancements towards a national theatre with the appearance of Gélinas's French-Canadian characters on the burlesque stage. Gélinas's efforts resulted in a yearly vaudeville review of French-Canadian types called *Les Fridolinades* and what has been called the founding play of Québécois theatre, *Tit-Coq* (first performed in 1948). Marcel Dubé's psychological realist texts of the 1950s and 1960s pick up the gauntlet thrown down by Gélinas. But it is Michel Tremblay's 'miroir effrayant' of *Les belles-sœurs* that signals the end of colonial theatre for Weiss. Tremblay's major contribution to the national cause, in this narrative, is his inspiration for a new school of national and theatrical realism. This is not to say that this narrative is not accurate in many ways concerning the history of theatre in Quebec. That this progress narrative is repeated so frequently in the scholarship is testament not only to the persuasiveness of its contours, but also to its widespread academic acceptance. Rather, it is simply to say that tying the theatre's development to the development of the state limits the scope of theatrical activity to reflection.

6 Radio-Canada's *Première chaîne* summer morning radio broadcast, 'Pour la suite des choses,' hosted by Patrick Masbourian in the summer of 2006, played wittily on the frequent recurrence of a limited pool of first and last names in Quebec with its Friday series, 'Deux pour un' (Two for One). In this segment, Masbourian would interview two people of very different persuasions who shared the same first and last names.

7 The theatrical and editorial pages of *La Presse* would host a series of these '*crises de joual*' (joual crises): first, during the summer and fall of 1968; second, upon the opening of Tremblay's dark family tragedy *À toi pour toujours, ta Marie-Lou* in the spring of 1971; and then again, in the spring of 1973, coincident with the production of his transvestite tragedy *Hosanna*.

8 *Les belles-sœurs* would not travel to Paris until the following season, where it found an enthusiastic audience ('L'affaire des "Belles-Sœurs"' 1972; Dassylva 1972; Berthiaume 1972). Tremblay was already familiar with this kind of rejection; in 1965, the Festival d'art dramatique canadien refused his *Les belles-sœurs* because of its language (Robert 1991, 115).

9 Pierre Maheu's 'Œdipe colonial' (1964) pinpoints the origin of Quebec's national subjugation and individual alienation in the conquest of the French by the British in 1759, which forced Lower Canada into a federal system run predominantly by anglophone Canadians in Upper Canada. This usurpation of French Canada's sovereignty not only establishes the relations of dominance and submission for the following 200 years, but, as Pierre Lefebvre's and Paul Chamberland's contributions argue, it also permanently scars the Québécois psyche, marking it as defeatist (Lefebvre 1964, 14–16; Chamberland 1963).

10 *Parti pris*'s publishing house put out Jacques Renaud's joual novel, *Le Cassé*, in 1964. Robert Major reports that Renaud 'confided that the *joual* came to him from researching adequating speech and social reality and that he trained himself to write in that way in reaction to the "spittoon of falsehood"' (R. Major 1979, 64).

11 For examples of interpreting *Les belles-sœurs* as marginal, see Usmiani (1979a) and Rocheleau (1995). This metaphorical reading also enables the play's cross-cultural uptake; it has had successful runs in Scots and Yiddish translation, for instance, which capitalize on a perceived shared marginality (Harvie 1995).

12 To be clear, Tremblay's utilization of the transvestite did not display the same homophobia as that in *Parti pris*. Schwartzwald recounts (1991, 180): 'When asked why there were no male characters in his plays, Tremblay responded "Because there are no men in Quebec," and this is perhaps the provocation to which many a revolutionary nationalist, but not Tremblay

himself, felt compelled to respond.' For Tremblay, his transvestite characters – be they *belles-sœurs* or male homosexuals – symbolized Quebec's
marginality, certainly, but also its specificity, its distinction from the rest of
Canada. However, Tremblay's intentions did not necessarily guide critical
interpretation, and his early comments about *Les belles-sœurs* did not oppose
readings of the good sisters as distorted self-images of *les Québécois* (male
gender implied).

13 Thanks to Derek Nystrom for this insight.

5 National Simulation: Marco Micone's *culture immigrée*

1 For instance, Sherry Simon's edited volume, *Fictions de l'identitaire au Québec*
(1991b), grew out of the Concordia University French Department's research group, 'L'Identitaire et l'hétérogène dans la prose romanesque
québécoise depuis 1940.'

2 Dates listed in the text are the dates of initial production or initial public
reading. In the instances where the texts are published, their publication
dates are given in the References. *Gens du silence* was first produced as a
reading at the Bibliothèque nationale in 1982 and was given full production
at La Licorne and at Le Théâtre de la Manufacture in 1984. The first version of *Addolorata* was produced at Le Théâtre de la Manufacture in 1983; its
second version also played at the same theatre in 1996. *Déjà l'agonie* received
its first production by Le Théâtre de la Manufacture in 1986, under the title
Bilico. The first two have been translated into English by Maurizia Binda
as *Voiceless People* and *Addolorata*; Jill MacDougall translated *Déjà l'agonie* as
Beyond the Ruins. Montreal's major regional theatre, known for its staging
of classics, Le Théâtre du Nouveau Monde (TNM), has produced most of
Micone's translations: *Six personnages en quête d'auteur* in 1992; *La Locandiera*
in 1993, which swept Quebec's theatre awards; *La mégère de Padova* in 1995;
La serva amorosa in 1997; and *L'oiseau vert* in 1998. *Les femmes de bonne humeur*
was mounted at Quebec City's Théâtre du Trident in 2000, *La veuve ruse*
was produced by Théâtre du Rideau Vert in April 2002, and his most recent
Goldoni translation, *L'imprésario de Smyrne*, opened in the spring of 2008 at
TNM. Of these translation/adaptions, *La Locandiera* and *Les femmes de bonne
humeur* have been published.

3 Interwar fascist governments were succeeded by a republican government
in 1946. Between 1946 and 1976, almost 7.5 million Italians emigrated,
approximately two-thirds of that total to elsewhere in Europe and approximately one-quarter to the Americas, predominantly the United States,
Canada, and Argentina. More than 60% of the postwar emigrants were from

the south of Italy, where unemployment and poverty were significantly more prevalent than in the northern or central regions. Almost 70% of all Italian immigration to Canada happened between 1946 and 1976 (Painchaud and Poulin 1988, 21–3). See Caccia (1988a, 7–17).

4 Part of this shift in immigration stems from improving conditions in southern Europe (see Painchaud and Poulin 1988), but more importantly, from the Quebec government's increasing control over immigration to the territory and its interest in bolstering the francophone population through selective immigration. Political scientist Michael Keating writes (1996, 105): 'By an arrangement with the federal government, [Quebec] is allowed to select a proportion of Canada's total immigration quota each year ... Selection of these immigrants is the responsibility of Quebec officials stationed in Canadian diplomatic missions, especially in French-speaking countries.'

5 With the Reorganization Act of 1875, the Council for Public Instruction was divided into Catholic and Protestant committees, which had the final word within their discrete educational systems (Magnuson 1980, 44–6). Micone's introduction to Montreal's linguistic fault-lines and their forceful impact occurred when he was turned away from the local French Catholic school in which he wished to enrol. In the all-or-nothing cultural logic of the period – which persists in the figural logic of national metaphor – if one was not francophone then one was, ipso facto, anglophone. In a recent reflection on the heterogeneity of Québécois culture, Micone pointed out that as late as the 1980s, no distinction was made between anglophones and allophone immigrants (1998/1999, 21). Although neither French- nor English-speaking, Micone, along with the generations of allophone schoolchildren before the passage of Bill 101, in 1977, was automatically shunted to the English side. He attended an English school for four years before adopting French as his vehicular language and studying Québécois literature at Loyola College and then at McGill University, where he wrote his M.A. thesis on the 1950s and 1960s dramas of Marcel Dubé. In 1998, a modification to the Law on Public Instruction rearticulated Quebec's Catholic and Protestant school boards into French and English school boards, making language, not religion, the criterion for differentiation in the public school system (Commission scolaire de Montréal 2004).

6 Micone has recounted the story of his education in countless interviews. His educational experiences in Quebec inform his critical reflections on integration policy in 'Immigrant Culture: The Identity of the Voiceless People' (1990a, 55–64) and 'De l'assimilation à la culture immigrée' (1990b, 151–60). He reprises his schoolboy experiences in *Le figuier enchanté* and fictionalizes them in 'Ces enfants d'ailleurs ...' (1979b, 4–20).

7 Throughout *Gens du silence*, Mario uses English for effect: his English-language sentences are littered with 'fuck' and 'Christ.' English also indicates affect: English-language sentences are frequently punctuated by exclamation points. He further associates English with the excitement of his Trans-Am and the freedom its speed and mobility connote: 'RICKY: *Fuck! What a beauty! Where are we going, Mario?* MARIO: *Anywhere, Christ! As long as we get out of here*' (Micone 1996c, 61).

8 In her translation quoted here, Binda elaborates somewhat on Micone's words. A literal translation of the last sentence in the quoted passage would read something like this: 'It's only by writing in French that you will have a chance of being understood and respected for what you are' (my translation).

9 In English-language Québécois theatre, David Fennario pioneered this same subject position in the 1970s in plays like *Balconville, On the Job,* and *Nothing to Lose.* Vittorio Rossi extends this dramatic depiction of anglophone Italo-Québécois in plays such as *Little Blood Brother, The Chain,* and *Scarpone* (Reid 2000, 177–94).

10 Micone further pries apart the presumed coincidence of language and national territory by introducing neologisms to the Quebec lexicon and through his translations of Italian dramatic classics. In *Le figuier enchanté*, for instance, Micone substitutes the Italianism *névasse* (drawn from the Italian *nevaccia*) for the common anglicism *sloche* (from slush) (14). In his translation of Goldoni's *La Locandiera*, Micone rewrote the asides in Italian with words that shared linguistic roots with words in French. As a result, the predominantly francophone Théâtre du Nouveau Monde audience was able to understand much of the asides' meaning at the same time that they were being spoken in an 'other' tongue. Micone discusses these strategies at length in S. Lévesque (1994, 17–30).

11 It has since been read as part of Radio-Canada's series 'Littératures actuelles' in 1991, reprinted as part of Micone's *Le Devoir* editorial entitled 'Speak What,' published by *Québec français* and the Quebec Ministry of Education, rendered in poster form by *Écrits des Forges* in 1992, and published in book form with a critical introduction by Lise Gauvin from VLB Éditeur as *Speak What.* The orthography of Micone's poem's title varies; in the body of the text, I shall follow that used in Micone 2001. In the notes, I shall follow the orthography of the version I am citing.

12 For 'text poélitique,' see Micone 'Le palimpseste' (1996b, 21). On Quebec's manifesto tradition, see J. Demers (1997, 25–9).

13 Quebec's declining birthrate since the late nineteenth century has reduced the percentage of the Quebec population vis-à-vis that of Canada as a whole

from 33.1% in 1871 to 25.4% in 1991. If Quebec wishes to maintain its relative weight vis-à-vis the rest of Canada, in terms of parliamentary representation and ideological clout, immigration is a necessity (Lacroix 1996, 169).
With neo-Québécois fully participating in the public life of French Quebec,
their numbers would ensure the perpetuation of French Quebec vis-à-vis
English Canada.

14 It was chanted at rallies militating for a French McGill University as well
as during the *Crise d'octobre* when the federal government imposed the
War Measures Act in Quebec, as a response to the Front de libération du
Québec's terrorist violence. Lalonde discusses these and other uptakes,
which she experienced as out of her control, with palpable bitterness in a
1999 interview with *Le Devoir* reporter, Manon Cornellier.

15 The transcultural project was most fully elaborated in the trilingual revue,
Vice versa, founded by Tassinari, Caccia, and Antonio D'Alfonso, published
from 1983 to 1994. For more on transculturalism, see Caucci (1992/1993)
and Verdicchio (1997).

16 The Front de libération du Québec (FLQ), founded in 1963, was a group of
left-wing activists that espoused violence as the means to achieving Quebec's
independence. Their activities included bank robberies, bombings, and
kidnappings generally targeting federal government institutions (like the
army), English-owned businesses, and engines of capital (like the Montreal
Stock Exchange). The 1968 'Poèmes et chants de la résistance' raised money for the legal defence of Charles Gagnon and Pierre Vallières, imprisoned
in New York City pending their trial for manslaughter.

17 All further references to the poem will appear in end-of-line citations.

18 For earlier considerations of the question, see Dorsinville (1974). Haitian-
born Québécois writer Gérard Étienne has produced an 'anthroposemi-
ological' accounting of representations of race in the Québécois novel
La question raciale et raciste dans le roman québécois: Essai d'anthroposémiologie
(1995).

19 Montreal attracts about 90% of Quebec's immigrant population. In 1989,
50% of immigrants to Quebec came from Asia, mostly Hong Kong and Vietnam; 8.2% of that year's immigrants hailed from Africa, largely northern
African countries like Morocco. The most significant influx of people of
African descent came from Haiti, which since 1977 has been the privileged
source-country, along with Vietnam, for Quebec immigration (Lacroix
1996, 174). According to Citizenship and Immigration Canada (2005),
25,430 Haitians immigrated to Quebec between 1986 and 2001 (of whom
83% lived in Montreal in 2001). Another 24,020 Haitians immigrated to
Quebec (again settling largely in Montreal) before 1986.

20 All subsequent citations will appear in the body of the text.
21 Following Alan Filewod's argument about national simulation in the English Canadian context (2002), Micone's simulations may also be read as exposing *as simulation* the notion of Québécois authenticity. With Micone, Québécois 'de souche' is revealed to be as much an *immigré* identity as that of the *néo-Québécois* with respect to Aboriginal peoples.
22 Even if they cannot reproduce themselves as unhyphenated Québécois, neo-Québécois nonetheless provide a kind of surrogate reproductive service for Québécois. With the fall of Québécois reproduction rates, neo-Québécois' presence, comparatively higher birthrate, and overwhelming *francisation* augments Quebec's French-speaking population, keeping Quebec as home to around 25% of Canada's population.
23 I thank Naomi Levine for pushing me on this point and for helping me formulate its terms.
24 For fuller elaboration of his argument and its potential, see Harel's four articles in *Liberté* (2004a, 2004b, 2005a, and 2005b). See also Mauricio Gatti's work (2004 and 2006) on Amerindian writers of Quebec.

6 National Metonymy: Arresting Images in the Devised Works of Carbone 14

1 The province-wide referendum took place on 20 May 1980. The Parti québécois's proposal to negotiate secession from Canada with the federal government on the behalf of Québécois was defeated by a 59.56% to 40.44% margin at the polls.
2 To date, little work has been done on solo performance in Quebec, notwithstanding Badir's article and a few scattered considerations of Pol Pelletier's three-play cycle of solos, whose work I also take up in the conclusion to this book. However, Gilbert David has a very promising research project underway, 'Formes et discours des spectacles en solo au Québec, 1980–2005,' from which we can expect important documentary coverage and analytical insights.
3 With 'visible grammar,' I am drawing on Sandra L. Bermann's analysis (1988, 22) of Petrarch's figural highlighting. I thank Naomi Levine for bringing this source to my attention.
4 Carbone 14's aesthetic goals also reflect Maheu's training as a mime with Étienne Decroux and Yves Lebreton, and his work with Eugenio Barba, all of whom elaborate the autonomous and distinct language(s) of the body.
5 Although 'image theatre' aptly describes Carbone 14 productions, Lévesque's reference to Bausch points to where Maheu's image-theatre

crosses with *la nouvelle danse* or *la danse-théâtre*. This concert dance style, developed in the 1980s, is known for its inventive choreography and imagery, its high-risk, often athletic physicality, its deeply personal themes, and its structural theatricality (Tembeck 1992, 231). Funnily, at the moment when theatre was divesting itself of text and voice, *la nouvelle danse* was appropriating them. Commenting on the crossover trend, André G. Bourassa writes: 'If dance and mime steal the text from the theatre and attribute more than ever an actantial function to the object ... the theatre steals from dance and mime the exclusivity of body language for "phrases," even entire scenes' (1985, 76). Some of *la nouvelle danse*'s most innovative and familiar proponents are the two Québécois companies I mentioned in chapter 1: Édouard Locke's La La La Human Steps and Ginette Laurin's Ô Vertigo Danse.

6 A notable exception to this rule is the young, francophone couple in *Les Âmes mortes* who spend most of their stage-time chasing each other through the doors. In *Le Dortoir*, the narrator who opens the piece and the nun who rules the dormitory's inhabitants make visible entrances and exits. The students, however, are in place from the beginning.

7 Artaud's influence on this project is evident and, indeed, readily acknowledged by Maheu. In his detailed performance analysis of *Pain blanc*, Gilbert David takes Artaud's precept, 'The actor is an athlete of the heart,' as his starting point. He situates Carbone 14 in 'a current of contemporary occidental theatre [that] has effectively looked for the "other stage" in the body's expressivity; battling against servitude to the (literary) text and to psychology, denouncing naturalist imitation, this "theatre of images," "body language," ("hieroglyphics" according to Artaud), most frequently presupposes a metaphysical, a-historical, not to say sacred, conception of the real' (1983, 90).

8 Thanks again to Naomi Levine for this language.

9 My sense of metonymy encompasses synecdoche, as per the *New Princeton Encyclopedia of Poetry and Poetics*.

10 This was, in fact, the second 'conscription crisis' in Quebec history. Conscription had been imposed on Quebec in 1917 and the army intervened to force the Québécois conscripts to go to war. Adding to Québécois frustration over conscription was the fact that 'the army was a means of Anglicizing Quebecers [*sic*], and Francophone Quebecers [*sic*] were the first to be sent to the front lines during the war' (Richard Desrosiers, quoted in Gougeon 1994, 76–7). In dramatic literature, the conscription crisis is also referenced in *Tit-Coq*, by Gratien Gélinas.

11 A 'cabane à sucre' is a cabin situated in or near a maple forest used to distil

sap from maple trees into maple syrup and maple sugar ('sugar shack,' in English). The action of 'sugaring off' the maple trees (drawing out their sap) is a season unto itself in Quebec, opened by the first day the sap runs in the maple trees.

12 *Le Dortoir*'s scenes of sexual experimentation involve dancers disrobing; *L'Homme rouge*, Maheu's one-man show, featured Maheu in black briefs; the contemporary, young couple in *Les Âmes mortes* are completely naked when they simulate sex, and the Edwardian women dance a sequence topless; etc.

13 Because Foster's and my uses of the word 'reflection' signify different relations to the world – hers signals a (self-reflexive) retreat from the world and mine signals a mirroring relationship to the world – I will use her definition of 'reflection' in this chapter but call it 'reflexion.'

14 Maheu speaks of his attraction to the new dance in Perelli-Contos and Hébert (1994, 67–70) and is interviewed as one of its choreographers in the *Jeu* special issue on *la danse-théâtre* (Lefebvre and Marleau 1984). In movement sequences like the ice-breaking one, Maheu choreographs in the tradition of postmodern choreographers like Yvonne Rainer or Merce Cunningham, who created dances by reframing pedestrian physical activity like walking or running.

15 More recently, Ann Cooper Albright has written of dance's ephemeral nature: 'Based on the motion of live bodies, the dancing "text" is singularly elusive' (1995, 159). Siegel (1988) critiques Susan Leigh Foster's *Reading Dancing* as a failed attempt at making a fundamentally visceral and cagey art form 'readable.' There is another critical tradition, spearheaded by Mark Franko's work (1993), which understands choreography as precisely a bodily technology of writing.

16 Inuktitut is the primary spoken and written language of Canada's Inuit population. The Nunavut government uses it, Inuinnaqtun, English, and French in its literature. Nunavut is the Inuit territory of 350,000 square kilometres of land in the eastern Arctic established in April 1998. Nunavut, which means 'our land,' represents the settlement of the largest land claims agreement negotiated in Canadian history ('Nunavut Kavamanga').

17 In the original production, it was a woman who entered the dormitory; she wrote on the blackboard, 'Jean a avalé la pillule amère.' See MacDougall (1991) and Lavoie (1989) for two academic-journal reviews of the original production.

18 I should mention here that two of the most striking bed-related images in *Le Dortoir* are themselves recycled from earlier Carbone 14 choreography. The dreamy bed-dance reworks *L'Homme rouge*'s solo *adagio* with a similar, twin-sized, iron bed of utilitarian design; the whirl-around sequence made

its first appearance using a wind-machine in *Peau, chair et os* (Skin, flesh, and bone) (1991).

7 National Affection: Céline Dion

1 According to Lawrence Grossberg, pop music's 'authentic' counterpoint is rock and roll. He writes, '"Inauthentic rock" is "establishment culture," rock that is dominated by economic interest, rock that has lost its political edge, bubblegum music, etc. "Authentic rock" depends on its ability to articulate private but common desires, feelings and experiences into a shared public language. It demands that the performer have a real relationship to his or her audience – based on their common experiences defined in terms of youth and a postmodern sensibility rather than class, race, etc.—and to their music – which must somehow "express" and transcend that experience. It constructs or "expresses" a "community" predicated on images of urban mobility, delinquency and bohemian life' (1992b, 206–7).

2 This cosmopolitan understanding of *québécité* may also be read in Dion's music videos. Her early videos feature her in a story, sometimes in fairy-tale-like fashion. Later videos focus almost exclusively on her, often in close-up, to the exclusion of visual story. Increasingly polished and decontextualized, more recent videos like 'If Walls Could Talk' depict the singer alone in a room that could be anywhere in the West.

3 The *accent aigu* over the *e* in 'Céline' was removed from English-language albums, starting with *Unison* in 1990. Of her eleven French-language albums, six retain the accent, three print her name entirely in capital letters and without the accent, one drops the accent but retains the usual orthography (*Celine: au coeur de stade*), and one uses only her last name in the title, thereby avoiding the issue (*Dion chante Plamondon*).

4 Thank you to Sara Warner for this reference and for our ongoing conversations on affect and performance.

5 This temporal lag between affect and qualification – 'the skin is faster than the word,' writes Massumi (2002, 25) – is so tiny (Massumi cites research putting it at about a half-second), it is barely if at all registered on the part of the sentient being adapting to its environment. For this reason, because affect is an event that that 'happens too quickly to have happened, actually,' it is *virtual*. In that virtual half-second lag, which has yet to qualify or determine a pathway of action and expression in relation to the environment (which might be external or internal to the body), Massumi finds the political potential of affect. Massumi's work represents one influential strand of 'the affective turn' in the humanities. For a more detailed parsing of 'affect'

and its kin (notably 'emotion') in relation to theatre and performance, see Ridout (2007) and Hurley (2010).

6 See, for instance, the largely cognitive approaches in Hjört and Laver (1997); Nussbaum's philosophical treatise linking emotion to ethical judgment (2001); in political science, Marcus (2002), which argues for emotion's centrality to rational democratic processes; and Edelman (1996).

7 Massumi gets to affect through Deleuze's exegesis of Spinoza's monist philosophy; Sedgwick follows the work of psychologist Silvan Tomkins (and as a response to Lacan's influence on post-structuralist theory in the humanities); Altieri pursues his inquiry largely via philosophy.

8 A brief note on method: The seventeen-question survey (of which six were demographic questions) was conducted in both English and French; respondents could choose the language in which they wished to take the poll. I solicited Québécois respondents specifically and left it to the respondents to self-identify. In other words, I did not furnish the definition of Québécois. I distributed the invitation to participate in the survey on academic and cultural list-servs, on Dion-related websites and bulletin boards, and on posters hung at musical outlets around Montreal and university campuses. It was also posted on my personal and departmental web-pages. I received ninety French-language responses and sixty-one English-language responses, for a total of 151. I do not interpret the survey results as quantitatively significant. My intention in executing the survey was to gather some qualitative data with some representative or indicative value. It is in that spirit that I use the survey responses here.

9 Straw is writing here about Montreal's disco scene of the 1970s. For a fuller elaboration of what he intends by 'scene,' see Straw (2004). For the classic statement on fans' production of alternate listening communities, see Hebdige (1979).

10 In his article on Russia's new national anthem, J. Martin Daughtry relates and applies Malcolm Boyd's categorization of national anthems: 'Malcolm Boyd (2003, 44) singles out two compositions as providing the generic foundation for the majority of the world's anthems: '"God Save the King/ Queen" (anthem-as-hymn model; "stately rhythmic tread and smooth melodic movement") and the "Marsellaise" (anthem-as-march model; a "rousing martial piece").'

11 This count is based on documentation by Beauregard (2002).

12 As of 1 July 1990, 'at least 65% of the vocal music played weekly by all Francophone AM and FM radio stations [in Canada], irrespective of format or market, must be French-language songs' by Canadian Radio-Television and Telecommunications Commission (CRTC) regulation (Grenier 1993, 119).

Anecdotal evidence gathered from Dion-related online chat rooms and bulletin boards also supports this contention; her U.S. fans complain that her
new music isn't played as frequently there as it is north of the 49th parallel.

13 Thirty-four per cent make music-purchasing decisions based on what they
have heard on the radio. Rap, hip-hop, and worldbeat are increasingly
popular in Quebec, according to data analysed by Pronovost (2005, 46). It
is these sounds, among others, that stand out against the tonic note of Quebec pop; they must also be read with it.

14 However, TeamCeline's male membership, while smaller in total, exceeds
female membership in this same 35-to-over-55 age range; 74% of male members are in that category, whereas 72% of female members place themselves
in that age range. Because of the way in which the data were presented to
me, in a 19 September 2005 letter from Jacky Magee of Feeling Productions, I have no way of correlating these statistics with her Québécois or
even Canadian membership. (Canadians comprise 11% of 'TeamCeline''s
total membership.)

15 According to the survey responses, negative affect vis-à-vis Céline separates
francophone from anglophone Québécois. Of the 90 French-language
responses to the poll, not one used the noun 'haine,' nor the verb 'haïr,'
although one indicated his 'repulsion.' Positive responses – ranging from
'respect' (7 responses) through 'admiration' (25), to 'fierté' (11), a tie
of kinship ('affection relative,' 6), to finally 'amour' and 'passion' (12) –
eclipse the responses with negative valence by a ratio of 3:1. The bulk of the
negative responses can be qualified as a combination of irritation (e.g., 4
'énnervemment,' 2 'agacement') and shame (e.g., 4 'honte,' 1 'embarras,' 1
'dédain'). On the other hand, the majority of the 61 English-language responses are negative, ranging from feelings of embarrassment (2) to irritation (9) to nausea (10) to hatred expressed in fantasies of sexually violating
and killing Dion (2).

16 See the Desjardins article (2005) and its 45 responses. Interestingly, the
journalist's wrath is reserved largely for what he perceives as the leftist
Québécois press's efforts at using her outburst as an opportunity to express
anti-American sentiments (this is the 'indecency' of the title). However, a
significant number of the responses focus their energies (positive or negative) on Dion herself, not her action's uptake in the media.

17 For instance, Roch Voisine, an Acadian-Québécois pop singer boasts a career path similar to, though not on the same scale as Dion's, without the
same kind of backlash. He records in French and English, performs in Las
Vegas, collaborates with David Foster, and has been made an Officer of the
Order of Canada.

18 All of survey respondents save one said 'Céline' is *Québécoise*. The industry, too, counts her music as *chanson québécoise*, as evidenced in her almost yearly nominations for the annual awards of l'Association québécoise de l'industrie de disque, du spectacle et de la video (ADISQ). In 2006, for instance, she was nominated in two categories ('chanson populaire de l'année' and 'interprète feminine de l'année'). She did not win in either category.

19 French songwriter Eddy Marnay penned most, when not all, of the songs for the following albums: *La Voix du Bon Dieu* (1981); *Tellement j'ai d'amour ...* (1982); *Les Chemins de ma maison* (1983); *Mélanie* (1984); and *C'est pour toi* (1985). Marnay also contributed several songs to *Incognito* (1987), his last collaboration with Dion. Luc Plamondon wrote several songs for *Incognito* and all the songs on *Dion chante Plamondon* (1991). French singer-songwriter Jean-Jacques Goldman penned *D'Eux* (1995) and *S'il suffisait d'aimer* (1998). Goldman, Gildas Arzel, Erick Benzi, and Jacques Veneruso wrote the songs on *1 fille + 4 types* (2003); the songs on *D'Elles* (2007) were written by French and Québécois women writers and set to music by Goldman.

20 On Québécois' 'Latin blood,' see Handler (1988, esp. 37–9). It should be pointed out that if Quebec's demands are excessive, English Canada's response to them is equally so and generally comes in the form of angry, self-righteous questions like 'What do they want?!'

8 Conclusion: Feminist (Re)production

1 Josette Féral clarifies the use of the term 'théâtre institutionnel' in Quebec as follows (2007, 21): 'they are called such in Quebec because they are the oldest and the most financed by the State. These theatres do not yet have the historical weight of certain large, European, even older theatrical institutions. Moreover, national theatres in the European sense do not exist in Quebec.' Here, she builds upon Gilbert David's typology of Quebec's theatre venues; he adds that institutional theatres also benefit from the greatest critical legitimacy (1994).

2 Gauvreau (1925–1971), an automatiste playwright and poet, is best known for *La charge de l'orignal épormyable* (1956) and *Les oranges sont vertes* (1971).

3 In fact, in a subsequent Tremblay play featuring Carmen, *Saint Carmen de la Main* (1976), Carmen's family name is replaced by the name of the street, signifying her identification with the street and all it represents.

4 As influential as Bélair's interpretations of Tremblay's early work were, Lucie Robert (1993), among others, has contested his optimistic reading of Pierrette and Carmen's futurity.

5 Readers may be understandably wary of such seemingly essentialist, because biological, notions of the female. Gould cautions, however, against such a stance (1990, 47–8): 'a closer look suggests that the theoretical considerations underlying these inscriptions of the female body are as firmly rooted in political analyses of the various forms of women's oppression as they are in some of the more essentialist paradigms of biological difference.'

6 Most recently, perhaps, Yves Jubinville, in his otherwise exemplary article on the authorial function and its redistribution among different theatre workers (dramatist, scenographer, director, actor, etc.) in modern Quebec theatre, notes in passing the 'heritage' feminist theatrical production might have left to notions of author. Their particular contributions are not, however, examined in this text; rather, they 'remain to be understood' (2009).

7 Where published texts for these plays exist, I list them in the References. Unfortunately, not all made it to print. For a more ample chronology of this period see Moss (1985), Pelletier (1979), Noël (1980), and Boyer (1988).

8 See, for instance, Jean-Marc Larrue's history of collective creation in Quebec from 1965 to 1985, 'La création collective au Québec' (2001).

9 In her exposé of the conditions of women's authorship, *La Terre est trop courte, Violette Leduc*, Marchessault surrounds the eponymous woman writer with sympathetic readers including Simone de Beauvoir, Clara Malraux, and Nathalie Sarraute. Women writers, in turn, must work to change the interpretive contexts in which and according to whose conditions women's words will be read. Marchessault's own contribution to this effort is revealed in the proliferation of 'paratexts' around her creative works of drama and fiction (Forsyth 1991). Her play, *La saga des poules mouillées*, for instance, directed by Pelletier for her collective le Théâtre expérimental des femmes is preceded by a foreword by Marchessault and a series of letters between Marchessault and American literary critic Gloria Orenstein. Revealing something of her creative process and more of her catalysts to write, these prefaces help to set the terms for entering the world of the play; they reset 'all that is pertinent to understanding an experience and the enunciation of that experience' (235). *Tryptique lesbien*, in which *Les Vaches de nuit* appears, is preceded by a drawing by Marchessault of a 'femme tellurique porteuse d'espérance' (telluric woman bearing hopefulness) and followed by an interpretive postface by Gloria Feman Orenstein.

References

Abrams, M.H. 1981. 'Metaphor.' In *A Glossary of Literary Terms*, 4th ed. New York: Holt, Rinehart, and Winston.

Ahmed, Sara. 2004. *The Cultural Politics of Emotion*. Edinburgh: Edinburgh University Press.

Aird, Robert. 2008. 'De Coutlée au stand up comique. L'évolution du monologue québécois, de 1900 à nos jours.' *Globe: Revue internationale d'études québécoises* 11(2): 23–41.

Albright, Ann Cooper. 1995. 'Incalculable Choreographies.' In Goellner and Murphy, 157–81.

Allwood, John. 1977. *The Great Exhibitions*. London and Toronto: Studio Vista.

Altieri, Charles. 2004. *The Particulars of Rapture*. Ithaca: Cornell University Press.

Anderson, John. 1967a. 'Matinee with Pat Patterson.' *CBC Radio*. (28 April). MPEG http://archives.cbc.ca/IDCC-1-69-100-550/life_society/expo_67/ (accessed 3 March 2007).

– 1967b. 'Hostesses with the Mostesses.' Matinee with Pat Patterson. *CBC Radio*. (28 April). MPEG http://archives.cbc.ca/programs/484/ (accessed 1 June 2009).

Andrès, Bernard, and Pascal Riendeau. 1997. 'La dramaturgie depuis 1980.' In *Panorama de la littérature québécoise contemporaine*, ed. Réginald Hamel, 208–39. Montreal: Guérin.

antiGUY. 1999. 'Top Five List of Uses for Céline Dion CDs.' AntiMUSIC Website. http://www.antimusic.com/top5/1999/aug/weektwo.shtml (accessed 19 Oct. 2006).

Arbic, Thérèse. 1975. 'Le théâtre de Michel Tremblay et la dégradation de la personne humaine en milieu ouvrier.' *Chroniques* 1 (Jan.): 54–7.

– 1976. 'Entrevue avec André Brassard et Michel Tremblay.' *Chroniques* 22 (Oct.): 14–31.

Arès, Richard, S.J. 1969. 'L'immigration et l'avenir du français au Québec.' *Action Nationale* 59 (Nov.): 209–27.

Badir, Patricia. 1992. 'Playing Solitaire: Spectatorship and Representation in Canadian Women's Monodrama.' *Theatre Research in Canada / Recherches théâtrales au Canada* 13(1–2): 120–33.

Balibar, Etienne. 1991. 'The Nation Form.' In *Race, Nation, Class: Ambiguous Identities,* ed. Etienne Balibar and Immanuel Wallerstein; trans. Chris Turner, 86–106. London and New York: Verso.

Balthazar, Louis. 1987. 'Québec Nationalism: After Twenty-Five Years.' *Québec Studies* 5: 29–38.

Banes, Sally. 1987. *Terpsichore in Sneakers: Post-Modern Dance.* Middletown, CT: Wesleyan University Press.

Baribeau, Jean-Serge. 2003. 'Rêves d'apothéose stellaire et machines à "starlettiser-starifier."' *Prisme* 41: 116–30.

Barish, Jonas. 1981. *The Antitheatrical Prejudice.* Berkeley: University of California Press.

Barthes, Roland. 1977. 'Musica practica.' In *Image, Music, Text,* trans. Stephen Heath, 149–54. New York: Hill and Wang.

Basile, Jean. 1972. 'Une Entreprise familiale de démolition.' In Tremblay, 135–8.

Baudrillard, Jean. 1983. *Simulations,* trans. Paul Foss, Paul Patton, and Philip Beitchman. New York: Semiotext(e).

Bauman, Richard. 1989. 'Performance.' In *International Encyclopedia of Communications,* ed. Eric Barnouw, 262–6. New York: Oxford.

Beauchamp, Hélène. 2003. 'Les théâtres. Lieux de représentation et lieux de création théâtrale au XXe siècle.' In Beauchamp and David, 33–58.

– 2005. *Les Théâtres de création, au Québec, en Acadie et au Canada français.* With Yves Raymond. Montreal: VLB.

– and Gilbert David, eds. 2003. *Théâtre québécois et canadiens-français au XXe siècle.* Ste-Foy: Presses de l'Université du Québec.

Beauchemin, Malorie and Tristan Péloquin. 'Les déclarations de Michel Tremblay font des vagues.' 2006. *La Presse,* 11 April, A13.

Beaunoyer, Jean. 1988. 'Carbone 14 de retour au bercail.' *La Presse,* 3 Dec., D5.

Beauregard, Sylvain. 2002. *Passion Céline Dion, The Book: The Ultimate Reference for the Fan.* Victoria: Trafford.

Bélair, Michel. 1971. '*À toi, pour toujours, ta Marie-Lou* ou quand Michel Trembay se permet d'espérer.' In Tremblay, 6–31.

– 1973. *Le nouveau théâtre québécois.* Ottawa: Leméac.

Benjamin, Walter. 1968. 'Unpacking My Library.' In *Illuminations,* ed. Hannah Arendt; trans. Harry Zohn, 59–67. New York: Schocken.

Bennett, Susan. 2000. 'Theatre History, Historiography and Women's Dramatic Writing.' In *Women, Theatre and Performance: New Histories, New Historiographies*, ed. Maggie B. Gale and Viv Gardner, 46–59. Manchester: Manchester University Press.

Bergeron, Léandre. 1980. *Dictionnaire de la langue québécoise*. Montreal: VLB.

Berland, Jody. 1998. 'Locating Listening: Technological Space, Popular Music and Canadian Mediations.' In *The Place of Music*, ed. Andrew Leyshon, David Matless, and George Revill, 129–50. New York and London: Guilford.

Bermann, Sandra L. 1988. *The Sonnet over Time: A Study in the Sonnets of Petrarch, Shakespeare, and Baudelaire*. Chapel Hill: University of North Carolina Press.

Berthiaume, Christiane. 1972. '"*Les belles-soeurs*" ne peuvent répondre à l'invitation de Paris (Michel Tremblay: "On passe pour des fous!").' *Dimanche-Matin*, 9 April, 49.

Berton, Pierre. 1970. *The Great Railway, 1871–1881*. Toronto: McClelland and Stewart.

Billig, Michael. 1995. *Banal Nationalism*. London: Sage.

Billy, Hélène de. 2004. 'Du rêve à la téléréalité.' *Sélection du Reader's Digest* 687 (Sept.): 42–9.

Birley, Shane. 2005. 'Live 8: Celine Dion, You Need Some Work.' (12:46 p.m., 2 July). http://www.shanesworld.ca/live_8_celine_dion (accessed 9 July 2005).

Blackburn, Marthe, Marie-Claire Blais, Nicole Brossard, Odette Gagnon, Luce Guilbeault, Pol Pelletier, and France Théoret. 2006. *A Clash of Symbols*, trans. Linda Gaboriau. In Forsyth, ed., 287–329.

Boivin, Jean, and Patrick Hébert. 2000. 'Trois œuvres musicales québécoises marquantes, diffusées quotidiennement sur le site de l'Exposition universelle de Montréal en 1967.' *Les cahiers de la société québécoise de recherche en musique* 5: 1–2, 75–90.

Borduas, Paul-Émile. 1977. *Refus global & Projections libérantes*. Montreal: Parti pris.

Bouchard, Michel-Marc. 1987. *Les feluettes, ou, La répétition d'un drame romantique*. Montreal: Leméac.

Bourassa, André G. 1985. 'Scène québécoise: permutations de formes et de fragments en danse, mime et théâtre.' *Études littéraires* 18: 73–85.

Boyer, Ghislaine. 1988. 'Théâtre des femmes au Québec, 1975–1985.' *Canadian Literature / Littérature canadienne* 118 (Fall): 61–80.

Brisset, Annie. 1996. *A Sociocritique of Translation: Theatre and Alterity in Quebec, 1968–1988*, trans. Rosalind Gill and Roger Gannon. Toronto: University of Toronto Press.

Burger, Baudoin. 1974. *L'Activité théâtrale au Québec (1765–1825)*. Montreal: Parti pris.

Caccia, Fulvio, ed. 1998. *Interviews with the Phoenix: Interviews with Fifteen Italian-Quebecois Artists,* trans. Daniel Sloate. Toronto: Guernica.

– 1998a. 'Introduction.' In Caccia, 1998, 7–17.

– 1998b. 'Lamberto Tassinari: The Transcultural Project.' In Caccia, 1998, 211–221.

– 1998c. 'Marco Micone: The Emigrated Word.' In Caccia, 1998, 186–94.

Camerlain, Lorraine, and Pierre Lavoie. 1982. 'Études sur Tremblay et son oeuvre.' *Voix et images du pays* 7(2): 226–306.

Canning, Charlotte. 1996. *Feminist Theatres in the USA: Staging Women's Experience.* New York: Routeldge.

– 2001. '"I am a Feminist Scholar": The Performative of Feminist History.' *Theatre Research International* 26(3): 223–32.

Carel, Ivan. 2008. 'L'Expo 67 et la jeunesse.' In Monière and Comeau, 101–11.

Carle, Gilles. 1967. *Le Québec à l'heure de L'Expo.* (Videocassette). Quebec: Office du film du Québec.

Carlson, Marvin. 1989. 'The Iconic Stage.' *Journal of Dramatic Theory and Criticism* 3(2): 3–18.

Caron, Jean. 1968. '"*Les belles-soeurs*," une production de grande mérite.' *Le Soleil,* 31 Aug.; reprinted in Tremblay, 1972, 141–4.

Caucci, Frank. 1992/1993. 'Topoi de la transculture dans l'imaginaire italo-québécois.' *Québec Studies* 15 (Fall/Winter): 41–50.

'Céline Dion to Headline "One-Of-A-Kind" Theatrical Musical Spectacular At Caesars Palace.' 2001. Press release posted on the Official Celine Dion Website. (17 May). http://www.celinedion.com/anewday/english/pressreleases .cgi?id=1 (accessed 9 July 2007).

Chamberland, Paul. 1963. 'Aliénation culturelle et révolution nationale.' *Parti pris* 1–2: 10–22.

– 1964a. 'De la damnation à la liberté.' *Parti pris* 9–11: 53–80.

– 1964b. *Terre Québec.* Montreal: Librairie Déom.

– 1965. 'Dire ce que je suis.' *Parti pris* 2–5: 33–42.

Chamberlin, Anne. 1967. 'Expo 67: The Big Blast Up North.' *Saturday Evening Post* 240(8): 30–7.

Chartier, Daniel. 2002. 'Les origines de l'écriture migrante: L'immigration littéraire au Québec au cours des deux derniers siècles.' *Voix et images* 27: 304.

Chaurette, Norman. 1981. *Provincetown Playhouse, juillet 1919, j'avais 19 ans.* Montreal: Leméac.

Citizenship and Immigration Canada. 2005. 'Recent Immigrants in Metropolitan Areas: Montréal – A Comparative Profile Based on the 2001 Census.' Prepared by Strategic Research and Statistics in collaboration with Informetrica

Limited. http://www.cic.gc.ca/english/research/papers/census2001/montreal/partb.html (accessed 20 Dec. 2006).

Clarke, George Elliott. 2002. 'Liberalism and Its Discontents: Reading Black and White in Contemporary Québécois Texts.' In *Odysseys Home: Mapping African-Canadian Literature*, 163–81. Toronto: University of Toronto Press.

Clio Collective. 1978. *Quebec Women: A History*, trans. Roger Gannon and Rosalind Gill. Toronto: Women's Press.

Cloutier, Rachel, Marie Laberge, and Rodrigue Gignac. 1971. 'Entrevue avec Michel Tremblay.' *Nord* 1 (Autumn): 49–81.

Commission scolaire de Montréal. 2004. 'A propos de la CSDM.' (23 Feb.). http://www.csdm.qc.ca/CSDM/fr_a_propos.htm (accessed 13 April 2004).

Connell, John, and Chris Gibson. 2003. *Sound Tracks: Popular Music, Identity, and Place*. London and New York: Routledge.

Corbett, John. 1990. 'Free, Single and Disengaged: Listening Pleasure and the Popular Music Object.' *October* 54 (Autumn): 79–101.

Cornellier, Manon. 1999. 'Que sont-ils devenus? La vie derrière soi, Michèle Lalonde s'est presque totalement retirée de l'écriture. Mais son poème Speak White, lui, est resté.' *Le Devoir*, 5 July, B1.

Cotnam, Jacques. 1976. *Le Théâtre Québécois, instrument de contestation sociale et politique*. Études littéraires. Montreal: Éditions Fides.

Cuccioletta, Donald. 2000. '"Américanité" or Americanization in Quebec Public Opinion.' *Québec Studies* 29 (Spring/Summer): 1–53.

Curien, Pauline. 2003. 'L'identité nationale exposée. Représentations du Québec à l'Exposition universelle de Montréal 1967 (Expo 67).' Unpublished doctoral dissertation, Université Laval.

– 2008. 'Matérialisation et incarnation du grand récit du Québec moderne à l'Expo 67.' In Monière and Comeau, 93–100.

Dansereau, Jean. 1999. 'La politique linguistique du Québec: Vérités et mensonges.' *Globe: Revue internationale d'études québécoises* 2: 63–82.

Dassylva, Martial. 1969. 'L'amour du "joual" et des timbres-primes.' *La Presse*, 29 Aug.; reproduced in Tremblay, 1972, 133–5.

– 1972. 'Les "Belles-Sœurs": Protestations auprès d'Ottawa.' *La Presse*, 30 March, A16.

– 1975. *Un théâtre en effervescence: Critiques et chroniques 1965–1972*. Collection Échanges. Montreal: Éditions de La Presse.

Daughtry, Martin J. 2003. 'Russia's New Anthem and the Negotiation of National Identity.' *Ethnomusicology* 47 (Winter): 42–67.

Davey, Frank. 1983. *Surviving the Paraphrase*. Winnipeg: Turnstone.

David, Gilbert. 1983. 'Sur un théâtre traumatique, "pain blanc ou l'esthétique de la laideur" / carbone 14.' *Jeu* 28: 89–110.

– 1994. 'Une institution théâtrale à l'ombre des mass-médias.' *Théâtre/Public* 117 (Feb.): 10–15.

– 2008. 'Chassé-croisé autour du Canon québécois: une dramaturgie nationale à l'épreuve de palmarès.' Paper presented at the conference 'Le théâtre de répertoire: lieu de mémoire, lieu de création,' Société québécoise d'études théâtrales. Montreal, 30 May.

– and Pierre Lavoie. 1993. 'Introduction. Une écriture québécoise inattendue.' In Gilbert and Lavoie, ed., 7–21.

– and Pierre Lavoie, ed. 1993. *Le Monde du Michel Tremblay. Des Belles-Sœurs à Marcel poursuivi par les chiens.* Montreal/Carnières: Cahiers du théâtre Jeu / Éditions Lansman.

Davis, Tracy. 1991. *Actresses as Working Women: Their Social Identity in Victorian Culture.* New York: Routledge.

Deleuze, Gilles. 1990. 'The Simulacrum and Ancient Philosophy.' In *The Logic of Sense,* ed. Charles Stivale and Constantin V. Boundas; trans. Mark Lester, 253–79. New York: Columbia University Press.

Deleuze, Magali. 2008. 'Le Maghreb à l'Expo 67 (Tunisie, Maroc, Algérie).' In Monière and Comeau, 49–62.

'Demande d'emploi / Application for Employment.' Expo 67 Hostess Application Form. http://expolounge.blogspot.com/search/label/happening%20hostesses (accessed 30 May 2009).

Demers, Frédéric. 1999. *Céline Dion et l'identité québécoise: "La petite fille de Charlemagne parmi les grands!"* Collection Études Québécoises. Montreal: VLB.

Demers, Jeanne. 1997. 'Autour de la question linguistique: le manifeste québécois des années '60 –'70.' *Canadian Literature / Littérature canadienne* 152–3 (Spring/Summer): 17–35.

DeNora, Tia. 2000. *Music in Everyday Life.* Cambridge and New York: Cambridge University Press.

'Des hôtesses à la hauteur.' 1967. Les Archives de Radio-Canada. Société Radio-Canada. (24 June). [Originally aired on *Langue vivante* on the television of Radio Canada.] http://archives.radio-canada.ca/societe/celebrations/dossiers/21-13410/ (accessed 30 May 2009).

Desrochers, Nadine. 2001. 'Le théâtre des femmes.' In Lafon, 111–32.

Desaulniers, Jean Pierre. 2004. *Le Phénomène Star Académie.* Montreal: Saint-Martin.

Desjardins, David. 2005. 'L'indécence.' *Voir,* 8 Sept. http://www.voir.ca/actualite/ennemipublic.aspx?iIDArticle=37928 (accessed 18 Oct. 2006).

Dharwadker, Aparna. 2003. 'Diaspora and the Theatre of the Nation.' *Theatre Research International* 28(3): 303–25.

Diamond, Elin. 1997. *Unmaking Mimesis.* London and New York: Routledge.

Dickinson, John Alexander, and Brian Young, ed. 1993. *A Short History of Quebec.* Montreal and Kingston: McGill-Queen's University Press.

Dickinson, Peter. 1998. *Here Is Queer: Nationalisms, Sexualities and the Literatures of Canada.* Toronto: University of Toronto Press.

Dion, Celine. 2000. *Celine Dion: My Story, My Dream.* With Georges-Hébert Germain. New York: Morrow.

Dorsinville, Max. 1974. *Caliban without Prospero: Essays on Quebec and Black Literature.* Erin, Ont.: Press Porcepic.

Dostie, Gaëtan. 1974. '"Speak White" à L'Hexagone, Michèle Lalonde: "Le français c'est notre couleur noire."' *Le Jour,* 1 June, V3.

Drouin, Jennifer. 2005. '"To Be or Not to Be Free": Nation and Gender in Québécois Adaptations of Shakespeare.' Unpublished doctoral dissertation, McGill University.

Dubois, René-Daniel. 1984. *Ne blâmez jamais les bédouins.* Montreal: Leméac.

Dumont, Fernand. 1996. *Genèse de la société québécoise.* Montreal: Boréal-Compact.

Dupuy, Pierre. 1972. *Expo 67 ou la découverte de la fierté.* Montreal: Éditions de La Presse.

Duval, Étienne-F., ed. 1978. *Anthologie thématique du théâtre Québécois au XIXe siècle.* Montreal: Leméac.

Eco, Umberto. 1983. *Travels in Hyperreality.* New York: Harcourt Brace Jovanovich.

Edelman, Murray. 1996. *From Art to Politics: How Artistic Conceptions Shape Political Conceptions.* Chicago: University of Chicago Press.

Éditions Larousse. 1998. *Le Petit Larousse en couleurs.* Paris: Larousse.

Elam, Keir. 1988. *The Semiotics of Theatre and Drama.* New Accents Series. London and New York: Routledge.

Étienne, Gérard. 1995. *La question raciale et raciste dans le roman québécois: Essai d'anthroposémiologie.* Montreal: Balzac.

'Expo 17, a World's Fair in Montreal.' (1 Sept. 2007). http://www.expo17.ca/english/expo_proposal.pdf (accessed 1 June 2009).

Expo 67: A Virtual Experience. 'Introduction.' Library and Archives Canada in collaboration with La Section des archives de la Ville de Montréal. http://www.collectionscanada.gc.ca/expo/index-e.html (accessed 29 May 2009).

'Expo 67: An experiment in the Development of Urban Space.' 1966. *Architectural Record* 140 (Oct.): 170.

Expo 67: Back to the Future. 2004. Toronto: CBC Home Video, Morningstar Entertainment.

Faber, J.M. 1967. *Terre des Hommes = Man and His World.* Ottawa: Canadian Corporation for the 1967 World Exhibition.

Febvre, Michèle. 1987a. 'Les paradoxes de la danse-théâtre.' In Febvre, 73–83.

– ed. 1987b. *La Danse au défi.* Montreal: Parachute.

Femmes de Thetford Mines. 1980. *Si Cendrillon pouvait Mourir!* Montreal: Remue-ménage.

Féral, Josette. 1985. 'Pratiques culturelles au Québec: Le Théâtre et son public.' *Études littéraires* 18(3): 191–210.

– 1998a. *Mise en scène et jeu de l'acteur, entretiens,* vol. 2, *Corps en scène.* Montréal: Éditions Jeu-Lansman.

– 1998b. 'Denis Marleau: une approche ludique et poétique.' In Féral 1998a, 177–97.

– 2007. *Mise en scène et jeu de l'acteur, entretiens,* vol. 3, *Voix de femmes.* Montreal: Québec Amérique.

Ferraro, Alessandra. 1999. 'Palimpsestes, métissages, frôlements: Textes immigrants et littérature québécoise.' In *Palinsesti Culturali: Gli Apporti delle Immigrazioni alla Letteratura del Canada,* ed. Anna Pia De Luc, Jean-Paul Dufiet, and Alessandra Ferraro, 141–54. Udine: Forum.

Filewod, Alan. 2002. *Performing Canada: The Nation Enacted in the Imagined Theatre.* Kamloops, BC: Faculty of Arts, University College of the Cariboo.

Fiset, Édouard. 1965. *Introduction d'un concept urbain dans la planification de l'exposition / Introduction of an urban concept in the planning of the exposition.* Montreal: Canadian Corporation for the 1967 World Exhibition.

Fontenay, Danièle de. 1985. 'Une écriture de silence.' *Jeu* 34: 107–9.

Foster, Susan Leigh. 1986. *Reading Dancing: Bodies and Subjects in Contemporary American Dance.* Berkeley: University of California Press.

Forsyth, Louise H. 1979. 'First Person Singular: Monologues by Women in Several Modern Quebec Plays.' *Canadian Drama / L'Art dramatique canadien* 5(2): 189–211.

– 1991. 'Jouer aux éclats: l'inscription spectaculaire des cultures de femmes dans le théâtre de Jovette Marchessault.' *Voix et images* 16(2): 230–43.

– 2006a. 'About Jovette Marchessault.' In Forsyth, ed., 117–21.

– 2006b. 'Introduction: Québec Women Playwrights of the 1960s, 1970s and 1980s.' In Forsyth, ed., iii–xviii.

– ed. 2006. *Anthology of Québec Women's Plays in English Translation,* vol. 1, *1966–198).* Toronto: Playwrights Canada Press.

– ed. 2008. *Anthology of Québec Women's Plays in English Translation,* vol. 2, *1987–2003.* Toronto: Playwrights Canada Press.

Fournier, Marcel. 1986. *L'entrée dans la modernité: science, culture et société au Québec.* Montreal: Saint-Martin.

Francis, Daniel. 1997. 'Making Tracks: The Myth of the CPR.' In *National Dreams: Myth, Memory, and Canadian History,* 15–28. Vancouver: Arsenal Pulp Press.

Franko, Mark. 1993. *Dance as Text: Ideologies of the Baroque Body.* Cambridge: Cambridge University Press.

Fricker, Karen. 2008. 'À l'heure zéro de la culture (dés)unie: problématiques de représentation dans *Zulu Time* de Robert Lepage et Ex Machina.' *Globe: Revue internationale d'études québécoises* 11(2): 81–116.

Frith, Simon. 1996. 'The Voice.' In *Performing Rites: On the Value of Popular Music,* 183–202. Cambridge: Harvard University Press.

Gagnon, Alain-G. 1993. 'Quebec-Canada: Constitutional Developments, 1960–92.' In Gagnon, ed., 96–115.

– ed. *Quebec: State and Society.* Scarborough: Nelson.

Gagnon, Dominique, Louise Laprade, Nicole Lecavalier, and Pol Pelletier. 1979. *À ma mere, à ma mere, à ma mere, à ma voisine.* Montreal: Remue-ménage.

Galantay, Ervin. 1967. 'Expo 67, Space/Time in Montreal.' *Nation* 204(18): 557–62.

Gatti, Mauricio. 2004. *Littérature amérindienne du Québec: écrits de langue française.* Montreal: Hurtubise.

– 2006. *Être écrivain amérindien au Québec: indianité et création littéraire.* Montreal: Hurtubise.

Gauthier, Bertrand, Jean Royer, Jacques Lanctôt, André Vanasse, and Robert Soulières. 1993. 'Le mauvais prix à la mauvaise personne.' *La Presse,* 3 Dec., B2.

Gauvin, Lise. 1995. 'De *Speak White* à *Speak What?*: À propos de quelques manifestes québécois.' *Québec Studies* 20 (Spring/Summer): 19–26.

– 2000. *Langagement: L'écrivain et la langue au Québec.* Montreal: Boréal.

– 2003. 'Manifester la différence: Place et fonctions des manifestes dans les littératures francophones.' *Globe: Revue internationale d'études québécoises* 6: 23–42.

Gauvreau, Michel. 2005. *The Catholic Origins of Quebec's Quiet Revolution.* Montreal and Kingston: McGill-Queen's University Press.

Gélinas, Gratien. 1949. 'Pour un théâtre national et populaire – allocution prononcée à l'Université de Montréal le 31 janvier 1949.' *Amérique Française* 1(3): 32–42.

Gendron, Adeline. 2008. 'De la rue à l'usine. Les lieux de Carbone 14.' *Globe: Revue internationale d'études québécoises* 11(2): 61–80.

Germain, Jean-Claude. 1968a. 'J'ai eu le coup de foudre.' *Théâtre vivant* 6: 3–5; reproduced in Tremblay, 1972, 120–5.

– 1968b. '"*Les belles-sœurs*": une condamnation sans appel.' *Le Petit Journal,* 8 Sept.

– 1972. 'Quand un ex-critique critique le critique du Devoir.' *Le Devoir,* 11 March, 15.

- 1976. 'Théâtre Québécois or Théâtre Protestant?' *Canadian Theatre Review* 11 (Summer): 8–21.

Gilbert, Helen. 1998. *Sightlines: Race, Gender, and Nation in Contemporary Australian Theatre.* Ann Arbor: University of Michigan Press.

Gill, A. A. 2003. 'What Would Frank Say?' *Vanity Fair* (Oct.): 204–9.

Gingras, Claude. 1969. '"Mon Dieu que je les aime, ces gens-là!"' *La Presse*, 16 Aug., 26.

Glatzer, Jenna. 2005. *Céline Dion, Pour toujours ...* Trans. and adap. Georges-Hébert Germain. Bellevue, WA: Becker & Mayer.

Godard, Barbara. 1985. 'Flying Away with Language.' In Marchessault, 9–27.

- 1987. 'Comments in A/Part.' Paper presented at 1984 Ottawa Conference on Language, Culture and Literary Identity in Canada / La langue, la culture et l'identité littéraire au Canada. In *Canadian Literature, Supplement 1*, ed. J.M. Bumsted, 130–7.

Godin, Jean Cléo. 2001. 'Création et réflexion: le retour du texte et de l'auteur.' In Lafon, 57–71.

- and Laurent Mailhot. 1970. *Théâtre Québécois I: Introduction à dix dramaturges contemporains.* Quebec: Hurtubise.

- 1980. *Théâtre Québécois,*vol. 2, *Nouveaux auteurs, autres spectacles,* ed. Alonzo Le Blanc. Montreal: Bibliothèque québécoise.

- and Dominique Lafon. 1999. *Dramaturgies québécoises des années quatre-vingt.* Montreal: Leméac.

Goellner, Ellen W., and Jacqueline Shea Murphy. 1995. 'Introduction: Movement Movements.' In Goellner and Murphy, 1–18.

- eds. 1995. *Bodies of the Text: Dance as Theory, Literature as Dance.* Rutgers, NJ: Rutgers University Press.

Gold, John R., and Margaret M. Gold. 2005. *Cities of Culture: Staging International Festivals and the Urban Agenda, 1851–2000.* Aldershot: Ashgate.

Gougeon, Gilles. 1994. *A History of Quebec Nationalism,* trans. Louisa Blair, Robert Chodos, and Jane Ubertino. Toronto: Lorimer.

Gould, Karen. 1990. *Writing in the Feminine: Feminism and Experimental Writing in Quebec.* Carbondale: Southern Illinois University Press.

Graver, David. 2005. 'The Actor's Bodies.' In *Performance: Critical Concepts in Literary and Cultural Studies,* ed. Philip Auslander, 157–74. New York and London: Routledge.

Greenblatt, Stephen J. 1991. *Marvelous Possessions: The Wonder of the New World.* Chicago: University of Chicago Press.

Greffard, Madeleine. 1993. 'Le Triomphe de la tribu.' In *Le Monde de Michel Tremblay: des Belles-sœurs à Marcel poursuivi par les chiens,* ed. Gilbert David and Pierre Lavoie, 31–46. Montreal: Cahiers de théâtre Jeu / Éditions Lansman.

Grenier, Line. 1990. 'Radio Broadcasting in Canada: The Case of "Transformat" Music.' *Popular Music* 9 (April): 221–33.

– 1993. 'Policing French Language Music on Canadian Radio.' In *Rock and Popular-Music: Politics, Policies, Institutions,* ed. Tony Bennett, Simon Frith, Lawrence Grossberg, John Shepherd, and Graeme Turner, 119–41. London and New York: Routledge.

– 1997. '"Je me souviens" ... en chansons: articulations de la citoyenneté culturelle et de l'identitaire dans le champ musical populaire au Québec.' *Sociologie et sociétés* 29 (Fall): 31–47.

– 2001a. 'Global Pop on the Move: The Fame of Superstar Céline Dion within, outside, and across Quebec.' *Australian Canadian Studies* 19: 31–48.

– 2001b. 'Governing "National" Memories through Popular Music in Quebec.' *Topia* 6 (Fall): 11–19.

Grescoe, Taras. 2001. *Sacré Blues: An Unsentimental Journey through Quebec.* Toronto: Macfarlane Walter & Ross.

Grossberg, Lawrence. 1992a. 'Is there a Fan in the House?: The Affective Sensibility of Fandom.' In *The Adoring Audience: Fan Culture and Popular Media,* ed. Lisa A. Lewis, 50–65. London and New York: Routledge.

– 1992b. *We Gotta Get Out of This Place: Popular Conservatism and Postmodern Culture.* New York and London: Routledge.

Guilbeault, Luce, Marthe Blackburn, France Théoret, Odette Gagnon, Marie-Claire Blais, Pol Pelletier, and Nicole Brassard. 1992. *La Nef des sorcières.* Montreal: L'Hexagone.

Hajdukowski-Ahmed, Maroussia. 1984. 'La sorcière dans le texte (québécois) au féminin.' *French Review* 58(2): 260–8.

Hamelin, Jean. 1961. *Le renouveau du théâtre au Canada Français.* Collection les idées du jour. Montreal: Éditions du jour.

Handfield, Micheline. 1970. 'Fou ou génie? Michel Tremblay travaille en "joual" pour éveiller le peuple québécois.' *Sept-Jours* 26 (14 March): 27–8.

Handler, Richard. 1988. *Nationalism and the Politics of Culture in Quebec.* Madison: University of Wisconsin Press.

Hardt, Michael. 1999. 'Affective Labor.' *Boundary 2* 26(2): 89–100.

Harel, Simon. 1989. *Le Voleur de parcours. Identité et cosmopolitisme dans la littérature québécoise contemporaine.* Longueuil: Préambule.

– 2002. 'Une littérature des communautés culturelles made in Québec?' *Globe: Revue internationale d'études québécoises* 5: 57–77.

– 2004a. 'La chasse gardée du territoire québécois.' *Liberté* 46 (Sept.): 73–87.

– 2004b. 'La chasse gardée du territoire québécois 2: Un Québec palimpseste.' *Liberté* 46 (Nov.): 105–17.

– 2005a. 'La chasse gardée du territoire québécois 3: Braconnages identitaires.' *Liberté* 47 (Feb.): 110–28.

– 2005b. 'La chasse gardée du territoire québécois 4: À la manière des tageurs.' *Liberté* 47: 137–61.

– 2006. 'Perdre la carte: Braconnages et postcolonialisme dans la littérature québécoise.' Paper presented at the Fifteenth Biennial Conference of the American Council for Québec Studies, Les études québécoises: du colonial au postcolonial / Québec Studies: From the Colonial to the Postcolonial, Cambridge, Mass., 12–14 Oct.

Harvie, Jennifer. 1995. 'The Real Nation? Michel Tremblay, Scotland, and Cultural Translatability.' *Theatre Research in Canada / Recherches théâtrales au Canada* 16(1–2): 5–25.

– 2005. *Staging the UK.* Manchester: Manchester University Press.

– and Erin Hurley. 1999. 'States of Play: Locating Québec in the Performances of Robert Lepage, Ex Machina and the Cirque du Soleil.' *Theatre Journal* 51(3): 299–315.

Hébert, Chantal, and Irène Perelli-Contos. 2001. *La face cachée du théâtre d'images.* Saint-Nicolas: Presses de l'Université Laval.

Hebdige, Dick. 1979. *Subculture: The Meaning of Style.* London: Methuen.

Hendrick, Aude. 2008. 'Les pays africains à l'Expo 67: symbols du changement.' In Monière and Comeau, 79–92.

Hjört, Mette, and Sue Laver. 1997. *Emotion and the Arts.* New York: Oxford University Press.

Hochschild, Arlie. 2003. *The Managed Heart: Commercialization of Human Feeling.* 20th anniversary ed. Berkeley: University of California Press.

Hood, Sarah B. 1995. 'Theatre of Images: New Dramaturgies.' In *Contemporary Issues in Canadian Drama*, ed. Per Brask, 50–67. Winnipeg: Blizzard.

'House Passes Motion Recognizing Quebecois as Nation.' 2006. cbcnews.ca. (27 Nov.). http://www.cbc.ca/canada/story/2006/11/27/nation-vote.html.

Hunt, Nigel. 1989. 'The Global Voyage of Robert Lepage.' *TDR* 33(2): 104–18.

Hurley, Erin. 2004. '*Devenir Autre:* Languages of Marco Micone's *culture immigrée.*' *Theatre Research in Canada / Recherches théâtrales au Canada* 25(1–2): 1–23.

– 2009a. 'Céline Dion à Las Vegas ou les affects de la simulation.' *L'Annuaire théâtral* 45 (Spring): 21–44.

– 2009b. 'Original Versions: "*L'affaire Nancy Huston*" and Authorized Performance.' In *Changing the Subject: Marvin Carlson and Theatre Studies 1959–2009*, ed. Joseph Roach, 261–77. Ann Arbor: University of Michigan Press.

– 2010. *Theatre and Feeling.* Basingstoke and New York: Palgrave Macmillan.

– and Will Straw, eds. 'Are We American?' Special dossier. *Québec Studies* 48 (Fall 2009/Winter 2010): 3–66.

'In Depth, the 39th Parliament. Debate: The Motions on the Québécois Na-

tion.' 2006. CBC News. (24 Nov.) http://www.cbc.ca/news/background/
parliament39/motion-quebecnation.html.

Innes, Christopher. 2005. 'Puppets and Machines of the Mind: Robert Lepage
and the Modernist Heritage.' *Theatre Research International* 30(2): 124–38.

Ireland, Susan, and Patrice J. Proulx. 2004. 'Introduction.' In *Textualizing the
Immigrant Experience in Québec*, Contributions to the Study of World Literature
127, 1–7. Westport and London: Praeger.

Jackson, Shannon. 2003. 'Partial Publicity and Gendered Remembering: Figuring Women in Culture and Performance.' *Cultural Studies* 17(3): 691–712.

– 2004. *Professing Performance: Theatre in the Academy from Philology to Performativity*. Cambridge and New York: Cambridge University Press.

Jacques, Hélène. 2005. 'Projections de la mort, sur deux mises en scène de
Denis Marleau.' *L'Annuaire théâtral* 37 (Spring): 113–27.

– 2006. 'Un théâtre d'acteurs vidéographiques: *Les Aveugles* de Denis Marleau.'
Intermédialités 6 (Spring): 79–94.

Jameson, Frederic. 1984. 'Postmodernism, or The Cultural Logic of Late Capitalism.' *New Left Review* no. 146 (July/Aug.): 53–92.

– 1986. 'Third World Literature in the Era of Multinational Capitalism.' *Social
Text: Theory/Culture/Ideology* 15 (Fall): 65–88.

Jasmin, O.C., Yves. 1997. *La Petite Histoire d'Expo 67: L'Exposition universelle et
internationale de Montréal comme vous ne l'avez jamais vu*. Montreal: Québec/
Amérique.

Joseph, May. 1999. *Nomadic Identities: The Performance of Citizenship*. Minneapolis:
University of Minnesota Press.

Jubinville, Yves. 2003. 'Appel d'air. Regards obliques sur l'institution théâtrale
au Québec.' In Beauchamp and David, 325–39.

– 2009. 'Portrait de l'auteur dramatique en mutant.' *Voix et images* 34(3)
(Spring/Summer): 67–78.

Juéry, René. 1978. 'Michel Tremblay: une interpretation psychanalytique des
Belles-sœurs.' *Études littéraires* 11(3): 478–89.

Juneau-Garneau, Gabrielle. 1994. 'Speak White Speak What.' *Le Devoir*, 31 Jan.,
A6.

Keating, Michael. 1996. *Nations against the State: The New Politics of Nationalism in
Quebec, Catalonia and Scotland*. New York: St Martin's Press.

Killick, Rachel. 2006. 'In the Fold? Postcolonialism and Quebec.' *Romance
Studies* 24(3): 181–92.

Kramer, Lawrence. 2003. 'Subjectivity Rampant! Music, Hermeneutics, and His-
tory.' In *The Cultural Study of Music: A Critical Introduction*, ed. Martin Clayton,
Trevor Herbert, and Richard Middleton, 124–35. New York and London:
Routledge.

Kröller, Eva-Marie. 1997. 'Expo '67: Canada's Camelot?' *Canadian Literature* 152–3 (Spring/Summer): 36–51.

Kruger, Loren. 1992. *The National Stage: Theatre and Cultural Legitimation in England, France, and America.* Chicago: University of Chicago Press.

Labreque, Marie. 1998. 'L'hiver de force: Louis Robitaille.' *Voir,* 28 April.

Lacroix, Jean-Michel. 1990. 'Représentation de la parole immigrée dans l'espace théatral de Marco Micone.' In *Multilinguisme et Multiculturalisme en Amérique du Nord: Espace: seuils et limites,* ed. Jean Béranger, Jean Cazemajou, Jean-Michel Lacroix, and Pierre Spriet, Annales du Centre de recherches sure l'Amérique Anglophone 15, 193–208. Bordeaux: Maison des sciences de l'homme d'Aquitaine.

– 1996. 'Réalités démographiques et politiques de l'immigration au Québec: l'état des lieux au début des années 1990.' In *Études québécoises: Bilan et perspectives,* vol. 2, ed. Hans-Josef Niederehe and Lothar Wolf, 165–78. Tubingen: Max Niemeyer Verlag.

Ladouceur, Louise. 2005. *Making the scene: la traduction du théâtre d'une langue officielle à l'autre au Canada.* Montreal: Nota Bene.

Lafon, Dominique, ed. 2001. *Le théâtre québécois, 1975–1995.* Archives des lettres canadiennes, vol. 10. Ottawa: Fides.

Lakoff, George, and Mark Johnson. 1980. *Metaphors We Live By.* Chicago and London: University of Chicago Press.

Lalonde, Michèle. 1979. 'Speak White.' In *Défense et illustration de la langue québécoise: suivie de prose et poèmes,* 37–40. Paris: Seghers Laffont.

Lamonde, Yvan. 1996. *Ni avec eux ni sans eux. Le Québec et les Etats-Unis.* Quebec: Nuit Blanche Éditeur.

– and Esther Trépanier. 1986. *L'Avènement de la modernité culturelle au Québec.* Quebec: Institut québécois de recherche sur la culture.

Lamoureux, Diane. 2001. *L'amère patrie: Féminisme et nationalisme dans le Québec contemporain.* Montreal: Remue-ménage.

Lanctôt, Jacques. 1993. 'Cantique des plaines: Assez, c'est assez!' *Le Devoir,* 24 Dec., A9.

Lane, Jill. 2005. *Blackface Cuba, 1840–1895.* Rethinking the Americas. Philadelphia: University of Pennsylvania Press.

Laplante, Benoît. 1982. 'L'homme rouge.' *Jeu* 24: 107–9.

Larrue, Jean-Marc. 2001. 'La création collective au Québec.' In Lafon, 2001, 151–77.

Latouche, Daniel. 1983. 'The Power of Words: The State as a Literary Creation.' *Québec Studies* 3: 13–21.

– 1986. *Canada and Quebec, Past and Future: An Essay.* Royal Commission on the Economic Union and Development Prospects for Canada, vol. 70. Toronto: University of Toronto Press.

Lavoie, Pierre. 1977. 'Bilan tranquille d'une révolution théâtrale.' *Jeu* 6: 47–61.
– 1989. 'Le Dortoir.' *Jeu* 52: 201–5.
Le Canada reçoit / Canada at Home. Montreal: Compagnie canadienne de l'exposition universelle de 1967 / Canadian Corporation for the 1967 World Exhibition.
Le Devoir. 'L'affaire des "Belles-Sœurs"' 1972: Protestation de 83 artistes du Québec auprès de M. Sharp.' *Le Devoir*, 30 March, 11.
Le Dortoir [The Dormitory]. 1991. Produced by Niv Fichman. Toronto: Rhombus Media (videocassette).
'Le programme de recherche en démographie historique.' Université de Montréal. http://www.genealogie.umontreal.ca/fr/nomsPrenoms.htm (accessed 13 Sept. 2006).
Les arts de la scène, grands ambassadeurs de l'identité canadienne à l'étranger. Document présenté à M. Pierre Pettigrew, Ministre des Affaires Étrangères, Gouvernement du Canada. Condensé des réflexions du Conseil québécois du théâtre, du Regroupement québécois de la danse et du Conseil québécois de la musique, à l'egard de la situation financière des organismes organisant des tournées à l'éxterieur du Canada. Montréal, 14 Jan. 2005. Available at the website of the Conseil québécois du théâtre (CQT), http://www.cqt.ca/Dlls/Pdf.dll?DocumentId={23537FD5-E10B-40BE-AFEE-4A884E63B111}&Reference=634&TargetGroup=&. (accessed 24 Feb. 2009).
'Les 40 ans d'Expo 67: Les hôtesses.' 2007. By Anne-Caroline Crespel. Archives of Radio-Canada.ca. (11 April). http://archives.radio-canada.ca/fr/expo67/hotesses/index.asp (accessed 31 May 2009).
Lecker, Robert. 1995. *Making It Real: The Canonization of English-Canadian Literature.* Concord: Anansi.
– ed. 1991. *Canadian Canons: Essays in Literary Value.* Toronto: University of Toronto Press.
LeClerc, Patrice, and Lois A. West. 1997. 'Feminist Nationalist Movements in Quebec: Resolving Contradictions?' In *Feminist Nationalism*, ed. Lois A. West, 220–46. New York: Routledge.
Lefebvre, Paul, and Denis Marleau. 1984. 'Cet enfant incestueux, table ronde sur la danse-théâtre.' *Jeu* 32: 49–56.
Lefebvre, Pierre. 1964. 'Psychisme et valeurs nationals.' *Parti pris* 9–11 (Summer): 6–18.
Legault, Guy R. 2002. *La ville qu'on a bâtie: Trente ans au service de l'urbanisme et de l'habitation à Montréal, 1956–1986.* Montreal: Liber.
Leonardi, Susan J., and Rebecca A. Pope. 1996. *The Diva's Mouth: Body, Voice, Prima Donna Politics.* New Brunswick, NJ: Rutgers University Press.
Lepecki, André. 2006. *Exhausting Dance: performance and the politics of movement.* New York and London: Routledge.

Lesemann, Frédéric. 2000. '"Américanité" des Québécois passe par un rôle actif de l'État-providence.' *Québec Studies* 29 (Spring/Summer): 43–53.

Létourneau, Jocelyn. 1992. 'Le "Québec moderne": Un chapitre du grand récit collectif des Québécois.' *Revue française de science politique* 42(5): 765–85.

– 2006. *Que veulent vraiment les Québécois?: regard sur l'intention nationale au Québec (français) d'hier à aujourd'hui.* Montreal: Boréal.

Lévesque, Robert. 1984a. 'Carbone 14 se surpasse.' *Le Devoir,* 9 May, 8.

– 1984b. 'Le rail, un théâtre de l'intuition et de l'urgence.' *Le Devoir,* 27 Oct., 28.

– 1988. 'Le débarquement des Belles-Sœurs.' *Le Devoir,* 27 Aug.

Lévesque, Solange. 1994. 'Traduire, c'est émigrer: Entretien avec Marco Micone.' *Jeu* 70 (March): 17–30.

Levine, Mark V. 2003. 'Tourism-Based Redevelopment and the Fiscal Crisis of the City: The Case of Montréal.' *Canadian Journal of Urban Research* 12(1): 102–23.

Levinson, Jerrold. 1997. 'Emotion in Response to Art: A Survey of the Terrain.' In *Emotion and the Arts,* ed. Mette Hjört and Sue Laver, 20–34. New York: Oxford University Press.

Linteau, Paul André. 2000. *Histoire de Montréal depuis la Confédération.* Montreal: Boréal.

Lortie, André, Jean-Louis Cohen, and Michael Sorkin. 2004. 'Learning from Montreal.' In *The 60s: Montreal Thinks Big,* ed. André Lortie, 149–59. Montreal and Vancouver: Canadian Centre for Architecture / Douglas & McIntyre.

Lortie, Marie-Claude. 1989. 'Carbone 14 ou la parole donnée aux gestes et aux émotions.' *La Presse,* 22 April, D4.

MacDougall, Jill. 1991. Review of *Polygraph,* by Marie Brassard, Robert Lepage, and the Théâtre Repère of Quebec, and *Le Dortoir,* by Gilles Maheu and Carbone 14. BAM Next Wave/Next Door Festival, Brooklyn, New York. 26 Oct. – Dec. *Theatre Journal* 43(4): 252–5.

MacLennan, Hugh. 1945. *Two Solitudes.* Toronto: Collins.

Magnuson, Roger. 1980. *A Brief History of Quebec Education: From New France to Parti Québécois.* Montreal: Harvest House.

Maheu, Gilles. 1978. 'les enfants du paradis.' *Jeu* 8: 79–82.

– 1992. 'Gilles Maheu: l'espace vital.' *Jeu* 63 (June): 16–30.

Maheu, Pierre. 1963. 'De la révolte à la révolution.' *Parti pris* 1: 5–17.

– 1964. 'Œdipe colonial.' *Parti pris* 9–11 (Summer): 19–29.

Mailhot, Laurent. 1970. '*Les Belles-sœurs* ou l'enfer des femmes.' *Études françaises* 6(1): 96–104.

– 1973. 'Le monologue québécois.' *Canadian Literature / Littérature canadienne* 58 (Autumn): 26-38.

Major, André. 1964. 'Pour une littérature révolutionnaire.' *Parti pris* 8 (May): 56–7.

– 1968. 'Un exorcisme par le joual.' *Le Devoir*, 21 Sept., 14.

Major, Robert. 1979. *Parti pris: idéologies et littérature.* Collection Littérature. Lasalle: Éditions Hurtubise HMH.

Marchessault, Jovette. 1980. *Tryptique lesbien: Chronique lesbienne du moyen-âge québécois, Les Vaches de nuit, Les Faiseuses d'anges.* Montreal: Éditions de la pleine lune.

– 1982. *La terre est trop courte, Violette Leduc.* Montreal: Éditions de la pleine lune.

– 1983a. 'Letter to Michelle Rossignol.' In Marchessault, 1983b, 21–2.

– 1983b. *Saga of Wet Hens. A Play by Jovette Marchessault.* Trans. Linda Gaboriau. Vancouver: Talonbooks.

– 1985. *Lesbian Triptych.* Trans. Yvonne M. Klein. Toronto: Women's Press.

Marcus, George. 2002. *The Sentimental Citizen: Emotion in Democratic Politics.* University Park: Pennsylvania State University Press.

Marleau, Denis, and Stéphanie Jasmin. 2004. 'La non-action comme terrain fertile pour un travail d'acteur témoignage.' *Annuaire théâtral* 36 (Autumn): 95–102.

Marsan, Jean-Claude. 1981. *Montreal in Evolution: Historical Analysis of the Development of Montreal's Architecture and Urban Environment.* Montreal and Kingston: McGill-Queen's University Press.

Martel, Marcel. 1997. *Le deuil d'un pays imaginé: Rêves, luttes et déroute du Canada français, Les rapports entre le Québec et la francophonie canadienne (1867–1975).* Collection Amérique Française, vol.5. Ottawa: Presses de l'Université d'Ottawa.

Martin, Paul. 1968. 'Les conférences.' In *Man and His World / Terre des hommes: The Noranda Lectures Expo 67 / Les conférences Noranda L'Expo 67,* intro. Helen Hogg, 5–6. Toronto: University of Toronto Press.

Martin, Wallace. 1993. 'Metonymy.' In *New Princeton Encyclopedia of Poetry and Poetics,* eds. Alex Preminger, T.V.F. Brogan, Frank J. Warnke, O.B. Hardison, Jr, and Earl Miner. Princeton: Princeton University Press. http://gateway.proquest.com/openurl/openurl?ctx_ver=Z39.88-2003&xri:pqil:res_ver=0.2&res_id=xri:lion-us&rft_id=xri:lion:rec:ref:PEP0552 (accessed 19 June 2009).

Massumi, Brian. 2002. *Parables for the Virtual: Movement, Affect, Sensation.* Post-Contemporary Interventions. Durham: Duke University Press.

'Match the Hostess with the Pavilion.' *Expo 67: A Virtual Experience.* Library and Archives Canada in collaboration with La Section des archives de la Ville de Montréal. http://www.collectionscanada.gc.ca/expo/053302100101_e.html (accessed 29 May 2009).

Mathis, Ursula. 1996. 'Marco Micone et le dialogue interculturel.' *Cahiers francophones d'Europe Centre Orientale* 5(6): 227–89.

Mayer, Andre. 2005. 'The Barrie Blog.' (3:51 p.m., July 2). http://www.cbc.ca/arts/music/live8blog.html (accessed 7 Sept. 2005).

McClary, Susan. 2002. *Feminine Endings: Music, Gender, and Sexuality.* Minneapolis: University of Minnesota Press.

McConachie, Bruce. 2001. 'Social Practices and the Nation-State: Paradigms for Writing National Theatre History.' In *Theatre, History and National Identities,* ed. Helka Mäkinen, S.E. Wilmer, and W.B. Worthen, 119–39. Helsinki: Helsinki University Press.

'Michel Tremblay: "... les bibittes des autres."' 1972. *Magazine Maclean,* Sept., 20.

Micone, Marco. 1979a. 'Quelques notes sur l'immigration (inédit).' *Derives* 17–18: 4–20.

– 1979b. 'Ces enfants d'ailleurs, des enfants d'ici.' *Dérives* 17–18: 4–20.

– 1981. 'La culture immigrée réduite au silence.' *Dérives* 29–30: 87–93.

– 1989. 'Speak What.' *Jeu* 50 (March): 83–5.

– 1990a. 'De l'assimilation à la culture immigrée.' *Possibles* 14 (Summer): 55–64.

– 1990b. 'Immigrant Culture: The Identity of the Voiceless People.' In *Writers in Transition: The Proceedings of the First National Conference of Italian-Canadian Writers,* ed. C. Dino Minni and Anna Foschi Ciampolini, Essay Series 6, 151–60. Montreal: Guernica.

– 1992. *Le figuier enchanté.* Montreal: Boréal.

– 1993. *La Locandiera.* Montreal: Boréal.

– 1996a. 'La culture immigrée comme dépassement des cultures ethniques.' *Center for the Study of Canada, Occasional Papers* 6 (Feb.): 1–5.

– 1996b. 'Le palimpseste impossible.' *Jeu* 80 (Sept.): 20–2.

– 1996c. *Trilogia: Gens du silence, Addolorata, Déjà l'agonie.* Montreal: VLB.

– 1997. *Two Plays: Voiceless People and Addolorata,* trans. Maurizia Binda, Afterword by Sherry Simon. Drama Series 2. Toronto, New York, and Lancaster: Guernica.

– 1998/1999. 'Le Québec: une societé complexe.' *Québec Studies* 26: 21–2.

– 2000. *Les femmes de bonne humeur.* Montreal: VLB.

– 2001. *Speak What,* ed. Lise Gauvin. Montreal: VLB.

– 2004. *Silences.* Collection Théâtre. Montreal: VLB.

– 2005. *Migrances suivi de Una donna.* Collection Théâtre. Montreal: VLB.

Middleton, Richard. 1990. *Studying Popular Music.* Milton Keynes and Philadelphia: Open University Press.

Ministère de la Culture et des Communications. 1996. 'Remettre l'Art au monde.' Quebec. http://mcc.quebectel.qc.ca/sites/mcc/ClinStat.nsf/

5b2056a79fa8a7e785256b8200569d61/a6ace02b39333a9b85256b88006b2200 !OpenDocument (accessed 10 Oct. 2006).

Ministère des relations internationales du Québec. 'Offices Abroad.' http:// www.mri.gouv.qc.ca/en/ministere/bureaux_etranger/bureaux_etranger.asp (accessed 15 July 2008).

Modleski, Tania. 1997. 'Doing Justice to the Subjects, Mimetic Arts in a Multicultural Society: The Work of Anna Deavere Smith.' In *Female Subjects in Black and White: Race, Psychoanalysis, Feminism,* ed. Elizabeth Abel, Barbara Christian, and Helene Moslen, 57–76. Berkeley: University of California Press.

Molinaro, Ines. 1999. 'Contexte et intégration: les communautés allophones au Québec.' *Globe: Revue internationale d'études québécoises* 2: 101–24.

Monière, Denis. 2008. 'Expo 67, 40 ans plus tard.' In Monière and Robert Comeau, 13–14.

– and Robert Comeau, eds. 2008. 'L'Expo 67, 40 ans plus tard,' special edition. *Bulletin d'histoire politique* 17(1).

Morasse, Gemma. 2007. 'On voudrait que Montréal vive quelque chose d'aussi extraordinaire": Entrevue avec Gemma Morasse.' (13 April). In 'Les 40 ans d'Expo 67.'

Morissette-Michaud, Monique. 2007. 'Un pavillon controversé: Entretien avec Monique Morissette-Michaud.' By René Hormier-Roy. *Attendez qu'on se souvienne.* Radio-Canada (14 July). http://www.radio-canada.ca/radio/emissions/ document.asp?docnumero=40654&numero=1825 (accessed 29 May 2009).

Moser, Karen. 1967. 'Best-Dressed Girls Are Expo Attraction.' *Canadian Press* (2 June). http://expo67.ncf.ca/expo_hostesses.html (accessed 1 July 2006).

Moss, Jane. 1985. 'Women's Theatre in Quebec.' In *Traditionalism, Nationalism, and Feminism: Women Writers of Quebec,* ed. Paula Gilbert Lewis, 242–54. Westport, CT: Greenwood Press.

– 1986. 'Le Corps spectaculaire: le théâtre au féminin.' *Modern Language Studies* 16(4): 54–60.

– 1996a. 'Multiculturalism and Postmodern Theatre: Staging Quebec's Otherness.' *Mosaic* 29 (Sept.): 75–83.

– 1996b. 'Quebecois Theatre: Michel Tremblay and Marie Laberge.' *Theatre Research International* 21(3): 196–207.

– 1998. 'Staging the Act of Writing: Postmodern Theatre in Quebec.' *French Review* 71(6): 940–8.

Muñoz, José Esteban. 1999. *Disidentifications: Queers of Color and the Performance of Politics.* Minneapolis: University of Minnesota Press.

– 2000. 'Feeling Brown: Ethnicity and Affect in Ricardo Bracho's the Sweetest Hangover (and Other STDs).' *Theatre Journal* 52 (March): 67–79.

Nardocchio, Elaine F. 1986a. '1958–1968: Ten Formative years in Quebec's Theatre History.' *Canadian Drama / L'Art dramatique canadien* 12(1): 33–6.
– 1986b. *Theatre and Politics in Modern Quebec.* Edmonton: University of Alberta Press.
Nardout-Lafarge, Élisabeth. 2004. 'La valeur "modernité" en littérature québécoise: notes pour un bilan critique.' In *Constructions de la modernité au Québec,* ed. Ginette Michaud and Élisabeth Nardout-Lafarge, 285–301. Montreal: Lanctôt.
Nelligan, Émile. 1952. 'Soir d'hiver.' In *Poésies Complètes, 1896–1899,* ed. Luc Lacourcière, 82–3. Montreal: Fides.
– 1983. *The Complete Poems of Emile Nelligan,* ed. and trans. Fred Cogswell. Montreal: Harvest House.
Nietzsche, Friedrich. 2000 [1872]. *The Birth of Tragedy,* ed. and trans. Douglas Smith. Oxford: Oxford University Press.
Noël, Francine. 1980. 'Quelques sorcières par elles-mêmes.' *Jeu* 16: 44–56.
'Nombre d'emplois selon l'industrie et répartition selon le sexe, moyennes annuelles, Québec, 2000 à 2004.' 2005. Québec, Institut de la statistique. http://www.stat.gouv.qc.ca/donstat/societe/march_travl_remnr/cat_profs_sectr_activ/professions/pop_active/finali1_5.htm (accessed 18 Oct. 2005).
Nunavut Kavamanga, Government of Nunavut. http://www.gov.nu.ca/ (accessed 22 Jan. 2007).
Nussbaum, Martha. 2001. *Upheavals of Thought: The Intelligence of the Emotions.* Cambridge: Cambridge University Press.
O'Leary, John. 1967. 'The World at Six.' Reporting by John Sheltus. *CBC Radio,* (16 June). http://archives.cbc.ca/IDC-1-69-740-4524-11/on_this_day/life_society/expo_hostesses (accessed 3 July 2006).
O'Neill-Karch, Mariel. 1997. 'Drama in French 1981 to 1996.' *Oxford Companion to Canadian Literature.* Toronto: Oxford University Press, 169–82.
Ouellet, Fernand. 1985. 'La modernisation de l'historiographie et l'émergence de l'histoire sociale.' *Recherches sociographiques* 26(1–2): 11–83.
Pacheco, Patrick. 1974. 'Montreal's Michel Tremblay and His "Hosanna."' *After Dark* (Nov.): 55.
Painchaud, Claude, and Richard Poulin. 1988. *Les Italiens au Québec.* Montreal: Asticou & Critiques.
Paré, François. 1997. *Exiguity: Reflections on the Margins of Literature.* Trans. Lin Burman. Waterloo: Wilfrid Laurier University Press.
Parker, Andrew, Mary Russo, Doris Sommer, and Patricia Yaeger. 1992. 'Introduction.' In *Nationalisms and Sexualities,* 1–18. New York and London: Routledge.
Pavis, Patrice. 1982. *Languages of the Stage: Essays in the Semiology of the Theatre.* New York: Performing Arts Journal Publications.

Pavlovic, Diane. 1987. 'Gilles Maheu: Corps à Corps,' trans. Roger E. Gannon and Rosalind Gill. *Canadian Theatre Review* 52 (Fall): 22–9.
– 1992. 'Gilles Maheu: l'espace vital.' *Jeu* 63 (June): 16–30.
Pelletier, Pol. 1979. 'Petite Histoire du théâtre des femmes au Québec.' *Possibles* 4(1): 175–87.
– 1995. *Joie*. Montreal: Remue-ménage.
– 2008. *Joy*, trans. Linda Gaboriau. In Forsyth, ed., 107–71.
Perelli-Contos, Irène, and Chantal Hébert. 1994. 'Les voix multiples de la scène, Gilles Maheu et Carbone 14.' *Nuit blanche* 55 (March–May): 67–70.
Petrowski, Nathalie. 1993. 'Bar Payant.' *La Presse*, 18 Nov., D3.
Phelan, Peggy. 1993. *Unmarked: The Politics of Performance*. London and New York: Routledge.
Piccione, Marie-Lyne. 1983. 'De Michel Tremblay à Élizabeth Bourget: images de la femme dans le théâtre québécois contemporain.' *Études canadiennes* 15 (Dec.): 47–52.
Pivato, Joseph. 2000. 'Five-Fold Translation in the Theatre of Marco Micone.' *Canadian Theatre Review* 104 (Fall): 11–15.
Pontaut, Alain. 1972. '*Les belles-sœurs* de Michel Tremblay cinq ans après.' In Tremblay, 1972, i–vii.
Potvin, Claudine. 1991. 'Entrevue avec Jovette Marchessault.' *Voix et images* 16(2): 218–29.
Pratt, Mary Louise. 1997. 'Arts of the Contact Zone.' In *Mass Culture and Everyday Life*, ed. Peter Gibian, 61–72. New York: Routledge.
Probyn, Elspeth. 1996. 'Love in a Cold Climate: Queer Belongings in Quebec.' In *Outside Belongings*, 63–92. London and New York: Routledge.
Program from the theatrical production of *La Forêt*, 1994.
Program from the theatrical production of *Le Dortoir*, 1996.
Program from the theatrical production of *L'Hiver–Winterland*, 1998.
Pronovost, Gilles. 1989. 'L'écoute musicale.' In *Les comportements des Québécois en matière d'activités culturelles de loisir/1989*. Quebec: Les Publications du Québec.
– 2005. *Les enquêtes de participation culturelle. Une comparaison France-Québec-États-Unis*. Rapport remis à l'Observatoire de la culture et des communications, de l'Institut de la statistique du Québec et au Ministère de la Culture et des Communications du Québec. http://www.stat.gouv.qc.ca/observatoire/publicat_obs/pdf/RapportGP.pdf (accessed 17 July 2008).
Purkhardt, Brigitte. 1994. Review of *La Forêt*. *Jeu* 70: 162–4.
Radio-Canada.ca avec Presse canadienne. 2009. 'Bataille des Plaines d'Abraham. La reconstitution est annulée." http://www.radio-canada.ca/nouvelles/National/2009/02/17/001-plaine-reconstitution-annul.shtml (accessed 9 May 2009).

'Recent Immigrants in Metropolitan Areas: Montréal – A Comparative Profile Based on the 2001 Census.' 2005. Citizenship and Immigration Canada, prepared by Strategic Research and Statistics in collaboration with Informetrica Limited, April. http://www.cic.gc.ca/english /research/papers/census2001/ montreal/partb.html (accessed 20 Dec. 2006).

Reid, Gregory J. 2000. 'Face to Face: A Conversation with Vittorio Rossi.' *Theatre Research in Canada / Recherches théâtrales au Canada* 21 (Fall): 177–94.

Renaud, Jacques. 1964. *Le cassé*. Montreal: Parti pris.

Richards, I.A. 1950. *Philosophy of Rhetoric*. New York and London: Oxford University Press.

Richards, J.M. 1967. 'Design Commentary.' *Architectural Review* 142 (Aug.): 155–66.

Ridout, Nicholas. 2007. *Stage Fright, Animals, and Other Theatrical Problems*. Cambridge: Cambridge University Press.

Roach, Joseph. 1996. *Cities of the Dead. Circum-Atlantic Performance*. New York: Columbia University Press.

Robert, Lucie. 1991. 'The New Quebec Theatre,' trans. David Homel. In Lecker, 112–23.

– 1993. 'L'impossible parole des femmes.' In David and Lavoie, 359–76.

– 1995. 'The Language of Theater.' In *Essays on Quebec Theater*, ed. Joseph I. Donohoe and Jonathan M. Weiss, 109–29. East Lansing: Michigan State University Press.

– 2000. 'Une carrière impossible: la dramaturgie au féminin.' In *Trajectoires au féminin dans la littérature québécoise (1960–1990)*, ed. Lucie Joubert, 141–55. Quebec: Nota Bene.

– 2004. 'Le grand récit féminin ou de quelques usages de la narrativité dans les texts dramatiques de femmes.' In *La narrativité contemporaine au Québec*, vol. 2, *Le théâtre et ses nouvelles dyamiques narratives*, ed. Chantal Hébert and Irène Perelli-Contos, 61–80 . Quebec: Presses de l'Université Laval.

Robertson, Strowan. 1972. 'Tremblay's comedy at Le Rideau Vert.' In Tremblay, 1972, 153–4.

Robichaud, Michel. 2007. '"Je voulais que l'uniforme soit facile à porter et moderne": Entrevue avec Michel Robichaud.' By Anne-Caroline Crespel. (12 April). In 'Les 40 ans d'Expo.'

Rocheleau, Alan-Michel. 1995. 'Visages montréalais de la marginalité québécoise dans l'œuvre de Michel Tremblay.' *Tangence* 48 (Sept.): 43–55.

Rosaldo, Renate. 1995. Foreword to *Hybrid Cultures: Strategies for Entering and Leaving Modernity*, by Néstor García Canclini, trans. Christopher L. Chiappari and Silvia L. Lopez, xi–xvii. Minneapolis: University of Minnesota Press.

Rosenberg, Marthe. 1985. 'The Development of a Lesbian Sensibility in the

Work of Jovette Marchessault and Nicole Brossard.' In *Traditionalism, Nationalism, Feminism: Women Writers of Quebec*, ed. Paula Gilbert Lewis, 227–39. Westport, CT: Greenwood.

Roy, Louise. 2007. '"C'était la beauté, l'audace, l'innovation et la connaissance du monde entier": Entrevue avec Louise Roy.' By Anne-Caroline Crespel. (2 May). In 'Les 40 ans d'Expo.'

Rubin, Don. 1996. 'Creeping toward a Culture: The Theatre in English Canada Since 1945.' In *Canadian Theatre History*, ed. Don Rubin, 318–31. Toronto: Copp Clark.

Rudin, Ronald. 1992. 'Revisionism and the Search for a Normal Society.' *Canadian Historical Review* 73 (March): 30–61.

Ruprecht, Alvina. 1985. 'Le discours dramatique de la femme: langage et identité chez Jovette Marchessault et Denise Boucher.' *Québec Studies* 3: 169–83.

Rydell, Robert W. 1984. *All the World's a Fair: Visions of Empire at American International Expositions, 1876–1916*. Chicago and London: University of Chicago Press.

– 1993. *World of Fairs: The Century-of-Progress Exhibitions*. Chicago and London: University of Chicago Press.

Ryngaert, J.-P. 1971. 'Du réalisme à la théâtralité: La dramaturgie de Michel Tremblay dans les Belles-Sœurs et À Toi pour toujours, ta Marie-Lou.' In *Livres et auteurs québécois 1971: revue critique de l'année littéraire*, 97–108. Quebec: Presses de l'Université Laval.

Saint-Martin, Lori. 1991. 'De la mère patriarcale à la mère légendaire: *Triptyque* [sic] *lesbien* de Jovette Marchessault.' *Voix et images* 16(2): 244–52.

– 1992. 'Introduction.' In Guilbeault et al., 21–41.

Salter, Denis. 1991. 'The Idea of a National Theatre.' In Lecker, 71–90.

Sauers, Don. 2004. 'The Birth of Girlwatching.' http://www.vintagegirlwatchers.com/birth-of-girlwatching.htm (accessed 29 June 2006).

Schechner, Richard. 1985. *Between Theatre and Anthropology*. Foreword Victor Turner. Philadelphia: University of Pennsylvania Press.

– 1988. *Performance Theory*. Rev. and expanded ed. New York and London: Routledge.

Schwartz, Huguette. 2007. '"On était comme sur une autre planète (…) C'est après l'Expo, qu'on s'est rendu compte qu'il y avait un vide": Entrevue avec Huguette Schwartz.' In 'Les 40 ans d'Expo 67.'

Schwartzwald, Robert. 1991. 'Fear of Federasty: Québec's Inverted Fictions.' In *Comparative American Identities: Race, Sex, and Nationality in the Modern Text*, ed. Hortense Spillers, 175–95. New York and London: Routledge.

– 1993. '"Symbolic" Homosexuality, "False Feminine," and the Problematics of Identity in Québec.' In *Fear of a Queer Planet*, ed. Michael Warner for the Social Text Collective, 264–99. Minneapolis: University of Minnesota Press.

Sedgwick, Eve Kosofsky. 1990. *Epistemology of the Closet.* Berkeley and Los Angeles: University of California Press.

– 2003. *Touching Feeling: Affect, Pedagogy, Performativity.* Durham, NC: Duke University Press.

– and Adam Frank. 1995. 'Shame in the Cybernetic Fold: Reading Silvan Tomkins.' *Critical Inquiry* 21 (Oct.): 496–522.

Sénécal, Gilles. 1992. 'Les idéologies territoriales au Canada Français: entre le continentalisme et l'idée du Québec.' *Journal of Canadian Studies / Revue d'études candiennes* 27(2): 49–62.

Servos, Norbert. 1987. 'Le corps est une fabrique d'émotions.' In Febvre, 1987b.

Sheltus, John. 1967. 'Expo hostesses and Canadian men.' *The World at Six.* CBC Radio. (16 June). MPEG http://archives.cbc.ca/society/celebrations/clips/536/ (accessed 1 June 2009).

Siegel, Marcia B. 1972. *At the Vanishing Point: A Critic Looks at Dance.* New York: Saturday Review Press.

– 1988. 'The Truth about Apples and Oranges.' *TDR* 32 (Winter): 24–31.

Siemerling, Winfried. 2005. *The New North American Studies: Culture, Writing and the Politics of Re/cognition.* London and New York: Routledge.

Simard, Monique. 2007. '"L'Expo, c'était le premier voyage de leur vie": Entrevue avec Monique Simard.' By Anne-Caroline Crespel. (11 April). In 'Les 40 ans d'Expo.'

Simon, Sherry. 1984. 'Écrire la différence: La perspective minoritaire.' *Recherches sociographiques* 25 (Sept.–Dec.): 457–65.

– 1985. 'Speaking with Authority: The Theatre of Marco Micone.' *Canadian Literature* 106 (Autumn): 57–64.

– 1991a. 'Culture and Its Values: Critical Revisionism in Quebec in the 1980s.' In Lecker, 167–79.

– 1991b. *Fictions de l'identitaire au Québec.* Montreal: XYZ.

– 1994. *Le Trafic des langues: Traduction et culture dans la littérature québécoise.* Montréal: Boréal.

– 2006. *Translating Montreal: Episodes in the Life of a Divided City.* Montreal and Kingston: McGill-Queen's University Press.

Sloan, Johanne. 2007. 'Humanists and Modernists at Expo 67.' *Revista Mexicana de estudios canadienses* 13 (Spring/Summer): 79–87.

Sommer, Doris. 1994. 'Love and Country: Allegorical Romance in Latin America.' In *Reading World Literature: Theory, History, Practice,* ed. and intro. Sarah Lawall, 177–202. Austin: University of Texas Press.

Sommer, Sally. 1991. 'Something Reckless, Something French.' *Dance Magazine* (March): 90–2.

States, Bert O. 1985. *Great Reckonings in Little Rooms: On the Phenomenology of Theater.* Berkeley: University of California Press.

Sterne, Jonathan. 2006. 'The mp3 as Cultural Artifact.' *New Media & Society* 8: 825–42.

Stockfelt, Ola. 1993. 'Adequate Modes of Listening,' trans. Anahid Kassabian and Leo G. Svendsen. *Stanford Humanities Review* 3: 153–69.

Straw, Will. 2004. 'Cultural Scenes.' *Loisir et société / Society and Leisure* 27 (Autumn): 411–22.

– 2005. 'Pathways of Cultural Movement.' In *Accounting for Culture: Thinking through Cultural Citizenship*, ed. Caroline Andrew, Monica Gattinger, Sharon Jeannotte, and Will Straw, 183–97. Ottawa: University of Ottawa Press.

Taussig, Michael. 1993. *Mimesis and Alterity: A Particular History of the Senses.* New York and London: Routledge.

Taylor, Diana. 1997. *Disappearing Acts: Spectacles of Gender and Nationalism in Argentina's 'Dirty War.'* Durham and London: Duke University Press.

Tembeck, Iro. 1992. *Danser à Montréal: Germination d'une histoire chorégraphique.* Quebec: Presses de l'Université du Québec.

Théâtre des cuisines. 1976. *Môman travaille pas, à trop d'ouvrage.* Montreal: Remue-ménage.

– 1980. *As-tu vu? Les maisons s'emportent!* Montreal: Remue-ménage.

'Theme.' 1964. In *Le Canada reçoit / Canada at Home.* Montreal: Compagnie canadienne de l'exposition universelle de 1967 / Canadian Corporation for the 1967 World Exhibition.

Thériault, Marie José. 1993. 'Faux original et copie authentique. Pour en finir avec le feuilleton Huston – Gouverneur général.' *Le Devoir,* 10 Dec., A11.

Thérien, Jean-Philippe, Louis Bélanger, and Guy Gosselin. 1993. 'Quebec: An Expanding Foreign Policy.' In Gagnon, ed., 259–78.

Thério, Adrien. 1972. '*Les belles-sœurs.*' Reproduced in Tremblay, 1972, 149–51.

Therrien, Ève Irène. 2008. 'De l'inanimé à l'*anima*: le fil conducteur entre l'acteur et le spectateur chez Denis Marleau.' *Globe: Revue internationale d'études québécoises* 11(2): 117–33.

Tremblay, Michel. 1968. *Les belles-sœurs.* Montreal: Holt, Rinehart and Winston.

– 1971. *À toi, pour toujours, ta Marie-Lou.* Montreal: Leméac.

– 1972. *Les belles-sœurs*, ed. Yves Dubé. Collection Théâtre Canadien. Montreal: Leméac.

– 1974. *Les Belles Soeurs. A Play by Michel Tremblay*, trans. John Van Burek and Bill Glassco. Vancouver: Talonbooks.

– 1976. *Saint Carmen de la Main.* Collection Théâtre Leméac. Montreal: Leméac.

– 1987. *Le vrai monde?* Montreal: Leméac.

– 1994. *Forever Yours Marie-Lou. A Play by Michel Tremblay,* trans. John Van Burek and Bill Glassco, 2nd ed. Vancouver: Talonbooks.

Trépanier, Esther. 1998. *Peinture et modernité au Québec, 1919–1939.* Quebec: Nota Bene.

'Usine C: Carbone 14.' Usine C: Centre de création et de diffusion pluridisciplinaire. http://www.usine-c.com/fr/carbone14 (accessed 11 Jan. 2007).

Usmiani, Renate. 1979a. 'The Tremblay Opus: Unity in Diversity.' *Canadian Theatre Review* 24 (Fall): 12–25.

– 1979b. 'Where to Begin the Accusation? Interview with Michel Tremblay.' *Canadian Theatre Review* 24 (Fall): 26–37.

Vaïs, Michel. 2005. *L'accompagnateur: Parcours d'un critique de théâtre.* Montreal: Varia.

– and Philip Wickham. 1994. 'Le brassage des cultures: Table ronde.' *Jeu* 72: 8–38.

Vallières, Pierre. 1968. *Nègres blancs d'Amérique: Autobiographie précoce d'un 'terroriste' québécois.* Montreal: Parti pris.

– 1971. *The White Niggers of America,* trans. Joan Pinkham. Toronto: McClelland and Stewart.

Vassaramva, Theodora. 1994. 'Speak Whatever.' *Le Devoir,* 28 Jan., A9.

Vennat, Pierre. 1994. 'Y a-t-il une littérature néo-québécoise?' *La Presse,* 22 May, B4.

Verdicchio, Pasquale. 1997. 'Subalterns Abroad.' In *Devils in Paradise: Writings on Post-Emigrant Cultures,* 7–26. Toronto: Guernica.

Vigeant, Louise. 1991. 'Du réalisme à l'expressionisme: la dramaturgie québécoise récente à grands traits.' *Jeu* 58: 7–16.

– 1994. 'Les dessous des prefixes ...' *Jeu* 72: 39–48.

Villeneuve, Isabelle. 1984. 'Mettre en scène des fantasmes.' *Spirale* 48 (Dec.): 13.

Wallace, Aurora. 2005. 'The Geography of Girlwatching in Postwar Montreal.' Paper presented at the conference 'Montreal at Street Level,' Montreal, 1 April.

Warhol, Robyn R. 2003. *Having a Good Cry: Effeminate Feelings and Pop-Culture Forms.* Columbus: Ohio State University Press.

Weiss, Jonathan. 1989. *French Canadian Theater.* Twayne's World Authors Series: French Canadian Literature. Boston: Twayne.

Whittaker, Stephanie. 2007. 'A Summer Job They All Remember.' *The Montreal Gazette,* 24 Sept.

Williams, Dorothy W. 1997. *The Road to Now: A History of Blacks in Montreal.* Montreal: Véhicule.

Wilmer, S.E. 2002. *Theatre, Society, and the Nation: Staging American Identities.* Cambridge: Cambridge University Press.

– 2003. 'On Writing National Theatre Histories.' In *Writing and Rewriting National Theatre Histories,* ed. S.E. Wilmer, 17–28. Iowa City: University of Iowa Press.

Wilson, Carl. 2007. *Let's Talk about Love: A Journey to the End of Taste.* New York and London: Continuum.

Wolf, Stacy. 2002. *A Problem Like Maria: Gender and Sexuality in the American Musical.* Ann Arbor: University of Michigan Press.

Woolfson, Peter. 1984. 'Language Policy in Quebec: *La survivance,* 1967–1982.' *Québec Studies* 2: 55–69.

Young, David. 2001. 'Céline Dion, National Unity and the English-Language Press in Canada.' *Media, Culture & Society* 23: 647–63.

Yuval-Davis, Nira, and Floya Anthias, eds. 1989. *Woman – Nation – State.* London: Macmillan.

Yuval-Davis, Nira. 1997. *Gender and Nation.* London: Sage.

Index